Registered Charity Number: 326068

ISBN 1 85776 891 4

Published by The Book Guild Ltd for
AGENDA AND EDITIONS CHARITABLE TRUST,
Submissions should be sent, with a stamped, addressed envelope, to
Patricia McCarthy, The Wheelwrights, Fletching Street, Mayfield,
East Sussex TN20 6TL; Tel. 07870684549 (mobile);
e-mail agendapoetry@lycos.co.uk

Subscriptions to: Patricia McCarthy, The Wheelwrights, Fletching Street,
Mayfield, East Sussex TN20 6TL

Agenda gratefully acknowledges the financial assistance of the Arts Council South/
South East region, The Po-shing Woo Foundation and The Lottery Fund

Subscription Rates:

Inland
Private	£26
Concessions (students/OAPs:	£20
Libraries and institutions:	£30

Europe
Private:	£28
Libraries and institutions:	£32

Overseas
Private:	£30 (US$52)
Libraries and institutions:	£34 (US$62)

We accept VISA and MASTERCARD

Vol. 39 No. 4   Summer 2003

Typesetting in Baskerville by IML Typographers, Birkenhead
Printed in Great Britain by Athenaeum Press Ltd, Gateshead

CONTENTS

EDITORIAL

This celebratory issue for William Cookson is conceived as one long elegy and eulogy, the choric polyphony of voices, both established and little known, granting him a fitting send-off to a place where he is differently alive, as Rainer Maria Rilke says, extended 'into the infinite', 'into the great cycle', plunging 'into the eternal stream'.

All contributors, subscribers and readers of *Agenda* will want to join me in paying the homage that this deliberately large (supposedly single) issue proffers to a man who sacrificed his life for poetry and was perhaps the best, most single-minded editor of our day

As Peter Dale says so succinctly: 'A good poem is a word for which there is no other word'. It is hoped that poems approximating this exacting descripton within these pages will call out to William, reassuring him that he – or his work – will live on on this earthly plain, continuing to ignore the popular 'isms' so prevalent in our materialistic world. Reviews of chosen books received will appear in the next issue.

This has been a particularly difficult issue to assemble: haunting, respectful and driven by bereavement for a true friend and presence who ultimately preserved a childlike innocence deep within himself, despite his complexities, and the spirituality of a kind of pagan-mystic.

I share what Kathleen Raine wrote to me shortly after William's death, and only a few months before her own recent death: 'What I feel about him is pure affection and great admiration for his sheer appreciation of the beauty of poetry. Beauty is very unfashionable, but William knew what it is and its great value, that it is the divine imprimatur, the Good, Plato's other verities ... William's response to the sheer beauty of poetry is something very rare, almost awe-

5

inspiring. He was a very rare person and his untimely death is a tragic thing ... Although in one sense I did not know William well – I was never in his house – I really did love him and deeply mourn him because of what he was.'

Kathleen might never have visited William's flat on the Albert Bridge Road, very close to the Thames and overlooking Battersea Park, but William often went by bicycle, motor-bike or on foot to her Chelsea home for tea. Indeed, he took me there twice – where Kathleen appreciated what she called 'his discerning and richly-stored mind'. Stimulating conversations and mutual sympathies were accompanied by the savouring of her delicious cakes, memories of which linger like Proust's madeleines. It seems comforting that William is in good company now in the after-life with Kathleen and, of course, with Peter Russell who died just after him, Ian Hamilton and Ken Smith both of whom died recently too.

Because, in retrospect, William would have been unlikely to favour a lot of people, even sensitive close friends and colleagues, picking over his bones and would have agreed with Marvell that 'The grave is a fine and private place', I hope the writers of the moving memoirs/essays (Anita Money, William Bedford, Roland John, Peter Dale, Julie Whitby, Robin Buss, Alan Massey, Humphrey Clucas, Tania Waghorn, Stephen Lushington, Nancy Sandars) will forgive me for not giving much space to them here. I am hoping, however, that these, as well as the obituaries, will be published at a later date in a special Festschrift for which donations are welcome. I have chosen, rather, to promote William as another of those undeservedly neglected, unfashionable or underrated poets that he himself was intent on promoting. After all, his poems surely capture the essence of the man removed from nitty-gritty details of circumstances and daily survival tactics. As Milan Kundera says in *Life Is Elsewhere*: 'By means of his poetry' the poet 'creates his self-portrait.' William does this and also transcends such a limitation in the slim extant volume of his poetry.

It is precisely this transcendence over the mundane and popular polemic, this musical ability of poems which are necessities to transform themselves into meanings beyond ordinary meanings that Peter Abbs writes so articulately about in the recently published *Against The Flow: Education, The Arts and Post Modern Culture* (Routledge, £24.99 paperback).

In this personal, original, bravely outspoken and very readable treatise much concerned with poetics, Peter Abbs argues strongly for the importance of the arts, especially for the questing poet, in a shamanic role, to challenge, subvert, transform and heal the human predicament, freed from the bogus protection of postmodern irony and scepticism. He calls on readers and writers 'to place poetry under the sign of Orpheus again' and to bang – in prophetic warning – 'the metaphysical drum' already played for example by William Blake, Matthew Arnold, Lawrence, Eliot, Ted Hughes and Geoffrey Hill. Illustrating *Agenda*'s long-held and future refusal to 'go with the flow' i.e. the ephemerally fashionable, Peter Abbs writes most interestingly about 'the subverting nature' of Socrates' method of teaching in order to awaken, ultimately, to what amounts to Jungian individuation by means of the elenchus. The elenchus was the importance of refuting, undermining and questioning any conviction imbibed uncritically, any fashion, any fanaticism in order, perhaps, to start over and over again in a humble position of 'not knowing', akin to the proper darkness in Eliot's *Four Quartets*.

Internal darkness, deprivation
And destitution of all property,
Dessication of the world of sense,
Evacuation of the world of fancy,
Inoperancy of the world of spirit . . .
                              (*Burnt Norton*)

And the end of all our exploring
Will be to arrive where we started . . .
(*Little Gidding*)

Abbs' theories tally with Seamus Heaney's in *Feeling Into Words*, the first essay in *Finders Keepers: Selected Prose 1971–2001* (Faber and Faber 2002, £20 hardback) as Heaney, too, defines 'poetry as divination, poetry as revelation of the self to the self; as restoration of the culture to itself', poetry written by the kind of poets who, as Osip Mandelstam calls them, are 'stealers of air' that *Agenda* will continue to find and promote.

If, as Abbs suggests, Plato was shaped by his symbolic father, Socrates, who turned him, through a disturbing, transforming elenchus, from a brilliant prospective politician to the first systematic author-philosopher; if Stephen Dedalus in James Joyce's *A Portrait of the Artist as a Young Man* was shaped by his mythological father, Dedalus – 'Old father, old artificer, stand me now and ever in good stead'; and if, in turn, Ezra Pound came to be the main father-figure in William Cookson's life, then William himself must continue as founding father not only of the corpus of poetry he discovered, appreciated and promoted (evidenced here for readers not aware of, for example, the early issues of *Agenda*), but also in what one of my mentors, Rainer Maria Rilke, terms 'the heart-space' he leaves behind.

In turning William's death into an enrichment, a transformation of sorts, maybe we should all take the advice of Rilke in his letter to the Countess of Stauffenberg, 23 January, 1919, to strengthen our trust 'in Death and again to make him, who was never a stranger, more known and felt as the silent sharer in all life's processes'. Perhaps, we should also emulate the angels of the *Duino Elegies.*

all of the living
make the mistake of drawing too sharp distinctions.
Angels (they say) are often unable to tell
whether they move among the living or dead ...
> (*The First Elegy*, translated by J.B. Leishman
> and Stephen Spender)

Maybe we should even envy the dead:
Oh to be dead at last and endlessly know them,
All the stars! For how, how, how to forget them?
> (*The Seventh Elegy*)

I hope this issue, as Kathleen Raine hoped, 'comes to life' with its orchestral communion of voices: 'the complete consort dancing together' (Eliot's *Four Quartets*) to deserve, for William, the exclamation:

... What an epilogue
to mastery achieved
> (Rilke's *The Spirit Ariel* in *Miscellaneous Poems*
> *1912–1926 Turning Point* (Anvil Press, 2003, £8.95) –
> originally published under the title *An Unofficial*
> *Rilke*, selected and translated by Michael Hamburger,
> a very old friend of William, longstanding
> contributor to *Agenda* and foremost translator and
> scholar of Rilke).

Peter Abbs states: 'The ultimate silence Wittgenstein felt philosophy had to leave unviolated can be penetrated by all the arts', including poetry. Thus William Cookson, surely, can reciprocally transform into that music Rilke writes about in the poem *To Music* translated by Michael Hamburger, penetrating that 'ultimate silence' with an inner music that we will continue to hear, testified by this extract:

You stranger: music. You heart-space
grown out of us. Innermost of us

9

that, rising above us, seeks the way out –
holy departure:
when what is inward surrounds us
as the most mastered distance, as
the other side of air:
pure,
immense,
beyond habitation.

May the songs in this volume, chorused in unison from
England, including the South/South East region, Ireland,
Scotland, France, Russia, The U.S. and Canada, be the *song
alone* which cirdes *the land/hallowing and hailing* a very
considerable man.

Patricia McCarthy

Drawing by B.S. Andrews

AGENDA BROADSHEETS

This memorial/celebratory issue for William Cookson, Founder of *Agenda* marks, also the birth of the new *Agenda* broadsheets for young poets (sixteen to mid-thirties) which will be included (free to subscribers and free to chosen broadsheet poets) in each issue of *Agenda* from now on. One poet from each broadsheet will be selected for special inclusion in *Agenda* and highlighted by a spread of up to five poems in each succeeding issue.

Emma Cookson, William's 16 year old daughter, has kindly offered her painting to be the centre piece for this first broadsheet, linking William's death to the birth of this new venture for the future which concerns his own cherished daughter.

Young artists (paintings, drawings, lithographs, etchings) are invited, along with young poets, to send in work for the front of each broadsheet.

Young essay-writers and reviewers are also invited to send in submissions to *Agenda*. For example in this issue Glyn Maxwell's *The Nerve* is reviewed by twenty year old Lytton Smith and twenty-nine-year-old Gabrielle J. Reed has written an essay on Ovid about whom William Cookson wished to do an issue in the near future.

I wish to extend my warm thanks to all those who encouraged their students and friends to submit poems for the first broadsheet, especially Peter Abbs, Peter Carpenter, Mimi Khalvati, Glyn Maxwell, Patrick McGuiness, Jan Montefiore and Nigel Thompson. It is hoped that many more tutors, teachers, lecturers and mentors will encourage gifted, aspiring poets to send in their submissions accompanied by their name, address, age and place of work or study.

12

The inspiration for these broadsheets came from Hayden Murphy's famous Broadsheets produced with regularity and vigour in Dublin in the seventies, although they featured poets of any vintage. The age band, sixteen to mid thirties, as a definition of 'young' for the *Agenda* broadsheets is of course arbitrary. I remember a twelve-year old at school who was, even then, a veritable old matron, and there is no doubt that a poet can be 'young' at eighty if he has just found his voice. As Rainer Maria Rilke said in his *Letters to a Young Poet*: 'There is no measuring in time. Ten years are nothing. Being an artist means not reckoning and counting, but ripening like the tree that does not force its sap'. However, a boundary had to be drawn; hence the compromise. It is hoped that these posters will be pinned or stuck on notice-boards, walls, doors, and then turned around to the other side, or hung as mobiles when both sides can be viewed at once so that the young poets in print can gain exposure to as many readers as possible, even perhaps drawing in their peers from other faculties or with other interests to the world of poetry which is, after all, about communication in general and life.

It is planned to establish, in the near future, *Agenda* archives so that essays/reviews and poems in back and current issues of *Agenda* can be used for inspiration, information and research.

NOTES FOR YOUR OWN 'PECULIAR MUSIC'

The poet Emily Dickinson (b 1830) said, 'If I read a book and it makes my whole body so cold no fire can ever warm me, I know that is poetry. If I feel physically as if the top of my head were taken off, I know that is poetry.'

You might well agree with Emily Dickinson that a lot depends upon gut reaction. Charlotte Bronte said something similar

13

about her sister, the loner Emily's poems when she first came upon them.

Emily Bronte's poems stirred Charlotte's heart 'like the sound of a trumpet'. She admired the way they were: 'condensed and terse, vigorous and genuine. They also had a peculiar music – wild melancholy and elevating ... a condensed energy.'

Is this not what every poet seeks? That 'peculiar music' which means finding a voice of your own.

YOUR OWN VOICE

In *Finders Keepers* (Faber and Faber, £20 hardback), Seamus Heaney explains that you will know you have found your own voice if 'you can get your own feeling into your own words and your words have the feel of you about them'.

How to start, then, using your words to 'bring to silence what the great Gothic cathedrals did to light', as Peter Abbs suggests in his recently published book *Against The Flow?* Auguste Rodin certainly managed to use his hands to bring to stone what these great cathedrals did to light, infusing life into the lifeless maybe because he used his own experience – his passions, losses, hardships, celebrations. Indeed, 'the wound may well be the best hurting place to start from' (P. Abbs) in attempting to communicate, through poetry, what cannot be conveyed in normal speech.

Rainer Maria Rilke in *Letters to a Young Poet* pre-empts Abbs: 'Our sadnesses are special – for they are the moments when something new has entered into us, something unknown. We have changed as a house changes into which a guest has entered...'

14

Geoffrey Hill, in a radio broadcast, stated likewise: 'A poem is a sad and angry consolation.

YOUR THEMES

We all write best about what we have experienced and about what we know, even if we distance that experience from ourselves through the craft or form of the poem, or place the veil of mythology over it. Many of Yeats' poems addressed directly to Maud Gonne on the subject of his unrequited love were written as very personal poems. Some he left in their raw state to transcend the merely personal because they were so deeply lived; others he clothed almost apologetically in Classical or Irish mythology as a kind of mask for his vulnerable self. It must be remembered that many poems deeply felt expand beyond mere personal utterance and become universal e.g. Thomas Hardy's 1912–13 poems written on the sudden death of his wife expand into anyone's shocked bereavement, anyone's sense of irrevocable loss. It does not matter that the main drive behind them was guilt, for Hardy had not got on with his wife at all for most of their marriage (see John Montague's poem on this subject in this issue). The poems stand on their own, with a life of their own.

The American poet, Robert Frost, said: 'A poem begins as a lump in the throat, a homesickness, a lovesickness. It finds the thought and the thought finds the words.'

Rainer Maria Rilke, in his *Letters to a Young Poet* urged the uncertain young poet he was addressing: 'Seek themes your own everyday life offers you: describe your sorrows and desires, passing thoughts and the belief in some sort of beauty and use, to express yourself, the things in your

15

environment, the images from your dreams, and the objects of your memory. If your daily life seems poor, do not blame it. Blame yourself; tell yourself you are not poet enough to call forth its riches; for to the creator there is no poverty and no poor indifferent place ... Go into yourself and test the deeps in which your life takes rise.'

Rilke continues: 'Live your life like a painful and beautiful day in the history of a great gestation. For everything that happens keeps on being a beginning ... and beginning in itself is always so beautiful'.

Ruth Padel endorses what Rilke says in picking, for her detailed analyses, modern poems that 'were made from all the textures of life around us, from what we all see in newspapers and the home, on TV, on the street.' Her palatable, articulate book, *52 Ways of Looking at a Poem* (Chatto and Windus 20002 , £12.99) is an attempt to make modern poetry accessible to those locked out of it, and to show how poetry can 'transform real life imaginatively so we understand our lives new-paintedly, more fully; to make familiar things look strange so you see them new'. The poems she chooses for inclusion are on 'subjects that matter to all of us: memory, childhood, embarrassment; war, illness, death, love; dreams, art, jealousy, betrayal, loss. They are about cooking, rain at the bus stop, parents, defloration; about being unable to drive, being misunderstood. About cruelty ... identity, origin, landscape, home and hope, inequality and immigration; ambition, incest and failure, slavery and exile...'

THE MAGIC OF POETRY

Some poems, of course, can surprise even their creator when they take off as if with a life of their own and communicate, somehow, without being fully understood. As Don Cupitt

16

suggests in *After God*: 'Language speaks us ... It makes us; it makes the world; it makes and unmakes all things.'

Gerard Manley Hopkins (1844–1889), who burnt all his early poetry and went on to be innovative with his sprung rhythm, along with his definitions of *inscape* and *instress*, said: 'Sometimes one admires and enjoys the very lines one cannot understand', especially if one reads, as he advocated, 'with the ears, not with the eyes.'

Borrowing from other writers, painters or musicians, even tangentially, is no crime either (viz Pound and Eliot); and it is true that many good poets are kleptomaniacs, even subconscious ones.

Hopkins said more than a hundred years ago: 'that nothing should be old or borrowed ... cannot be.'

VERSIONS

Drafting and re-drafting poems is often an essential part of the process, as is the discarding of them in order, perhaps, to return to them with a fresher, lighter touch. After all, only very few poems arrive as special gifts, all of a piece, and these belong to what Hopkins called 'the highest (and rarest) kind of poetry'. The Welsh poet, Dylan Thomas, who recited his poems out loud while composing them, did not worry about having to 'grope', like Hopkins, 'for the tune' in order to thrum 'the sweetest and most secret catgut of the mind'. It is often precisely this 'groping' that perfects the final draft of the poem.

THE NECESSARY POEM

In aiming for the indispensable poem, the poem that is written because it has to be, because it is wrung out of the depths of your experience in whatever form, and has, as Rilke says, 'sprung from necessity', it is worth recalling Dylan Thomas's words of warning to the aspiring poet, Vernon Watkins, who was then only twenty-three: 'The words are lovely but they seem so chosen, not struck out … I cannot see the strong inevitable pulling that makes the poem an event, a happening, an action perhaps, not a still life or an experience put down…'

CRAFT

'An experience put down' … Transforming that raw experience into a poem means learning to use the technique and craft of poetry. Of course, unconscious effects can happen in a poem and be successful, especially if the poet has a natural, musical ear. Ruth Padel asserts: 'The poems chosen are carefully crafted and structured, but not all of the ways they get their effects will have been put there consciously by the poet. Some will have been, some won't. How conscious they were does not matter, and the same goes for the reader … Responding is what matters…'

Heaney defines craft as 'what you can learn from other verse: the skill of making' and he continues: 'Learning the craft is learning to turn the windlass at the well of poetry', using, often innovatively, the tools of the trade that concern pattern and sound. Ruth Padel lays down the simple ground rules to follow even before these tools are taken up: show, don't tell and, 'at the end, frisk every word to make sure it's necessary, that it's pulling its weight.' Then for the 'tools' that have evolved from poetry-making, the oldest of the literary arts, she adds: 'Part of the art is making the way you use these tools as invisible as possible in the finished product'. A fine example is Hardy's poem *The Haunter* in which he gives his dead wife the voice that he did not allow her to have while

18

she was alive. In each verse, every alternate line ends with 'know', 'go', 'do', 'thereto' so that the lines haunt one another throughout just as she haunts him, although when reading the poem, this pattern is so subtle that the rhyme and repetition can hardly be discerned.

Rilke might well add to Heaney's definition of craft that learning the craft is learning to turn the windlass at the well of your self. He advises the young poet: 'Works of art are of an infinite loneliness ... What goes on in your innermost being is worthy of your whole love.'

'Your innermost being' consists of your multiple selves, your instinct, your psyche, your subconscious as well as your conscious mind, your own experiences, the experiences of others you know, of previous generations, of the land, and of words themselves as 'bearers of history and mystery'.

TECHNIQUE

Technique, however, as Heaney puts it, 'entails the water-marking of your essential patterns of perception, voice and thought into the touch and texture of your lines'.

Technique comprises 'that whole creative effort to bring the meaning of experience within the jurisdiction of form.'

This 'form' need not be a daunting, tight corset around the content of the poem. It can entail free verse, (as Ruth Padel states, while allowing that – in modern poetry – free and formal methods are at work side by side – both of which she explains clearly and in context, with a useful, short glossary of poetic terms at the end of her book: 'There is a long and shining history of poetry that does not rhyme. Homer did not rhyme, nor did classical Greek or Latin poetry – rhymed poetry in Greek or Latin is late classical and medieval'), but somehow the style of the poem needs to match or illuminate its content. For example, if the poem describes a jarring relationship between a mother and daughter, then the form to illuminate this might well be free verse, with broken lines within a line, enjambement and no rhyme since the mother and daughter are not rhyming with each other.

'Philip Larkin said a poem is a knife and fork partnership. The fork identifies an emotion: spears it, lands it on the poem's plate. The knife is analytical and technical, wants "to sort out the emotion, chop it up, arrange it and say either thank you or sod the universe for it". The fork is what makes readers (and writers) reach for poetry in a crisis.' (Ruth Padel)

It is this matter of 'technique', to be learnt by long, strict study, sometimes as long as twenty years, and harsh discipline in the ancient Bardic schools, that Caesar reported in his *De Bello Gallico* and Strabo in his *Geographica.* The Celtic Bards were regarded as superior to the Vates or natural philosophers and diviners, and to the Druids. For, as singers and poets, the Bards had 'the mystic import of words' (*The Empty School*), 'The Light of Foresight' (*The Train*) and were seen as guides and judges as Taliesin testifies in his *Riddle Song.*

The danger in over-concentrating on technique is that the technique can, in not very able hands, override the content and become just a technical exercise, reducing the poem's impact. The master craftsman Peter Dale, who wrote the invaluable *An Introduction to Rhyme* (Agenda/Bellew, £13.95 hardback) has agreed to write on the multiple and complex uses of technique in a future issue of AGENDA. Limited copies of AGENDA, Vol. 28 No. 4, *A Survey on Rhyme*, are still available at £4 plus postage. Other regular essays will focus on the art of poetry.

THE READER

In analysing how you write poems – and Ruth Padel emphasises that 'analysing' differs from 'dissecting' which 'destroys a dead animal's body' while 'analysing a poem is more like turning a spotlight on a living creature', the 'living creature' being the poem – you will need to consider why you read poems and what poems do for you, whether they are cathartic, celebratory or act as mirrors wherein you can see confirmed your own emotional or actual state. Larkin said that poetry begins with emotion in the poet and ends with the same emotion in the reader, the poem being the instrument that puts it there.

The reader's role certainly must not be underestimated, nor your own role as reader/poet. However, I would disagree with Larkin, for, although the reader can be seen to complete the poem once it has been relegated, in its elastic form (stretching different ways in accordance with different interpretations and according to the different experiences and echoes that each reader brings to the poem) to the market place of the page, each reader surely makes that poem specifically his or hers in the light of his or her own unique, hermetic interpretation. John Luis Borges seems to endorse this view: 'Poetry lies in the meeting of the poem and reader ... What is essential is the thrill, the almost physical emotion that comes with each reading'. 'Each reading' endorses the proposition that one poem can be a hundred thousand poems interpreted in myriad ways by a hundred thousand readers from differing cultures, backgrounds, upbringings, education and influences.

Furthermore, at one moment the reader can be highly receptive yet at another moment numb and barely responsive at all to the same poem, the reaction therefore

21

dependent to some extent on the pervading mood of the reader.

Gerard Manley Hopkins recognised this: 'You know well how deadened, as it were, the critical faculties become at times, when all good poetry alike loses its clear ring and its charm; while in other moods they are so enlivened that things that have lost their freshness strike you with their original definiteness'.

Hence the need to give each poem its chance and to look at it several times, allowing for the variant inadequacies in one's response.

THE ROLE OF POETRY

However, vacillating moods aside, poetry can serve the reader as a strong life force in many ways: as a life-saver, confidant(e), consolation, refuge, interpreter, instructor, tranquiliser, thinker, questioner, challenge, intensifier, goader, chastener, music-maker ... the list is endless.

Iris Murdoch, wife of former long-standing trustee of *Agenda*, John Bayley, who was William Cookson's tutor at New College, Oxford, declared firmly in an essay: 'Art should not console'.

But, as Ruth Padel contests, 'sometimes it is the only thing that can console, and people often turn to poetry in a crisis.' There is no doubt that poetry, and poets, help us not to feel so lonely. An example of this happened to me in my twenties when I arrived in Washington DC to take up residence and discovered that my father had been knocked down by a Volkswagon and killed. As an outsider in an alien culture, in a foreign world, a tattered copy of Rilke's *Duino Elegies*

22

(Leishmann, Spender translation, with the German on one side and scribbled upon by some anonymous student in smudged, looped writing) fell into my hands in a second-hand bookshop and became my life-support, sustaining me in that traumatic shock, and making Rilke at once, with a flash of recognition, a true, lasting friend.

SOLITUDE

Whether you are a writer or a reader, or both, as Ruth Padel says, 'you have to have time and something like solitude to go in and out of a poem, to turn it over'. . .

Rilke stressed: 'The necessary thing is ... great inner solitude. ... Works of art are of an infinite loneliness ... Patience is everything'.

It is within this 'great inner solitude' that Rilke urged the young poet he was addressing, Franz Xaver Kappus, and all of us now to 'assume our existence as broadly as we in any way can; everything, even the unheard of, must be possible in it'. What he goes on to say applies as accurately today as when he wrote the letters from 1902 to 1908, and indeed finds an echo in Peter Abbs' *Against The Flow*. The experiences that are called visions, the whole so-called 'spirit world', death, all those things that are so closely akin to us, have by daily parrying been so crowded out of life that the senses with which we could have grasped them are atrophied.'

THE ROOM OF YOUR LIFE

A memorable image Rilke uses to urge us to be daring and experimental with our lives is 'the room': 'If we think of this existence of the individual as a larger or smaller room, it appears evident that most people learn to know only a corner of their room, a place by the window, a strip of floor on which they walk up and down ...'

Rilke's advice to 'let life happen to you...' and 'change' ('Everything that makes more of you than you have heretofore been in your best hour is right') is paralleled by Carol Ann Duffy in her buoyant poem *Away and See*. Here, as in many of her poems, she involves the readers directly, making them active participants as she undermines prejudices and closed minds, urging people, with gentle imperatives, not to live dead lives but to be inquisitive, to experiment and to expand. Her avowal of language is epiphanic:

Away and see things that words give a name to, the flight
of syllables, wingspan stretching a noun. Test words
wherever they live; listen and touch, smell, believe.
Spell them with love.

The final verse shows her affirmation in the wonder of life:

Nothing's the same as anything else. Away and see
for yourself. Walk. Fly. Take a boat til land reappears,
altered forever, ringing its bells, alive. Go on. G'on.
　　　　　Gon.
Away and see.
　　　　　(*Selected Poems*, Penguin Poetry, £7.99)

YOUR ROLE

'Nothing's the same as anything else' matches Hopkins' definition of *inscape*, the distinctive quality of every single thing. His other term, *instress*, that quasi-mystical, Platonic illumination felt by the perceiver in viewing the *inscape*, seems to be what Carol Ann Duffy, in her own 'popular' voice, Ruth Padel and Peter Abbs, despite different standpoints, (e.g. Peter Abbs views irony as an unnecessary block to the spiritual whereas Ruth Padel admires the irony and implication in much poetry today) are all advocating in order that, through poetry, the reader might feel, behind 'the dull, dense world', that deeper pattern, order and unity which gives meaning to external forms. Here you the poet can retain that privileged, shamanic role both of 'walker between the worlds' and 'weaver of spells.'

Patricia McCarthy

The following poem seems particularly appropriate for welcoming young poets to the *Agenda* broadsheets:

NANCY SANDARS

To Poets Not Yet Born

Day after day that turns down, folds down leaves,
dry days without creation,
days that are only falling sap. Suns that have risen
because the world has made one revolution
upon imaginary poles, nights that are only shadow
out of a lesser shadow, the backside view of the universe.

Such days the matrix out of which
one is created, sapphire from silicate
such difference between causation and creation,
The jewel is harder than the matrix which
a cunning chemist can annihilate.
The day, the word, created and not made,
other-world felt, otherwise heard.

The long day of the saints
and their absurd lovely miracles
is past, the day of the poets now is passing
soon to be extinct. Their absurdities
equally lovely and obsolete
their anachronistic organs.
Act of faith, jump in the dark
dazzle of hope through drizzle of dispair

Poet, she is dying, your one and only Procris,
dazzling the eyes of death, your Last Duchess,
your sorrowing Eurydice, medium of your common language.
Dear body of your only usage lies on the ground

anaesthetised while the murderers gather round
First the logician with his little scalpel
to lecture on the humorous corpse,
he separates the bundles of the veins
within the body of the old magician
saying it was too inexact to live,
the dearness or the loveliness he does not reckon,
while in the brain the conscientious analyst
probes living matter with a deadly hand.
The man of calculation is the last to come,
when the white sinews are all unstrung,
neatly he removes the tongue and writes an X
upon the bleeding root, a Y upon the quivering heart
and Z upon the guts and with the sum
of each dissected part he formulates fresh form.
Communication must not cease.
Communication conquers all!

Poets, you are not concerned with truth,
laws of the Internet are not for you.
Some have claimed gods, or maidens did inspire,
tongs lifted altar-coals, tongues of fire,
stigmata, words from mountains, birds in flight.
There is no cause in reason why this should be,
but yet it is, therefore turn down this page,
the branch breaks here, upon creation.

William George Cookson

8th May 1939 - 2nd January 2003

St. Mary's Church, Battersea
Wednesday 22nd January, 2003
2.15pm

ADDRESS BY THE EARL OF GOWRIE

When people die, we like to say nice things about them and accompany their coffin with the verbal equivalent of Philip Larkin's 'wasteful, weak, propitiatory flowers.' Or if saying nice things proves difficult, we resort to code, as in the case of reminding friends of someone pompous or self-centred that he could not suffer fools gladly.

William Cookson had beautifully old-fashioned manners and the dignity of those who are innately shy. But what I most admired and envied in him had little to do with the sweetness of his nature. It was ferocity, the ferocity of his purpose. He had a custodial influence on literature in English for more than 40 years. You do not achieve that through niceness, or without cost to yourself or those close to you.

William discovered his calling when he was a schoolboy, in 1956, and he stuck with it. As someone who has worked in public life, I know what it is to trim; to adapt any intuitions I might have to the inevitable dilution that putting them into practice involves, maybe, but also to convenience of compromise and career. William was having none of that. And he was the custodian of a poetry which would have none of that – even, as his impressive obituaries reminded us, when it was submitted by poets of talent and renown.

To edit a magazine for more than 40 years is a remarkable achievement. To do so without compromising your vision of what poetry is, and what poetry is for, is a heroic one. William's good manners kept him patient when you disagreed with him. My reference to Larkin at a Cookson memorial service is in the nature of a posthumous tease and recalls old arguments. None of the dead poets whom I knew as friends, not Olson, nor Lowell, nor Ted Hughes had William's complete self-confidence in his own judgement and his own ear. He had, after all, come into the business of making, knowing and judging under the influence of *il miglior fabbro*, the exemplary Ezra Pound, whom, in his dedication to the most celebrated poem of the 20th century, T.S. Eliot dubbed the better craftsman. As William said in the introduction to his *Agenda* Anthology, 'My touchstone has been material that has stayed in my mind.' The reason *Agenda* worked, against all material odds, was that Cookson's mind had moved like a long-legged fly on the silence, the terror almost, that lies at the heart of all great poetry and makes it, however secular the context, akin to a form of prayer: whether of lament or celebration or both.

We are here to do honour to a purposeful man like his peers. One of the high points of my own life was when William asked me to write a foreword for that *Agenda* anthology and thereby rub shoulders, however briefly, with writers I revere and who sustain me, and I believe all those with eyes and ears, to read and hear them, through drought and flood. It would be invidious to mention the living. But look at the roll call of *Agenda*'s great dead: Pound, David Jones, Basil Bunting, William Carlos Williams, Theodore Roethke, R. S. Thomas. One of the low points of my own life was arriving at The Arts Council just as it ended its support for *Agenda* of 27 years, admittedly the longest contribution of this kind it ever made. I am sad at my failure to reverse the decision.

Heroism requires a fight against odds. William fought and won. *Agenda* lives and a tribute to him must be to try and nourish its survival. He was faithful to his quest and so must we be. William published in England William Carlos Williams' 'Asphodel, That Greeny Flower' which Auden thought one of the greatest love poems ever written. As Williams' wrote in *Asphodel*:

It is difficult
to get the news from poems
        yet men die miserably every day
                for lack
of what is found there.

Thank God William did find what there is to be found in poetry.

William died before he should have done. His prodigious service to poetry took a terrible toll on his own well-being and the well-being of Margaret and Emma, to whom he dedicated that anthology of his life's work. I once asked Robert Lowell who were his favourite 20th-century poets, expecting that he would cite his friends Eliot and Elizabeth Bishop. 'Oh, Hardy and Ezra,' he answered, 'because of the heartbreak.' Although great art must dance and celebrate and even shake the fist from time to time, there is always, at the core, that curious consolation of tragedy: the consolation of facing up to things as they are rather than as we would like them to be. Beethoven made his name by the way he played the slow movements of his concerti; the music from a further room of the 20th century is the Blues. William could not have been the editor he was without writing poetry himself. An imagist in the line of Pound and our own T. E. Hulme, he knew that if a poem lets the object of its attention provide the words, the emotional radiation will follow. His own poems, too, are like secular prayers. They ring true for us and ring now on the other side for him. Thank God for William Cookson, for his life and achievement. God comfort with pride in that achievement all who mourn him.

WILLIAM COOKSON

VESTIGES

&

VERSIONS

1955-2002

Dream Traces

A Sequence

I

Ancient sadness

Rumours of the death of Pan

Wept on the forest moss
        in the dawn

II

Rattle of thunder

I dreamt
        from a window
cirrus-cloud
        receding from blue quietude

Distant thunder today
The great trees
        beyond the pane
stir
        in the dream wind

III

Sequoia
        storied
                into timeless blue

IV

On a corner, near Battersea Bridge,
a faint moon
               almost full
                           low over the road
which leads south-west.

I waited long.

Dusk.

Turning away,
I noticed to the north
a rising wood
               tangled in mist.

V

Boles red gold in a late sun.

A place far back.

That avenue ended in a blue waste

VI

Grey day and your hair wild.

Walking back
      while you journey underground
I see your face again
      in moist gusts of river wind.

Years back, a girl's face
      contoured by long black hair
appeared through the grey rain
      on a tract of barren land.

You connect now
      with this trace of an old dream.

VII

Dappled grey and umber white
      the cloud-crags sail . . .

VIII

Life would have stopped, you said.

Now in the study you made
I think of the sycamore we planted.

It will survive a few more years,
      its roots boxed in.

We could still take it to Surrey
and plant it in woodland I knew.

Too late to shed
        the encrustations of the years.

*

Birches quiver in blue air
Woods dashed with rain

*

But the landscape you first saw in a dream
        we suddenly found.
That sloping wood
        half-lit by a low sun
lives now in my mind
as it survived in yours from a child.

*

Those dusty leaves on the balcony
        will soon fall.

And old knotted walls I'd built in the mind
        I could not break down.

Tonight, while you journey to Wales
I think of the dark tracts of wild and field
        widening between us.

IX

Sunlight beyond the pane
Trees stirring
        old green in gold

A wraith of spring

The past flashes
        on a drift of wind

X

I wake to find you gone.

An undercurrent of sound:
wind in the great planes
brings peace.

At six
I watch their dusky green
tossing against a rain-grey dawn.

XI

Lying awake
I've reached the woodland of your dream
searching...
Long since we walked under those boughs.

It's clear tonight.
Out there,
where gnarled roots grip the dank earth,
the wind sways dying leaves
across the scattered stars.

XII

Roots of old pain.

The cold would suit their need.

Journeying back
            to a remote place
I've come past two spruce firs
            over heather
and a tract of wild grass
            to the edge of a wood
where three silver birches
            sprung from a single root
gleam in the winter dusk

The bleak sky
            set for a night of snow.

XIII

Sun-shaft on the wall

Through trunks of planes
            a vista of faint green
shines in the new air

*

Wept on the forest moss
            at dawn

Three Poems of Childhood

Legends

(i)
Engraved in an ancient book
grey horses drew a chariot in the sky
above the gnarled bole of a shattered tree

(ii)

Those mounds of luminous grey
      in the north-east sky
recall a recurrent dream:

a house with towers
      above a twilit valley
where soft grass gleamed
      buried in blue mist

Fox

Dusk-star
      over bracken hills
by wayless woods

A glimpse of rusty fur
      crossed the lower track
into the tangled dark

An Old Panic

The pale lineament of veins
       in a child's palm
formed a nameless fear

by a concrete wall
       jagged, war-riven

on a sandy waste
       one summer day

False Spring

Wind strong from the south
brings spring in autumn
this bright day

the room in shade

Quicksilver, gold –
forms move in radiance
beyond the horizon
of my mind

Five Poems for K.

who sheds such light in the air

Two Dreams, Years Apart

(i)
caligine densus opaca

I reached the station at the end of the line
and walked a short distance
for a purpose since forgotten.
Going back
I skirted a small wood
of dingy, stunted firs.
Half-charred
their dusty boughs
moaned in the deepening dark.

(ii)
When you entered my sleep, I saw
a long tract of water, glass-still
reflecting lakes in the sky:

white-yellow, faint green, translucent blue.

In the Morning
You Always Come Back

Dawn
      at the end of empty roads
breathes with your lips.
Grey light
      your eyes
soft drops of dawn
on the dark hills
Your step
      your breath
like the dawn wind
submerges the houses.
The town shudders
      the stones smell –
you are life;
      awakening.

Fading star in the dawn-light
      creak of wind
first warmth, breath –
      the night gone.

You are the light
      and the morning.

(After Pavese)

Night Letter

Early this year
    I watched most of one night
your image in my mind.

Cloud-rift of pale green
    behind the winter planes
their grey entanglements
    against the dawn.

For a week or two
    the air alive –
common light transfigured.

And so in distant flashes
    your shadow went with me
till summer's end.

Then all lines severed.

Old leaves swayed in a watery sun.
Rain-bearing winds tonight
    sweep them to the ground.

I rake in the dark past:

*

Star over wind-torn moor.
Tattered heather.
Moon-smouldering sky.

*

Against sunrise
a forest of oak birch
beyond gleaming lawns.
Undergrowth glistens.
Chill moss.
Toadstool half-hidden
and lichen on a stump
ruined and overgrown.

*

The caverned face
        of a black stone
my father found
        beside a grass-choked ditch.
He said it must have fallen
        from the sky.

*

The battered woods sough.

Giant trees of childhood
        cataracting
in the wind-flood.

Bright fragments melted
        when it died

*

My friend you made me live again this year
so I send you this handful of old images.

Jumbled and broken,
they shone again
        in the early hours
drawing back to the dull rush of the rain.

Drops shake crinkling leaves
        in the bleak dawn.

Darkness slowly gathers in my mind.

Spring Night

Walking back from you
          near April's end
over petals scurrying like snow
it s your light that has taken
          the live winds.

Remembering an Old Letter

In touch again
          after years
I return to an autumn night
when I sat by a window in Wales
          writing to you

Copper half-moon
          low over valley wood
owl's cry, dim sound of a stream

The vast stillness of the mountains –
          the journeying stars

Soon after dawn
          an orange sun
near where the moon had been
lit frail tops of trees
          above bright mist

Where?

Eyes brown-topaz
  sheer brow
cascading hair

Twigs stir
  by a garden gate
half-shadowed at sunrise

Dim cries
  of winter birds

Autumnal

Between stunted trees
a rutted track
choked with withered leaves.

*

Last March
brown eyes shed love
on a station platform
but by the evening
you were gone.

Your water-colour
in my study –
the wraith of a flower
wafted on blue air...

The recognition came
too late.

Winter

Soon after sunrise
trudging snow
I search for the heron
but the lake is frozen
where we saw him fish.

On his island
black boughs
against a sky
of lead and rose.

Spell

A Sequence For P.

Al poco giorno ed al gran cerchio d'ombra

Dis

I dreamt when our love began
we sat on a common, at dusk.

Heather, bronze-gold.

I was beckoned
but wanted to stay.

You looked aside.

'My name is Dis', he said
'we'll grow to love each other'.

He led me down many stairs.

Love, lie again in my arms.
Lay the dust of that dream.

Five Haikus

(i)

Did you take me
      into the gentleness of your hands
just to shatter?

(ii)

Cool air – a leafy dawn.

I need your pale eyes
to lead me back to light.

(iii)

Behind my eyes
      skeletal boughs
a leaf-strewn forest
      torn by autumn gales.

(iv)

I've been falling
      layer by layer
to the black pit where nothing is.

(v)

In far regions
      too near and void of light
I fear the universe.

Fall

I tried to share my world with you.

It took fire
     toward light and air.

When you withdrew
     it knotted into grief.

Stilled

The rugged, ancient boughs
of your tulip tree
in the deep garden
where we walked.

No more frantic calls
no more blind visits.

I thought we had changed eyes.

Now I send you love
in token of your gentleness
for a few enchanted weeks:

In the waves
your drifting red-brown hair.
Wild woodlands where we strayed.
Under an oak
that thrust in ecstasy
no words can spell.

Memories etched
on a blank London day.

I have had my earthly joy.

Spell

A cirrus wing
        webbed in the dawn wind.

Months since you fled
        pale eyes draw me
through heather, bracken
wind-riven woodlands
        desert places
the wilderness is your domain.

*

Frost-crust fades
        in a later dawn.

Pictures of our brief summer
        go with me

colour air
soft with an inkling of spring.

Slow detritus
        toward oblivion.

*

Elemental
you cannot break this spell.

Dream quest

Dreaming at dawn
I passed a white ruin
to walk through dusky gold
down a deep lane
knowing neither the place
nor the direction.

*

That dream shadows the day.

Journeying far
            I leave flowers
on the threshold
            of an empty cottage.

Then see your dull green car.
You're at the cottage window
            flowers gone.

*

Slant December gold.

We walk down a deep lane.

*

Grey London.
 Your presence
in the holly twigs
you wrenched
to give me.

Gifts

(Bonzai, opals)

I give
        stillness
in this spindly pine.

Stones
        to match colours
in your eyes.

A Little Light . . .

A hillside forest
        moss in tangled light
flickers
        in dark regions of the mind.

Night

Stillness of stone pines.

I clamber crumbling crags
searching for your return.

Coda

Occluded banks
        no grass-blade
nor stir of air

The darkness of time

What can I give you
but embers from the past?

*

In far woods
a room in shade
flood of sunlight outside

Through ruined oaks
            tangled twigs
search for the golden flower

Tracts of bright mist

The tower that shines
        in the sunrise

*

A solitary bird-cry
            before dawn
renews ancient pain

The Return

The Isabella Plantation, Richmond Park

For Margaret
alcun vestigio

You took me to this place
    eight years ago

Now a hurricane since
    from drifts of bluebells
under ancient boughs
    to giant birch
white gold
    their tracery
against blue air
    we walk with our child
in this quietude
    searching again
for a vestige of paradise

Monoceros

And if the stars be but unicorns

In a long drought
      on dusky grass
by a scrub path
      a unicorn
formed in a trace of air

My daughters tells
      of journeying in dreams
to count the stars

Out of the World, Out of Time

Shape shifting
    the cloud-ranges
        voyage

Tree-crests glitter in a late sun

That green-gold light
    those air-drawn forms

I search for a land beyond death
where old loves, familiar things
    are strange and new

Walk

Crossing a long marsh
    beside black pines
I came to a group
    of broken trees
sapless, shell-riven
    on a low plateau
at the limits of a waste of sand

New Fires, Old Fires

A Sequence

Indian Summer

To the north
  beyond the city roofs
White turrets of cloud
  in the soft air

You stir
  sheer colours, lights
  far woods and hills
from remote regions
  in my mind

Autumnal

Western wind, when wilt thou blow...

I part from you
  into sunburst
and gusty shower
  the Western wind of the fall
lit by your sea-green eyes

Early Hours

But nothing save the slippry aire (unhappy man) he caught

I dreamt I almost held you in my arms

Waking to the blank dark
the mind moves
        through trackless woods
into thickets drenched with dawn

April

Red strays of ruined springs

Bird-cries hurt
            this grey morning
in the park

Now you're far over the waters
            in a foreign town
there's magic where we walked
            your presence in the air

*

You've stirred
            loves lost down the years
shadows of ancient pain

Remnants of Fifty Years

(i)

Sunset
    a furnace
beyond heather-brown hills

(ii)
Above a bank
beside that drab branch-line
    in thunder-wind
those leaves were wild
when I walked by the borders
    of another world

(iii)
Wind-cry
and sound of woodland horn –
a shaft of sun
    upon a stuccoed wall

(iv)
Passing Augustan houses
    in a different season
gold cross-lit London rooms
    at ebb of day

(v)
Sounds muffled by sleep
travelled from sunlit distances

In Battersea Park

A Sequence (1957–1994)

The Wilderness Survives

The Old English Garden

In autumn and especially September
we feel the nearness of Erebus
the flowers withering back to earth
and the departure of Proserpine.

*

In this sunken garden
        the birds call
and what they say
        you will never understand
though you imagine
        satyrs in the underbrush
or nymphs dancing
        through the fleckered shade
for even in Battersea Park
        the gods exist.

Mist's Pitch, in Two Seasons

A radiant tract at dawn
where laden twigs
    an hour before the thaw
held stillness
    in each particle of snow.

*

In a later year
    by the wood path
nettles in thundery light
    stir under leaden air.

Note *Mist's Pitch* is a small plateau in a copse that was turned into a nature
reserve by Brian Mist (1937–2002) in 1976.

A Spring

FROM THE WATERS UNDER THE EARTH

The borehole

In today's dream
          by a wooded island
it flows from the realm of the dead.

The sun's disc
          on the dark lake
dazzles and slides.

*

I return one night
to find the spring is stilled.

Full moon
          behind the island trees
a pale filament
          upon the lake's black glass.

Local Epiphanies

Thou shalt not always walk in the sun

Particles of light
      in Battersea Park
where live air moves
      through new leaves

In long grass
dandelion, white nettle, buttercup
      picked by my daughter

She's laid them
      in a 'secret place'
close to a silver birch

Once
   crossing the Albert Bridge
the sunlit wind
      opened a garden

The mind should hold
      moments like these
until
   in the end
from the long dream of the years
      we awake to death

VERSIONS

A Fragment out of Homer

(*Odyssey*, XIII, 96–112)

Between two craggy headlands
sheer to the sea
    a haven
sacred to Phorkys
where ships ride unmoored
safe from the surging breakers

At the harbour's head an olive
    extends its rugged boughs
above the cave of the Naiads' spring

Cool, shadowy light
    the haunt of bees

Jars, bowls, looms of stone

The nymphs weave
    sea-purple webs

The springs never fail

Two gates face the winds:
    the north for mortals
from the south
    only the gods can enter

DANTE

Fortuna

(*Inferno,* VII 73–96)

He whose wisdom transcends everything
   made the heavens and gave them guides
   so that each part to each part shines
equally distributing the light.
   Likewise, for the earth's splendours
   he appointed a general minister – a leader
who shifts vain wealth in season
   from nation to nation, kindred to kindred
   beyond human wit's prevention.
So one people rules, another languishes
   and they obey her judgement
   that's hidden like a snake in the grass.
Your wisdom cannot withstand her:
   she foresees, judges and maintains
   her realm just as the other gods do theirs.
Her permutations know no truce
   – necessity impels her speed –
   as fast as men crowd to their turns.
She is the one most reviled
   even by those who should praise her
   blaming her in twisted, evil words.
But she is in bliss and does not hear them:
   joyful with the other primal beings
   she turns her sphere and tastes her blessedness.

EZRA POUND

Passages from Italian Drafts

from Canto 74

Cunizza, tell your lover[1]
    his song still lives

Sound of the turn of the wave
    I saw only the cocoon
    colour of sun-ray
the sacred silk
    a thread of sun

Above are thrones
    supporting the lotus
where are Buddha and Confucius
    who lived on the earth
    already blessed

Gautama in his eternal dream
and Kung
    of the eternal law
founding enduring dynasties

Above that water forever unsullied

Eternal fountain
    Zenofonte
    Demofonte

the living, the subversives

---

[1] Sordello.

The thrones are two:
    the Indian
in the beauty of his eternal dream
    and the fine actions
the party of Confucius

Down, down run the girls from Ida
gentle spirits of ancient Greece
    Demofonte
who from love's pain
    can never rest

Douz brais e critz[1]
    sing the troubadours
among the birds
    of the eternal forest.

Queen Yrmindrudis[2] knitted
    'the gold thread in the pattern'[3].

---

[1] 'Sweet cries and cracks' (Arnaut Daniel on birdsong).
[2] See 'the queen stitched King Carolus' shirts or whatever/While Engena put greek tags in his excellent verses' (Canto 83). Queen Ermintruda was the wife of Charles the Bald (823–877 A.D.) who made Erigena his court scholar.
[3] I've used this phrase from Canto 116 to translate 'col filo d'oro'.

from Canto 75

The sun, great admiral,
    conducts his fleet
        under our craggy cliffs

Thus Anchises heard
        the girls singing
keening for the dead spring

You who draw near our meadows
    hear the voices
        of the joyful nymphs

Now he grazes our bright plains
gathering the boats of his planets
    to our shores

Blood shed by thousands
        by thousands they fall
in mist and snow

Flakes fall and melt
        melt and fall under April
whom Eurus brings
    or indeed Vulturo
as the Latins say, 'Some time'

. . .

Grazing our coasts
        the wide plain
full of meadows and so many flowers

With joyful songs and words of love

I was called Quintilia (Calvus and Gallus, Lycoris)[1]
this one is Lycoris

He grazes these shores and the wide plain
. . .

Cunizza's light overcame me
        throned
                with shoulders no longer bent
her hair the colour of copper and gold

Then she ascended
        and I saw only the cocoon
colour of light
        colour of sun
. . .

Ave Maris Stella sounds in my ears
        through the evening air
With a branch I saw her
        like Kuanon, with branch of willow.

She took form: the mother of pity
        protectress of the sea
succour in shipwreck
        manifest
seen again always at Prato and Monte Rosa

Fano destroyed
        my refuge at San Pantaleo
from La Dorota
        always an outcast
vaga, invicta Lucina dolentibus

----

[1] See the closing lines of Pound's *Homage to Sextus Propertius*. Poet friends
of Propertius – Cornelus Gallus sang of his girlfriend Lycoris – Licinius
Calvus of Quintilia.

Thus I am lunar
        protectress of cocoons
            humble, enduring

The little boy is my friend
        whom I feed
I am the moon
        I am not Sophia
I even fear her
        hieratic, mosaic'd.

Nor do I know Sophia Hecate
        ever uncrowned
in the high sphere
        hieratic, remote
injured, lacerated,
        an image of terror.

I am the outcast.
        Io, beloved of Jove,
miserable, wandering
        I am called Europa
under the stars of Argos

Under the olives
        that you once saw
my husband dug the earth
        near the olive tree
my new bridegroom.

I sat by the little boy.
        You have seen me
I am not Sophia, I even fear her.

The dogmatic are not my friends
    I am the outcast
not even Artemis is my friend.

The little boy is my friend
    whom I feed.
I am the moon and the milk
Too much explanation
    would be presumptuous
I am also called Pièta.
    My son is dead.
I am the assumption.
. . .

One beautiful December
    the sea bronzed
sun-hammered
    a blinding mirror.

Each soul brings its own heaven
    on which it depends
from which comes its happiness and power
at one with itself and everywhere

The ray of Cythera
    becomes a star
at the point where it converges.

Sun servant of nature.[1]

Cunizza's clear form
    became wrapped
then I saw only the cocoon
    rising slowly like a cloud

---

[1] In English in the original.

moving without fret, without haste
in the azure calm

The more beautiful
the greater the peril

Neschek[1] the serpent
destroyed paradise
such great harm from small talk
and how little truth
in the cries of the damned
making mystery where no mystery is
great darkness where no mystery existed
putting aside fact to spread destruction
to bestow and propagate
poison and pandemonium

Harmony distinguishes
dividing note from note
none losing its quality nor its own being
never blending
but the contrary

Erigena, Dante,
Lorenzo, St. Ambrose
. . .

Lorenzo against violence and cunning

Usury doesn't help commerce
quick profit loses the looms

---

[1] Usury.

Sigismundo not from usury
   nor from money-changing

Our sun in his periplum
Admiral of the planets, servant of nature
   grazes our cliffs
He draws his fleet, his ship over our plateau
crossing the open plain and the rocks
   coming close to our borders
now staying out at sea
   and now nearer

He gathers his fleet to our plateau
the bright plain where we walk singing
   over Gea, now the star of Mars
The blood calls to us, as it is spilled now

You need no explanation from me
   nor do I seek yours

By thousands
   under snow and mist
      men fall and lie.

Note: I chose these passages from Pound's Italian drafts myself. These cantos were written towards the close of the Second World War (1944–5) at a time when it seems Pound intended to write an entire section of *The Cantos* in Italian. My attempt is more in the nature of a homage than a formal translation although I have tried to remain faithful to Pound's Italian and add nothing. My renderings are far from complete – I indicate my omissions by three dots.

Ô Saisons, ô Châteaux

After Rimbaud

Ah seasons, towers at dawn
what spirit is unstained?

I've made a magic joy
no one can destroy

It renews each day
on the crowing of the cock

All striving ceased
I'll need nothing more –

that spell has taken
body and soul

Yet the hour of its flight alas
will be the hour of death

Ah seasons, towers at dawn

CESARE PAVESE

Sei La Terra E La Morte

You are earth and death.
Your season is darkness
and silence. No living thing
is more remote from the dawn.

When you seem to wake
it is only pain
in your eyes and blood
but you don't feel it. You live
as a stone lives,
as the hard earth.
You are wrapped in dreams,
movements, spasms of weeping,
which you ignore. Sorrow
like lake-water
trembles and surrounds you.
Rings on the water.
You let them fade.
You are earth and death.

ANTONIO COLINAS

Four Poems

Balafia

The enemies of radiant poverty
have filled every road of the island
with crosses and saints' names
turning their blood into merchandise.

But here Balafia still preserves
its beautiful Arab name.
In the farmyard cocks crow
under climbing vines and pomegranates
and the pigeons and stone of the old tower
defeat the black age of dogmas.
To be a man is to walk
noticing the sweat of the olive field
recently worked –
your solitude sweetened
by the scent of the locust tree:
between necessary labour, inexorable fate.

The friend of the fisherman
could be born again in
Balafia.

Encounter with Ezra Pound

you have to go on a Sunday evening
when Venice dies a little less,
despite the solitary children,
the half-ruined rosy walls,
the acid gardens' shadows,
you have to look for him
although he may not talk to you
(you'll forget that the sea
behind your back will drown
the islands, the churches, the palaces,
the most beautiful cupolas on earth,
don't let the sea
nor its sirens charm you)
remember: *Fondamenta Cabala,*
somewhere there's a glazier from Murano
and a café with the sweetest music,
ask in the pensione named Cici
where the American lives,
stiff and with snowy beard,
who came to Venice
mainly for its people,
then cross the stone bridge
beside puddles, gulls and black cats,
there, next to the canal of green waters,
full of orange blossom and rotten fruit,
you'll hear Vivaldi's violins,
stop and be silent while you look:
Ramo Corte Querina, that's the name,
in that side street with flowerpots
and no exit but death,
lives Ezra Pound.

Autumnal

Deep in the forest, the owl's call
empties the night, empties the world.
A river of stars flows between trunks
over the river bed of shadow
and the locust tree's overpowering scent
     kindles our blood.

Silence, only a black silence
follows the inhuman panic
     of the owl's cry.
Drawn by the journeying stars
     night after night

The vast silence
     and emptiness of the world.

Deep in the forest the owl's call
is an invisible thread
     binding divine and human.

It is death flowing
     in the river of wisdom
wisdom flowing in the river of death.

Lake Trasimeno

... 16,000 romani perirono
malgrado i presagi funesti

You shone for a moment
    in the dank, thundery dusk
like a flash of green lightning
    over the dripping gloom
of the olive wood
    cold emerald under black light

JONATHAN BARKER

William Cookson, *Vestiges & Versions: 1955–2002*, Agenda Editions, £8

Certain men move in phantasmagoria; the images of their gods,
whole countrysides, stretches of hill land and forest, travel with them.
Ezra Pound, *Selected Prose*

The first epigraph to William Cookson's collected poems, re-printed shortly before his too early death, provides us with a key which enables us to read some of them better. These are the poems of a man with a very wide literary frame of reference and for whom the classics were a part of his imaginative landscape. In his poems we recognise two worlds: the actual physical world we all inhabit but we also glimpse a personal Arcadian landscape too. Sometimes the sense of Arcadia is provided through memories of childhood or of love; at other times through moments near to Wordsworth's 'spots of time' when the veil of reality goes and wherein 'our minds/Are nourished and invisibly repaired'. Cookson certainly had a strong Wordsworthian sense of the wonder, the 'glory and the dream', the 'visionary dreariness' which lies just beneath the surface of everyday reality. So the phantasmagoria, the image of the god Pan, the countryside of Arcadia, hill land and forest indeed travel with Cookson and appear in his poems. But the sense of Arcadia is not a retreat from an unpleasant everyday reality; it is the opposite – an attempt to reach a deeper sense of reality within the human consciousness, as the painter Henri Rousseau's painting 'The Walk in the Forest' – a copy of which hung in Cookson's home – is both an actual portrait of a woman alone in a forest and a symbolist vision of a mental state too. But this world is not like that of, say, Edgar Allan Poe's poems in which a specific dream world is consciously constructed.

Rather, Cookson meditates on fragments of memories, which seem to enable him to connect up different parts of a past self with a present self, or to reconnect an emotion in the present with one from the past. Cookson's poems express a strong dream-like atmosphere where images connect with a tangential dream logic, which recreates a sense of mystery heavy with emotion. It is essentially also a poetry meditating on the past, or of several pasts – both a personal past consisting of memories – and a literary historical sense too.

The sequence 'Dream Traces' has haunted me since I read it in Roland John's Hippopotamus Press edition of 1975. At first reading it can appear slight, even wistful, but this is in fact a poetry of integrity and depth:

Ancient sadness

Rumours of the death of Pan

Wept on the forest moss
    in the dawn

Cookson refers in his notes and acknowledgements to Walter De La Mare's poem 'They Told Me' first published in 1906 as 'Tears', a poem in which:

They told me Pan was dead, but I
Oft marvelled who it was that sang
Down the green valleys languidly...

De la Mare's poem ends:

But even where the primrose sets
  The seal of her pale loveliness,
I found amid the violets
  Tears of an antique bitterness.

Cookson's reference to the poem changes 'antique bitterness' into 'Ancient sadness' and evokes a sadness inherent in the heart and memory of man. The assumption is that Cookson can also hear Pan playing on his pipes perhaps the 'still, sad music of humanity'. The sequence is made up of individual poems interlinked by feeling:

Journeying back
    to a remote place
I've come past two spruce firs
    over heather
And a tract of wild grass
    to the edge of a wood
where three silver birches
    sprung from a single root
gleam in the Winter dusk

This poem brings a mood to life but with imagistic precision. The memory seems specific and actual, as shown by those 'three silver birches', yet it has the intense brooding colours of a dream too. This is fine writing in the sometimes melancholy English meditative line wherein the past informs the present of a place, linking the Anglo-Saxon 'The Wanderer' to George Herbert, Alfred Tennyson's 'Mariana', Thomas Hardy and Edward Thomas.

The verse is cleanly expressed with few words. Stylistically it is clear that Cookson learnt a great deal from the Imagists yet his reference in 'Dream Traces' is to a Georgian poet, thereby connecting the styles of the two leading movements of the early part of the previous century.

Memory is a strong theme, both as a type of racial memory of 'Ancient sadness' and as a personal memory of an event or a dream as in the 'Three poems of Childhood'

Those mounds of luminous grey
    in the north-east sky
Recall a recurrent dream:

A house with towers
    above a twilit valley
Where soft grass gleamed
    buried in the blue mist

A meaning is not stated; rather the poem attempts to create
an emotion through specific images. These dream images
were perhaps a way for Cookson to make contact with an
older Arcadian world which he felt existed beneath the
scenes of the everyday world around us and also perhaps with
a part of himself which was out of reach during his waking
life. The dreamer is left with 'dream traces' or 'vestiges' on
waking. The dream randomly allows connectedness with
'Ancient sadness' or 'Roots of old pain'. These are poems of
strong emotions. The poem 'Dream Quest' further enables
the writer to find himself, but through finding himself lost:

Dreaming at dawn
I passed a white ruin
to walk through dusky gold
down a deep lane
knowing neither the place
nor the direction.

The mood here is of meditative reverie nearest in feeling,
perhaps, to that handful of visionary poems by D G Rossetti
including 'Sudden Light' and 'The Woodspurge', in which
memory and a mysterious present come together.

Elsewhere in 'Dream Traces' we find:

But the landscape you first saw in a dream
    we suddenly found.
That sloping wood
    half-lit by a low sun
lives now in my mind
as it survived in yours from a child.

This is a poetry in which trees are a constant source of reference. The sounds of trees, the religious feeling which trees can inspire as they did in old Cretan religion, the groves of the Greeks who saw trees as holy, the oak, the laurel, the plane, the myrtle of old Greece.

Distant thunder today
The great trees
    beyond the pane
stir
    in the dream wind.

or:

In far woods
a room in shade
flood of sunlight outside

Through ruined oaks
    tangled twigs
search for the golden flower

We have literary precedents in the 'dark forest' of the opening of Dante's Inferno and the religious awe of trees in the opening and closing lines of Ezra Pound's very early poem collected in *Personae*, 'The Tree':

I stood still and was a tree amid the wood,
Knowing the truth of things unseen before;
Of Daphne and the laurel bow . . .
. . . Nathless I have been a tree amid the wood
And many a new thing understood
That was rank folly to my head before.

I certainly remember a conversation with Cookson where he
stressed to me his feeling – a sense I have always felt – that
trees were living spiritual presences. So Cookson's poems are
informed by a number of highly unfashionable and strongly
held convictions. We are told by rationalists that the god Pan
is dead yet we hear his pipe music in the movement of the
leaves on trees. We have a sense of another good place,
Arcadia, and where trees are inhabited by benevolent spirits.
There is a danger here, perhaps, that I might appear to be
presenting Cookson as a person with cranky ideas; far from it
– his feet were firmly on the ground – but I am presenting
him, I hope, as a man with a profound imaginative response
to the world. We live in a rational and sceptical age which
doubts our spiritual insights, but Cookson is insistent that a
sense of wonder should be preserved as Blake and Coleridge
preserved a sense of imaginative wonder in an earlier
rational age. No good asking Blake if the angels he saw were
'real' or De la Mare if Pan really was playing his pipes; both
live within the imaginative spiritual world of these writers.
Cookson was a great admirer of C H Sisson's poem 'In Flood'
(first published in Agenda) a poem linking a sense of a
specific place to the figures of the Arthurian court as they
exist in Malory's poem:

There is the winter sunshine over the water,
The spirits everywhere, myself here.

Do you know it? It is Arthur's territory

Agravaine, Mordred, Guenivere and Igraine –
Do you hear them? Or see them in the distant sparkle?
Likely not, but they are there all the same.

William Cookson lived in a roomy flat near to the Thames
and across the road from Battersea Park. To him this park
was to provide another link to a personal Arcadia, as in the
sequence 'In Battersea Park'. In these poems Battersea Park
itself is to form a key part of his sense of Arcadia in a poem
which predates 'In Flood' and reflects its concerns with the
mythologised past existing in the present:

In this sunken garden
        the birds call
and what they say
        you will never understand
though you imagine
        satyrs in the underbrush
or nymphs dancing
        through the fleckered shade
for even in Battersea Park
        the gods exist.

A late poem, 'Local Epiphanies', looks at Battersea Park as a
blessed place valued in the memory, which provides a
doorway to a deeper reality. In fact here Cookson agrees with
Lewis Carroll – another favourite author – that life might be
a dream and death might just perhaps be another life:

The mind should hold
        moments like these
until
    in the end
from the long dream of the years
        we awake to death

Some readers will see this as a pessimistic comment, but I see in it an optimistic view of life, wherein the Wordsworthian 'spots of time' become 'local epiphanies' perhaps opening out onto a glimpse of a personal Arcadia. Given this, the 'Ancient sadness' is, in fact, one half of the story and its opposite is the Joy in William Blake's lines from 'Auguries of Innocence':

It is right it should be so
Man was made for Joy and Woe
And when this we rightly know
Thro the World we safely go.

I have referred to the poet throughout as Cookson, but to me he was actually William, a friend of twenty-five years, a fellow lover of Swinburne and hot mustard, a lover of beauty and a man of a rare generosity of spirit.

W S MILNE

William Cookson, *Vestiges & Versions,*
(Agenda Editions, £8)

As might be expected from a long-time devotee of Ezra Pound's work, the influence of the American poet is evident in a number of the poems in William Cookson's *Vestiges: 1955–1996* (Poets and Painters Press, 1996). The name of the press itself is significant, as many of these poems possess a 'painterly' quality, but although the images in particular are like this, the structure of the book overall is sculptural; coloration is important to Cookson, the gods of the natural world – sun, moon, trees, wind, light, flowers – these are his gods of colour. Pound's influence is noticeable in terms of open acknowledgment through quotation (mainly in the form of epigraphs, both from Pound's poetry and prose) and, less obviously perhaps, through a tone of 'gentleness and quietude' maintained throughout the book, qualities hymned or praised in 'Dedication for Margaret', the voice that poetry makes in the air:

Remember
        reading these lines
for distant loves
        your gentleness
and quietude
        bind me to you . . .

The re-working of phrases from Cookson's favourite authors, including Dante, Malory, Pound, Ovid, Shakespeare, Ibsen, Strindberg, de la Mare and Keats, also indicates the hand of the American master. The first epigraph (from Pound's 1917 review of Marianne Moore and Mina Loy's work) seems to

97

signpost Cookson's preference, or predilection, for imagism, and an anticipation that the poet will be moving in a landscape of 'phantasmagoria', not taking refuge in scenery for its own sake but as a foregrounding for the human condition. A full reading of the book proves this to be so. The use of space and light on the page, with the complete avoidance of commas, semi-colons and colons and any form of halting punctuation hints at a working method associated with Elizabethan printed poetry where attention is often concentrated on the openness to experience (the music of the language, not the stops of the mind, as in Sir Walter Raleigh's 'As you came from the holy land of Walsinghame', one of William's favourite poems) rather than a limiting 'caging' of it (paradoxically, you might say, given that a good deal of it was written behind bars!) In any case, I know that Cookson thought such an approach better 'captured' the mind's torsions, and I think his argument is vindicated in the reader's experience of this volume. At the heart of the method then (if that is the correct word, carrying as it does unintended connotations of rigidity, the last thing one associates with Cookson's poetry) is the image and music (melopoeia), the rhythm and consciousness of the awakened mind, concisely portrayed:

I tried to share my world with you.

It took fire
    toward light and air.

When you withdrew
    it knotted into grief.

The title *Vestiges* is again from Pound (openly acknowledged – see also Basil Bunting's poem of the same title, although on quite a different theme) – vestiges/traces/wraiths/dreams/distant flashes/remnants/shadows/

fragments 'jumbled and broken'/detritus/evanescent 'air-drawn forms' – these are the bundles of apperceptions that hold the artist's imagination, particularly in his use of the definite adjective, e.g. 'late sun', 'blue waste', an internal landscape of memory and forgetting, of vistas and tracts, distances, precise description, and a dream quality as in the late work of Strindberg or Bergman (two of William's favourite artists):

When you entered my sleep, I saw
     a long tract of water, glass-still
reflecting lakes in the sky:

white-yellow, faint green, translucent blue...

The poetic background to this spareness of description is to be found in the likes of Wordsworth's 'the round earth and the blue sky', Dante's 'dove il sol tace' ('where the sun is silent') and 'l'aura morta' ('the dead air'):

Dawn
     at the end of empty roads
breathes with your lips.
Grey light
     your eyes
soft drops of dawn
on the dark hills...

You are the light
  · and the morning...

Time's physical burden weighs the poet down, the gravity of 'the encrustation of the years', 'a sky of lead and rose', loss and recovery, fear, panic, 'roots of old pain', these are the perceptions 'storied' through the image and the grace of the artistic endeavour, contrasting with all that is 'jagged' and 'war-riven':

Ancient sadness

Wept on the forest moss
in the dawn...

In this sunken garden
the birds call
and what they say
you will never understand
though you imagine
satyrs in the underbrush
or nymphs dancing
through the fleckered shade...

It is this sort of strange (or mystical, if you like) experience, an intuition that the gods 'are just around the corner' somehow but at the same time so distantly removed from humankind, feelings that move 'beyond the horizon of the mind' to widen the field of speculation, that holds Cookson's imagination in *Vestiges*:

The borehole

In today's dream
by a wooded island
it flows from the realm of the dead.

The sun's disc
on the dark lake
dazzles and slides...

Cookson's verse is full of feeling and emotion, then, of that which is fully living, 'life-awakening', 'the air alive', 'common light transfigured', this last phrase being poetry's 'purpose', if again that is not too categorical a word for the intellectual process described. The main driving force of the book is love:

You are earth and death.
Your season is darkness
and silence. No living thing
is more remote from the dawn . . .
You are earth and death . . .

The battered woods sough.

Great trees of childhood
          cataracting
in the wind-flood.

Bright fragments melted
          when it died...

with, at times, a surreal quality, dream-like, involved, as in Donne's poetry:

The rugged, ancient boughs
of your tulip tree
in the deep garden
where we walked.

No more frantic calls
no more blind visits.

I thought we had changed eyes...

The shifting perspectives of the book enable the poet to incorporate his deep sense of awe in the presence of life (and at times the 'vestiges' left by the departing gods) with an equal sense of intellectual proportion and artistic tact:

Sequoia
    storied
        into timeless blue . . .

Boles red gold in a late sun.

A place far back

That avenue ended in a blue waste . . .

So it is that the Greek gods, Dis, Erebus, Prosperpine, come to the fore at times in poems with an unparaphraseable quality which the best poetry often possesses, although the 'black pit' of despair, 'the darkness of time', overwhelms the poet's sense of grace intermittently:

In autumn and especially September
we feel the nearness of Erebus
the flowers withering back to earth
and the departure of Proserpine . . .

I have had my earthly joy . . .

A sense of love helps us to interpret the data of the natural world in a more understanding light, and the intellectual ground for this is a 'searching again for a vestige of paradise', straining, as Keats has it, at 'particles of light':

A radiant tract at dawn
where laden twigs
    an hour before the thaw
held stillness
    in each particle of snow.

Many of the poems are situated at dawn, when the
dichotomies of presence and absence, light and dark, come
into play, and poetry's gift of lighting the mind overcomes, if
only temporarily, life's 'entanglements', its 'ancient pain':

Dreaming at dawn
I passed a white ruin
to walk through dusky gold
down a deep lane
knowing neither the place
nor the direction.

The dream shadows the day ...

    Poetry for Cookson is like alchemy, sharing in a similar
'search for the golden flower', 'the tower that shines in the
sunrise':

I search for a land beyond death
    where old loves, familiar things
        are strange and new...

Elemental
you cannot break this spell ...

There is little point in writing poetry if you are not
attempting to do something new or different, and I feel that
Cookson is extending novel frontiers here, following
experience to its limits, to the abyss, to the precipice of

103

being, 'the borders of another world', 'remote regions in my mind':

'My name is Dis', he said
'we'll grow to love each other'.

He led me down many stairs.

Love, lie again in my arms.
Lay the dust of that dream.

The volume is one poem really in which the right epithet, the right word for the intellectual concept, always seems to be correctly in place:

Did you take me
        into the gentleness of your hands
just to shatter?

You are the light
        and the morning...

If Cookson's poetry can be said to have a credo, then it would be 'Imagism Updated'; his precise and definite language works, in Pound's words, 'to find new beauty in natural things', to escape metaphysical terms and concentrate on the here-and-now, the apprehensible, transitory world, 'to describe the actual sensation with intensity'. Adjectives of pure or comparative quality, plain but eloquently stated phrasing, a glorying in the quotidian, vivid colouring, no conceding to received opinion – these qualities all combine to create a distinctive and clear poetic voice:

Gifts

(Bonsai, opals)

I give
    stillness
in this spindly pine.

Stones
    to match colours
in your eyes.

Each poem for Cookson is a 'fresh splendour' in which 'the ancient sound' of the gods is heard echoing; a place where 'words of praise arise, like flowers'. Here we can find (if we look closely enough, and with confidence) 'a trace of the fugitive gods', and we 'who must live in their absence' find 'eternal clearness' and 'patience, hope and quietness' in 'the holy hours, the days' of their vestiges:

You took me to this place
    eight years ago . . .
Against blue air
    we walk with our child
in this quietude
    searching again
for a vestige of paradise . . .

My daughter tells
    of journeying in dreams
to count the stars . . .

There is a dimension of stillness in *Vestiges* which is rare today, and an alertness to colour perspectives of a subtler sort, fusing, tempering and shaping experience to a sharp outline:

I wake to find you gone.

An undercurrent of sound:
wind in the great planes,
brings peace.

At six
I watch their dusky green
tossing against a rain-grey dawn.

As for structure, as Pound has written, 'Form may delight by
its symmetry or by its aptness' and I would say this is certainly
true of *Vestiges* in which we find not only Pound's desiderata
of accuracy of thought, graceful learning and poetry's
'dynamic particles', but also that acute apprehension of God
as 'an eternal state of mind':

Once
        crossing the Albert Bridge
the sunlit wind
                opened a garden

The mind should hold
                moments like these
until
        in the end
from the long dream of the years
                we awake to death...

William was very fond of the sayings of Richard of St. Victor
as translated by Pound (see his *Ezra Pound: Selected Prose 1909-
1965*, Faber, 1973, pp.73–75), particularly his 'The essence of
religion is the present tense', 'To love is to perceive', 'Who
composes words, as the heart dictates', 'Happy who can
gather the heart's fragmentations into unity' and 'Without

good intention, the mind dies'. These *aperçus* are as good a guide to a reading of his poetry as any critical analysis of the content. Not only in his editing of *Agenda*, but also in his poetry, one finds the establishment of William Cookson's true self, his repeated avowals of faith in poetry as a gift and as a task. To read this book again is to discover that William Cookson was a craftsman of the subjective lyric discovering tranquillity and quietus in the midst of a hectic, busy and generous editorial life.

Young William

Margaret and William Cookson on their wedding day

Early reviews by William Cookson

July 1957 (from *The Trifler*)
Section: Rock -Drill

A note

*' To replace the marble goddess on her pedestal at Terracina is worth
any metaphysical argument.'*

In 1942, Mr. Pound wrote in one of his *Six Money Pamphlets,*
in many respects his most important collection of essays: 'For
forty years I have schooled myself ... to write an epic poem
which begins 'in the dark forest', crosses the Purgatory of
human error and ends in the light "*fra i maestri di color che
sanno*". ' The latest instalment of the *Cantos, Section: Rock-Drill
85–95 de los cantares* was first published in Italy in 1953.

The new *Cantos* can be divided into two parts: 85–89 are
historical, didactic; 90–95 is an immense lyric, the first time
that the great tradition of the 'undivided light' of Erigena,
Avicenna, Dante and Richard of St. Victor has found
expression in the English language. These two parts inter-
inanimate each other. It is consequently impossible to
understand one without the other; 85–95 provide a historical
basis for 90–95.

There is more Chinese than in previous cantos, especially
in 85 ('the basic principles of government') and the
ideograms act as an important means of creating the general
effect of irradiation which pervades *Rock-Drill.* In fact, there is
much appeal to the eye; more than with any other poet,
beauty is conveyed by the layout of the words on the page.
Much of the metre, especially in 86 and 87, is almost bumpy
as each fact of the argument is rammed home, and there is a
new precision different from anything we find in earlier
cantos. It is, of course, impossible to enumerate the themes

109

of the first half of *Rock-Drill* but they deal chiefly with the 'two forces in history: one that divides, shatters and kills, and one that contemplates the unity of the mystery' which is best summed up by the phrase:

'Bellum cano perenne . . .
　　　. . . between the usurer and
　　any man who wants to do a good job'

followed by Mr. Pound's definition of usury:

'without regard to production –
　　　　　　　　　　a charge
　for the use of money or credit.'

The importance of the *Money Pamphlets* in explanation of the political, historical and economic thought contained in these cantos cannot be overstressed; they and the *Guide to Kulchur* (for the earlier parts of the work) are the essential companion volumes. *Rock-Drill* taken with the *Pamphlets* contains all Mr. Pound's conclusions now that his long economic studies are completed. Earlier passages in the *Cantos* which had caused confusion in the past are clarified, the account of Van Buren and the Bank War is seen in the light of Thomas Hart Benton's great speech against the renewal of the U.S. Bank Charter here summarised in 88. 85 enables us to appreciate the China Cantos (52–60) to a finer degree. It is no longer possible, as so many critics have done, to dismiss the Adams cantos as 'dull'. Thus the whole of the poem is coming into shape, showing a massive construction which it was not possible to perceive, even from the Pisan Cantos. Incidentally, this latest volume, as is only right, is more carefully constructed than any previous one; it also introduces us to some very important, though neglected, works of literature, which has always been a major function

110

of the *Cantos*; some of these are: Thomas Hart Benton: *The Thirty Year's View*, Alexander Del Mar: (i) *Barbara Villiers* or a *History of Monetary Crimes*, (ii) *Roman and Muslim Moneys*, and Philostratus: *Life of Appollonius of Tyana*.

Mr. Denis Goacher, in his interview with Ezra Pound published in the winter number of *Nimbus* quotes Mr. Pound as saying that 'it takes fifty years for a man to write poetry, most of 'em give up long before then. Very few people work hard enough – poets least of all'. He himself did not start writing his epic until he was thirty and he has now been at work on it for over forty years. He began writing the most difficult part of the work, the 'Paradiso' (it is almost impossible not to become involved in analogies with Dante) amid all the ruin of the war, in the *Pisan Cantos*. 'To build the city of Dioce, whose terraces are the colour of stars' (Canto 74), and much of his finest poetry can be found in this volume and *Rock-Drill*. It is very different from the lyricism of *A Draft of Thirty Cantos*, which were written between 1916 and 1930. Some of the old themes are taken up. For instance, John Heydon, 'servant of God and secretary of Nature', who first appeared in the rejected *Three Cantos* published in 1917, now plays a prominent part:

'monumenta in Nature are signatures
    needing no verbal tradition,
oak leaf never plain leaf.' John Heydon (Canto 87)

The whole of Mr. Pound's 'Paradiso', as in the case of Dante, coheres in a way in which, intentionally, the earlier portions of the poem did not. It is, though far from complete, much more of a whole than anything that the author has written previously; and this is because these cantos grow out of the highest use of the intellect, 'contemplatio' as defined by Richard of St. Victor in *Benjamin Major*. Beginning in Canto 90 we are in what Mr.

111

Pound once called 'the radiant world where one thought cuts through another with clean edge, a world of moving energies ... magnetisms that take form or that border the visible...' or in the words of Richardus: 'contemplation, guided by a ray of vision, sheds light over numberless things.' Thus innumerable themes are formed in the mind 'to remain there resurgent': the sea caves out of whose green depths rise the eyes of Aphrodite, which are the same colour as the holly leaf that St. Hilary may have looked at, 'manifest and not abstract'; first the crystal river and then the sapphire of divine contemplation over which the Princess Ra-Set voyages, which is the same as that of the blue serpent that 'glides from the rock pool'; what Mr. Hugh Kenner calls the 'now permanent sea ... that contains and requires all orderly movement'; the fountain of Castalia; the invocation to Diana (compare Canto 30); Odysseus who moves through Canto 94 in the form of Apollonius of Tyana, and thus the raising of the spirits of the dead, now with incense and myrrh: 'It was not by ditch digging and sheeps' guts'; the *terzo cielo* to set down a few of the themes which taking light from each other 'build' this now coherent 'permanent' sea ('crystal waves weaving together towards the gt/healing') with its roots extending through the poem from the beginning and by the birth of Venus, *Dea liberatis*, gives form, 'which is both orderly and free' to the whole work.

June 1960 *Editorial*

Attempts to define poetry lead nowhere but certain things often forgotten can be restated.

Poetry (and all the arts for that matter) and religion are one and the same thing.

Poetry is a science: it is the fundamental science on which, in an ideal state of the world, all the other sciences would be based because it is the instrument that makes language precise: the history of poetry shows how language has been purified by the poets into a condition capable of defining their successive discoveries.

In our day, poetry in England has shown an increasing lack of awareness of the poet's responsibilities; indigenous English poetry has made no progress since the nineties; nearly all the great poetry in English has been written by Americans, Irish and Scots while the English have remained amateur and provincial. There has been little of really creative value in *English* poetry since the continuous excellence of Hardy's collected edition.

What is needed urgently in the nineteen-sixties, is for the discoveries of the great poets of the twentieth century to be built upon scientifically and it is to this that *Agenda*, in its new form, exists. Current literary periodicals and the book review pages of our leading newspapers present us with a complete absence of literary values: witness the recent consideration, in feature articles, of Mr Priestley's views on 'Literature and Western Man' and the overestimation of the poetry of Mr Robert Graves while a re-issue of Wyndham Lewis' *One Way Song*, the only satirical poem of importance that this century has produced, is received with general disapproval.

The poet is the most responsible member of the community; poetry is concerned with facts, details, emotions, every side of human activity: history, theology, science, the mysteries, economics, politics: the poet handles the sum of human knowledge as a scientist handles significant data and by defining his perceptions of these things with ever greater precision, the field of human understanding is widened: language becomes a subtler instrument of communication, intelligence is made active, but if poetry ceases to be con-cerned with things of vital importance, or, as has happened in England, becomes the domain of amateurs and of no possible significance to anything, everything declines, and disintegrates.

Reviews are useless unless they point to books of importance and get them read. We shall only mention work of really creative value in these articles: that is, the few books that it is essential that those actively interested in poetry should read that have appeared in the last two or three years.

The important recent literary event has been the publication of Ezra Pound's new Cantos *Thrones*. It is Mr Pound's most considerable historical achievement. These are some of the most lucid Cantos that he has written and it is by their *lucidity* that they have a paradisal effect on the mind'. As there has hitherto been no 'Paradiso' in English poetry (after the signal failure of Milton) there is nothing in English with which to compare these Cantos and the preceding twenty: the language has here been made to do things which it has never done before or seemed capable of doing. The detailed examination of historical evidence (there are major historical discoveries in *Thrones*) makes most poetry seem the work of amateurs.

Ronald Duncan, in his introduction to *Rochester* (one of the finest literary essays of the century) traces the decline of the love poem by quotations from Rochester, Wordsworth and Tennyson (in that order) and his new volume of poems *The Solitudes* marks the end of that decline and the rebirth of the form with a vitality that has not been seen since Rochester. A revival of verse as *song* in English, this is really creative work, one of the few books that stand out from all the tide of rubbish that passes for poetry in this country: the most exciting new volume by an English poet anyway since the war.

William Carlos Williams' *Paterson Five* is an advance in the art of poetry generally (which it illuminates in every line) and of vers libre in particular. All those interested in poetry should possess it.

Thomas Cole's *A World of Saints* has an excellence and beauty that makes it one of the best small books of poems of this century.

The most serious poetic achievement by a poet under forty has been Alan Neame's translation of Jean Cocteau's *Leoun,* first published in Noel Stock's *Edge* (the most vital periodical of the 1950s). It will come to be recognized as one of the great English translations that comprise some of the finest poems in the language.

Castle Wynd Printers, Edinburgh are to be congratulated on reprinting most of Hugh MacDiarmid's poetry in cheap editions. Younger poets have a lot to learn from MacDiarmid whose greatest contribution to literature has been his vision of internationalism rooted in locality and nationalism. The provincialism of modern English poets has been caused not by too much sense of locality but by too little.

September–October 1961 *Editorial*

In a magazine mainly concerned with the publication of poetry, all that an editorial can do is to put forward a few ideas that may be of use to poets writing in England and America today.

We have already noted, in an earlier issue, that religion and the arts are one and the same thing; it is when attempts are made to divide them that they both forfeit their true nature and meaning; then, religion may become perverted into a negative upholder of conventional 'morality' and the arts may cease to have anything but the most marginal and amateur significance, as is the case with the greater part of poetry published in this country today.

In the moral sphere, both poetry and the church should concern themselves to a more active degree with economic justice and all things related to it.

The most essential element in the arts and religion is myth, or the many stranded tradition that has gone to create what David Jones describes as the 'Western Christian *res*' and the poet would do well to incorporate in his work, as Hugh

115

MacDiarmid has done in the poem we publish at the beginning of this issue, some aspects of these living roots of the civilization of these islands.

The Centaur Press announces a reprint, in October, of Arthur Golding's translation of Ovid's *Metamorphoses*. This is an important event; apart from it being one of the great translations that have done so much to enrich the English language, it is one of the most complete sources of the Western pre-Christian mythological tradition and, in this connection, we might note the words of Thaddeus Zielinski in his essay *The Sybil:* 'We find in ancient religion the genuine Old Testament of our Christianity.'

But we are not dealing only with a Western tradition. In 'The Great Trade Route' Ford Madox Ford wrote: 'The great will, as we have adumbrated, is an afflatus that runs over the regions of the earth, manifesting itself at rare intervals, for one or several reasons, influencing humanity for several lustres or for several centuries and slowly or swiftly exhausting itself on the extreme limits of the world.' And, in another sentence: 'or, of Christ, who, like their own Confucius, gathered together their traditions that still remained on a ruined road, and made them into a per-durable book.'

In an age when things have a tendency to 'fall apart', it is one of the poet's tasks precisely to gather, not to exclude, but to reconcile, all the traditions of this 'great will' that together, stretching from China to America, make up civilization, the art of living and great works of art and to restore, to quote Ford again, 'the cult of joy and rhythm'.

February–March 1962 *Editorial*

Nothing has been produced in poetry since 1920 that is coherent with contemporary sensibility other than by poets who reached their maturity at about that date and each successive group since (apart from isolated exceptions) has fallen into the category of dilution and deterioration. The weakness of the thirties is now apparent while the forties and fifties with their cliques of minor versifiers have made nothing worthy of the name of poetry.

If a further decline is not to take place in the sixties, a thorough study and rethinking of the great poetic movement of the first quarter of this century will have to come about in the context of the 'living whole of all the poetry that has ever been written.' 'Tradition is growth' as Professor Hugh Kenner has recently written, or, to quote a well-known essay of Mr Eliot: 'The historical sense compels a man to write not merely with his own generation in his bones. but with a feeling that the whole of the literature of Europe from Homer and within it the whole of the literature of his own country has simultaneous existence and composes a simultaneous order.'

One facet of this tradition that has received inadequate attention recently is the relation that ought to exist between poetry and music; perhaps the reason that so much contemporary poetry is mediocre is because many poets are unaware that such a relationship exists. The publication of an excellent study: *Ezra Pound and Music* by Murray Schafer the *Canadian* should be read by all those interested in writing poetry today. The divorce of poetry from music, although it was liberating to the latter, was, in most respects, detrimental to poetry. To see what was lost it is only necessary to compare English lyrics written at the time when poets and musicians worked in close collaboration with lyrics written at a later date by poets uninterested in music. An important event in 1962 will be the performance in the spring by the B.B.C. of Mr Pound's opera 'Villon', a work which is analysed at length in Mr Schafer's essay.

Many of the technical advances started by Ezra Pound ('absolute rhythm' and 'great bass' for example) were

117

conceived because he was also a musician. If a poetry is to be written that is not mere retrogression, but truly belongs to the second half of the twentieth century, it will be by poets who are involved and not out of touch with music. As Mr Pound has said: 'It is not intelligent to ignore the fact that both in Greece and Provence the poetry attained its highest rhythmic and metrical brilliance at times when the arts of verse and music were most closely knit together, when each thing done by the poet had some definite musical urge or necessity bound up within it.'

March–April 1963

Poetry, even epic, in this century at any rate, is particular and personal, generalizations don't fit it and reviews are only useful if they get people to buy and read it. If the poems are good they will express adequately what the comments of a critic merely weaken and dilute. Peter Dale's *Walk from the House* is such a book. Its quality can best be shown by the title poem . . . This is a poetry of actuality. It would not be possible to express this more directly, or in any other way. The form is not forced on to the words. but they, and the experience, are *of* the form. That the rhyme is so often on a noun, rather than on a preposition or an adverb, goes to illustrate this. The tone of voice belongs to no-one else.

Not all the poems are up to this standard. There is a certain limitation of theme. Some of the shorter lyrics, though competent, are insignificant. At least five, and two of these are of considerable length, are of achievement, not promise. The finest, like *Just Visiting* (a patient in hospital) are accurate renderings, free from metaphorical para-phernalia, of a unique experience, a moment of meditation, or to quote Rilke, 'not feelings I have had, but things felt' . . .

The positive qualities that Dale shows himself to possess in such poems are an ability to fix experiences permanently in

118

words that are unalterably part of them, without twisting any facet for the words' sake, understanding of people – not only himself (one of the best things here is a dramatic monologue of a middle-aged surgeon), and the power to control complex metrical patterns throughout nine or ten stanzas with rhythmic variations not only in single lines but half way through a line; on the negative side, it is evident that he does not know much about music, and, in consequence, his rhythms at times show too great a degree of uniformity of tone. None of these poems would find themselves in music.

The pamphlet is technically interesting throughout. 'Technique is the test of sincerity' and a new technique comes into being when a poet has something to say that will not fit the already existing idioms and forms. A lot has been written, most of it true, to the effect that the English have failed to utilize the advances made by American poets nearly fifty years ago. There has been a return to more or less regular, often iambic metre, and the natural speech and variety of rhythm made possible by *vers libre* has been largely ignored. The central prosodic quality of *Walk from the House* is freedom within form. We have here classic English stanza forms, notably those of Chaucer and Spenser, used in an uniambic way with natural rhythms and contemporary syntax: ... *Unaddressed Letter* is the finest poem in this little book. As an Elegy and a Letter it is deeply moving ... it has the lucidity and simplicity of an experience recorded with complete integrity of style. Unlike most recent work, one is certain that this poem *had* to be written and that ought to be sufficient comment. Incidentally, it exemplifies, *within a strict form*, in almost every particular, Ezra Pound's three requirements for good poetry. As they are short, and seem frequently to be ignored now, it may be worth quoting them again in full: '1. Direct treatment of the "thing" whether subjective or objective. 2. To use absolutely no word that does not contribute to the presentation. 3. As regarding rhythm:

119

to compose in the sequence of the musical phrase, not in sequence of a metronome.' With Dale's poetry we would have to substitute 'spoken' for 'musical phrase'

The type of rhyme used in much of *Walk from the House* was invented or re-established by Wilfred Owen and is sometimes known as pararhyme. There is little point in making a detailed metrical analysis, but it is worth noting that this bears no relation to the various forms of assonance that are so in vogue today. Its chief advantage is that its strictness tends to remain concealed.

But all this technical achievement would be as straw if these were not genuine poems, the best stand the acid test that, once read, they remain in the mind, and when re-read they do not bore, but gain in strength. How seldom could it have been possible to say this of poetry written at any time in the last or present decade? Of the subject matter, let it suffice that the writer has contrived to identify himself with human suffering and he has been able to write of it with consummate ease and without affront.

Bunting issue, Spring 1978

Editorial

This issue is intended to mark the publication of Basil Bunting's *Collected Poems.*
Criticism is most worthwhile if it leads readers to its subject and is then forgotten. Bunting's poetry has greater variety and scope than is often realised.
'Only emotion endures.' Basil Bunting is one of the few English poets of the twentieth century who has written durable pages. His finest work has a hardness and wit, a unity of sound and sense, and a quality which is perhaps best defined by Coleridge's phrase, 'more than usual emotion, more than usual order.'

September 1960 *Editorial*

It is the function of poetry to enable the potentialities of the brain to be realised to an ever greater extent. Vital thought which is the substance of poetry derives from the external world of phenomena, particulars and facts.
The poet in finding truth must, to use the language of Lord Herbert of Cherbury *(translated 1937* – a book that anyone learning to write poetry should possess), 'bring the faculties into conformity with their objects.' As Lord Herbert demonstrated, we have innumerable faculties (most of them in a state of disuse), each corresponding to some facet of external reality; the poet should see that these faculties do not become dulled and bring as many new ones into use as possible. 'There are as many faculties as there are differences of things and vice versa'.
This is the kind of poetry that Hugh MacDiarmid has written in his 'In Memoriam James Joyce' and no work of comparable importance has been produced in the British

Isles in recent years. As MacDiarmid says in this poem:

'There lie hidden in language elements that effectively
  combined
Can utterly change the nature of man.'

Our education system, and through this every sphere of human activity, is today directed towards preventing people using more than a fraction of their mental potentialities, while they are constantly desensitized by clichés emanating from most public means of communication. Unless a gradual decline in human intelligence is to come about, poetry will have to take a more significant place in human society as the most effective means of awakening human beings out of their present deluded condition. Any poem that achieves definition of an emotion or idea to some extent sensitizes the mind to some aspect of reality of which it has previously been unaware.

It is one of the tasks of poetry to affirm the existence of paradise.

KATHLEEN RAINE

In Praise of William

What was it that for me made William so special? What made him such a fine editor of a poetry review, and so discriminating a publisher? The 'literary world' is full to overflowing with writers, one or two good ones, many mediocre. William wrote some graceful poems, but essentially he was a reader. I have the impression that in my time there have been more writers than significant readers of literature, and that to be a gifted reader is a rarer talent, at least in the present state of culture. Yet there have to be readers as well as writers in order to sustain civilization. They are not always the same people, although we tend to suppose that good writers are likely to be discerning readers. On the contrary, perhaps writers are the least likely to be concerned with the work of others. William was, I think, the most gifted reader I have ever known. And this makes me ask myself, what makes a good reader?

A good knowledge of literature past and present is of course essential. This is a matter of education, but even more it is a matter of love. Not all who have read Homer or Shakespeare, or Ezra Pound derive pleasure or wisdom from having done so. William certainly received the best possible education at school and at Oxford, but self-education is the best of all. William described his discovery of Pound as being like falling in love. He had an amazing gift of imaginative empathy. How many readers of Martin Hammond's translation of the *Odyssey* have read it six times with increasing pleasure at each reading? How many of us have managed to read Pound's *Cantos* from beginning to end, even once? I myself have started many times with enthusiasm but never read them from beginning to end, still less with the insight and appeciation that made William one of Pound's few total readers. In a lesser degree he certainly brought to the reading of manuscripts for *Agenda* a generous openness and expectation of some degree of pleasure, or at least expected to find the glass half full, and not half empty. After all, even the worst poems must have originated in some experience of living delight, and unless there are readers open to receiving that delight, there can be no shared culture and civilization dries up.

Literary criticism is too often arid and censorious, treating the writer rather as a prisoner on trial than as the bringer of a gift. William's delight in the beauty of a work was his contribution to civilisation, to keeping alive experience of a certain kind and quality, at the highest level. 'Beauty' is a word seldom used in the discussion of the arts, for in this materialist civilisation it is a value not quantifiable. Truth and Goodness, Plato's other two verities, can at least to some small degree be quantified, but Beauty not at all. It is therefore deemed valueless, or unreal, in terms of current standards of evaluation. And yet Beauty has from time immemorial been the measure of all the arts, not least poetry. I see Beauty as the divine *imprimatur*, indeed the divine signature itself, but of course a civilization that denies divinity knows nothing of such a value.

Solzhenitsyn, speaking at Harvard in 1987, four years after coming to the West from the Soviet Union, passed his judgement on Western values as being no better than those of the Soviet East and for the same reason: the absence of a spiritual dimension. Atheism in the USSR was an article of faith, but in the West 'the calamity of a despiritualised and irreligious humanistic consciousness' and 'an atmosphere of moral mediocrity paralysing man's noblest impulses.'

Of these noblest impulses Beauty is surely a necessary measure, and whereas from time immemorial and, from the humblest crafts to the highest vision, Beauty has been the mark of all the arts, the twentieth century has sunk into a joyless and beautiless state of mind all but universally prevalent.

William had a natural and unerring sense of that Beauty whose verity, like Truth and Goodness, has, in all civilisations before our own, been held to be self-evident. He did not talk about it, but it seems to me to be always present in his evaluations. Just before his death, William had reproduced in *Agenda Editions* a reprint of Laurence Binyon's fine translation of Dante's *Divine Comedy*.

For what William has stood for, and achieved in his work, I am deeply grateful.

Drawn by William

Howard, William and Edmund

EDMUND GRAY

Recollections of friendship with the youthful Poundian

I first met William at Westminster School in the autumn term of 1952 – his first term, my second. We were in the same day-boy house (Wren's) and met at lunch, which we shared with the Queen's scholars in College Hall, the late medieval chamber originally built as the dining hall of the abbots of Westminster. Already quite tall and strongly built, his florid countenance, curly hair, pink cheeks and ready smile still gave him something of the cherubic appearance of his childhood photographs. He was in a different form from me, and shy, as he always remained, but we were free to sit where we liked at the table for our year, and he soon came to sit next to Howard Burns and myself, who were already lunchtime companions, being in the same 'A' stream. We were all dissidents from the predominant sporty philistinism of our thirteen-year-old contemporaries – in return mildly derided by many of them (in defensive parlance) as 'pseudo-intellectuals'. William differed from other boys additionally in his innocence, even naivety, which in some ways was lifelong, attributable in part to an isolated early childhood and to the liberal regime at his excellent prep school, The Hall, Hampstead. He was also not of conventional academic ability, hence his assignment to the 'C' stream.

Our conversation was not always on a very high level. Early on, I used sometimes to pose general knowledge questions to the other two – such as: 'What were the capitals of ancient Egypt?' William was not good at giving answers to these, but one day came back at me with the question: 'Who was Bjørnstjerne Bjørnson?' This put me in my place. I hadn't the least idea. We weren't above a bit of levity either. Later,

127

for instance, we devised a comical mock-doctrine of 'Itism', chiefly elaborated by Howard, I think (but possibly originating in my grandfather Laurence Binyon's reference to philosophers puzzling over the 'very itness of the it' in his play *Sophro the Wise*). I fancy we worked this up as a contribution to the house magazine.

The three of us at first shared no other school activities. William's sport was rowing – at which, if he'd bothered, he could have shone. He once caused a sensation in the annual sculling race by almost beating some top oarsman. All three of us must briefly have been in the school cadet corps, but after the minimum period I left for the Scouts and William was wisely released to study in the library. However, we regularly met during the mid-morning break for conversation, as we strolled round Little Dean's Yard or sat on the bench in one corner, generally with me in the middle, as I was somewhat the link between the other two, and tended to take the lead, at least initially. Quite soon I was often going to tea with William at the flat in the small mansion block overlooking Battersea Park and the Thames, where he lived with his mother Rachel. She gave me a warm welcome. A complete contrast to him in appearance, she was small and very sparely built, with a pale, bespectacled face, delicate features and rounded brow. Though now apparently frail, she must have had considerable wiry strength, since she had taken William on her bicycle twice a day to and from his first school six miles away. She had been a fine pianist, but had given up playing, perhaps after a serious illness she had suffered. I remember her talking of Beethoven's late quartets as the supreme musical profundity. Also welcoming was the smallish, coarse-haired and very mongrel dog Jack – who had fits. He used to accompany William and me on walks in the park.

The bay window of the front room looked across the road into the plane trees of the park. Books and quiet watercolours lined the walls of this room and the dining room through an archway beyond it. They were furnished with good, well-worn old furniture, including a chair inherited from Wordsworth, whose mother was a Cookson. Down the long corridor was the small kitchen with glass-fronted dresser, free-standing cooker and fridge, a geyser that supplied the flat with hot water and small balcony for the dustbin. Rachel was rather a good cook, though no great devotee of hygiene, and a little later earned money for a time by cooking for a well-to-do cousin.

Sometimes William and I would walk to Battersea from Westminster rather than waiting interminably for the rare 39 bus or taking the underground to South Kensington and walking from there. In those days he had a ferocious stride which reminded me of the nursery-rhyme character who walked so fast that gunpowder came from his heels. We also walked in the City, sometimes all three of us. I had long been fascinated by its historic churches, many then still standing as gutted ruins or in the midst of a blitzed wilderness, carpeted with wild flowers and seemingly unvisited by others. There was the allure of Lower Thames Street too, still with the scents of spices, furs and other exotic produce wafting from the warehouses. Memorably, we walked along the muddy black shore of the Thames below Blackfriars Bridge beneath the gaunt, romantic hulks of burnt-out wharves. Thirty years too soon I fancied taking up residence in one of those instead of boring Kensington. I took photos on a primitive box camera; later William celebrated the billowing smoke from the newly built Bankside Power Station in a poem.

He was fond too of Lots Road Power Station, especially as seen from Albert Bridge, its steep gable clasped by its four tall chimneys silhouetted against the glow of sunset – a subject he painted more than once. He made fascinating ink and watercolour drawings – highly romantic, in the spirit of Samuel Palmer's Shoreham period, which we both admired, though entirely in his own manner; always landscapes, as I recollect, of a magic complexity and usually back lit. He could well have gone on to be a fine painter.

His background, however, was literary, and his lifelong adherence to all that he knew and loved of that background steered him in a literary direction. His mother was also a powerful influence holding him to his background. Her life was focused almost exclusively on her only son, whom, as I gradually realised, she came to treat almost as a second husband. She had married the much older George Cookson, who had taught at Dartmouth Naval College and became one of H.M. Schools Inspectors. He also wrote two books of poetry ('published in Swinburne's lifetime', as William put it) and from 1936 was the founding editor of *English*, the magazine of the English Association. Rachel foreshadowed William in tending to live within a narrow range of a familiar world, and it was no doubt more than chance that she returned to London from a very rural part of Surrey to rent a flat in the very same block she and her husband had lived in before the Second World War. She also steered William towards the same life of editing (and teaching) as her husband.

William, however, was to strike out a much bolder literary path than his father. Ezra Pound, who was to be all-important in William's life, together with most of the other moderns, did not figure in his background, though he was fed a precocious literary diet in his childhood. He had no playmates in the isolated Limpsfield home in the woody heathlands of Surrey, but was read to by his parents: writers such as Dickens but also, I think, the great Russian novelists. At Westminster, aged 13 and 14, like me, he was reading Eliot, a poet who had, I think, an immediate resonance with both of us.

My grandfather, Laurence Binyon, the poet and curator at the British Museum, was a link with William and his mother from an early point. Both our families had been friends of William Pye and his family, who lived in Limpsfield until 1933. My grandfather had known the Pyes since 1893 and, before his marriage, was 'virtually adopted into this family, frequently staying with them and joining in musical evenings, poetry games and amateur dramatics.' Along with Thomas Sturge Moore, the two friends founded the Literary Theatre Club, dedicated to verse drama performed without scenery in a chanting, formalised style of which Yeats, another member of the circle, was a proponent. My grandfather's *Paris and Oenone* was an early production, with Sybil Pye as Oenone. Sybil Pye went on, under the influence of Ricketts, to become one of the great twentieth-century bookbinders, while Ethel was a sculptor. It was to the wider grouping of poets, artists, designers and musicians to which my grandfather belonged that Ezra Pound quickly gravitated on his arrival in London in 1908. From the prison camp at Pisa Pound was to look back nostalgically at what he called the 'B.M. era' and to gatherings of this circle at the Vienna Café close to the museum – at one of which my grandfather introduced him to Wyndham Lewis.

Very likely Pound's correspondence with my grandfather in the 1930s about his ongoing translation of Dante (published in the *Selected Letters* of 1950) came up in the manifold conversations I had with William, though I don't think I had read any of Pound's poetry before William bought a copy of *A Selection of Poems* 'probably early in 1955'. His commitment to Pound was almost immediate. A letter to me, dated September 7, 1955, starts by explaining, with quotations, how I have misunderstood Pound's *Odes of Confucius* – they were not folk songs but 'solid philosophy' and 'religion': 'so much for your ignorance'. It ends with a 'Pound Anthology' on a separate foolscap sheet, which consists of two examples of 'The Perfect Lyric': seventeen lines from Canto LXXIX, beginning 'O lynx, guard this orchard' and fifteen lines from Ode 23, beginning 'Lies a

131

dead deer on yonder plain'. He concludes by saying 'that is all I am going to give you save for 2 line[s] in which [Pound] sums up the whole situation of his internment in the D.T.C. at Pisa very movingly. The time [of] year was November. They are the close to all the Cantos so far written:

> 'If the hoar frost grip thy tent
> Thou wilt give thanks when night is spent'

At the bottom of the page, in bold capitals, William scribbled: 'REREAD THESE FRAGMENTS AND THEN READ MORE' [heavily underlined].

In the autumn of 1955 he gave or sent me a typed manifesto 'to teach yew verse.' Like Pound, he found that 'spellllingg wrong with a tipryter is more phunn than wif a penne' – but I will spare the reader this (and the capitalisation) in the following excerpts from these rules for writing poetry:

'I. Learn a few good poems ... II. No unnecessary words. Language as spoken. Forget Milton. No distortion of natural word order. Try and translate from good French poetry i.e. Rimbaud etc ... III. Regular metre. Don't use vers libre as 'a running dahn the road' ... Discipline ... 'Be influenced by as many great artists at one and the same time'. To be derivative is far, far, far, far better than to be original at start ... IIII. Don't ever be facile [quadruple underlining] ... IX. Try all difficult verse forms ... Sapphics good exercise i.e. examining thin syllabisation.' X. Dante, Ovid, Homer, Shakespeare, Cavalcanti, Pound, Odes, Sophocles (approved play), Villon, Daniel, Ibsen, Erigena????? etc. ... As ground to all intelligent study: Confucius.'

In December William followed up these rules with the injunction 'if you do try to write anything, remember: precise definition of inarticulate thoughts; it is the golden rule for really good work'. In the same letter he quoted Pound

132

disparaging Milton in favour of Dante, and also urged a visit to the current production of *The Wild Duck.* 'If you ever write plays, Ibsen is supreme, with, if you want verse, *Trachiniae*, but not Eliot. . .'

His commitment to Pound by no means curtailed his strong, existing enthusiasm for Ibsen, Strindberg, Chekhov and Hauptmann. He even laboriously began to translate one of Strindberg's plays of which no English version was available, from a German translation – encouraged by Dr H.F. Garten, a heavily academic German refugee, author of a study of Hauptmann and a somewhat improbable member of the Westminster staff. This was in spite of poor ability at languages. (He just managed French at O Level, but not German.) He strongly berated me for championing Shaw against Ibsen, showing his superior literary judgement, though I still value having been immersed in Shaw when very young as an influence towards independent-minded rationality – not a quality prized by William, whose cast of mind was independent in a quite different way.

This letter exemplifies William's abiding approach to the critical exposition of poetry very largely through quotation. As he says in the body of the letter, 'Neither Eliot nor Pound will bear analysis, nor will any poet for that matter ... Reading through study, getting by heart are the only methods of enjoying poetry. I got rid of Espey's book on Mauberley – it was a sort of analysis, mainly study of influences ... I didn't want to possess it.' It says much about him that he had himself the remarkable ability to have a poem by heart after a mere two readings. The way his mind was thus stocked with a huge range of literature, was just one aspect of a mental world that was quite different from most people in our modern rationalistic world. Like some other highly imaginative people, there always remained something childlike about him.

The instructional and well-nigh hectoring tone of many of

his early letters (which echoes that of Pound) does not reflect what was in fact a warmly amicable relationship, but had some counterpart in my letters to him: for instance, urging him to take an interest in the Bauhaus or to visit the Mondrian exhibition of 1955 at the Whitechapel Art Gallery, on which he replied on September 3, 1955: 'You will be pleased to hear that my mother and I have been reconciled to Abstract Art. I'm at the moment trying the catalogue cover up in my room, it's to look at one – rather than a lot. One must be progressive in all the arts (including Architecture); up to now I've been slow to see this.'

One admiration of mine which I passed on to William was for David Jones, who from 1929 had been a friend both of my mother and of Helen Sutherland, the patron of artists, poets and musicians with whom I stayed as a child of five for six months during the war. Her way of life in her house on the Lakeland fells was one of exquisite perfection, surrounded by a host of modern pictures, many by David Jones. He was also familiar in person from the time of his weekly supper visits to my parents in the mid 1940s and, as an author, from the Third Programme broadcasts of his *Anathemata*.

I took William to see David when we were both sixteen and they quickly took to one another. On January 7 1956, perhaps shortly afterwards, he wrote assuring me that he was buying the *Anathemata*, reciprocating my undertaking to buy the *Cantos*.

By now William, Howard Burns and I were together in the first year of the history side at Westminster. Oddly for a high-powered school, the history for that year was taught by a clapped-out cricket-lover whose lessons were well-nigh useless, while the highly intellectual history specialist Charles Keeley took us through a course of political theory in an endeavour to make sophisticates out of us. He encouraged Howard Burns on his way to his distinguished career as a scholar (in due course Director of the Instituto Palladiano in

134

Vicenza); William and I were less suited to his regime and were both recalcitrant pupils with ideas and methods of our own. In his essays, William set forth the Poundian view on every theorist. Keeley tried to wean him away from this tendency by mockery. ('Crikey!' was a favourite marginal comment.) It has to be added that both William and I were somewhat idle.

Quite at variance with our own abilities, along with Howard, we had a high-minded notion that the ideal education would consist of Latin, Greek, Chinese and Mathematics, but this was a bit tongue in cheek at least as far as I was concerned.

The three of us decided that we would like to revive the school literary magazine, *The Trifler*, which had temporarily lapsed. This plan was complicated by a similar plan by a group of partly more senior boys. In the subsequent manoeuvrings William's name in the list of editors was excluded (as was my somewhat ambitious theory of art and politics compressed into a couple of pages), but his 'Portrait, with a plea for the revival of the verse drama' took its place. The 'Portrait' consisted of 'fragments' of an intended longer work and was Canto-like in form, replete with literary references. Howard wrote a very erudite and intelligent editorial entitled 'The creed of unbelief' (too negative for William).

I was taken away from Westminster a year early by my parents and sent to Munich University as a preparation for training as an architect, but William and I corresponded quite frequently and often at some length. A topic of heated dissension was the Suez crisis, on which William was very pro-Nasser and I initially could not believe that Eden was lying over collusion with Israel. (When his perfidy became apparent, I took the view that he should be impeached.) On other matters we were in agreement. We both deplored the demolition of the Imperial Institute (except for the tower) and the planned demolition of Albert Bridge – just as back in 1954 we had been upset by the London County Council's wanton destruction of Holland House, which had been grievously damaged by fire in the war but the main rooms of which were all substantially intact. Characteristically, William was probably as much saddened by its park being tidied up for its opening to the public – he had delighted in its previous wild state.

From November 1956 onwards, William reported on the efforts being made to secure Pound's release from St Elizabeth's Hospital for the insane in Washington. He attended the London committee working to this end, and commented on the apparent reluctance of Eliot to put his full weight behind the campaign. He was also making friends with another campaigner, Peter Russell, the poet, editor of the noted literary magazine *Nine* and publisher of Pound's *Money Pamphlets*.

It was probably at about this time that he wrote two or three reviews for *Time and Tide*, through the good offices of Theodora Bosanquet, a friend of his mother and a director of the magazine (and once Henry James' emanuensis). Quite a coup for a mere schoolboy!

In June 1957 he wrote that he was 'busy reading Hugh MacDiarmid (the greatest living poet after Ezra). He is the *only* Communist poet and his communism is *good* – he's a Scottish nationalist, with a deep hatred of the English ... He works for setting up red gov't in Scotland, Ireland and Cornwall. The sad state of this country is no better shown than by the ABSOLUTE dearth of any great literary man this century. Wyndham Lewis was the *only* great English writer and now that he is dead there is NO-ONE. Much life in Scotland: Tom Scott, Sydney Goodsir Smith, etc, MacD all writing best work in Broad Scotch.' Later in the same letter he qualified his admiration: 'MAC D is very silly about religion. I have come upon the statement that 'Calvinism is just as good as any other religion' which displeases me a lot. However, he knows an immense amount and has a breadth of intellectual vision equalled only by E.P.'

By now William was in correspondence with Pound, having first written to him in 1955 (when he had been sent a copy of a Poundian newsletter by way of response); but it was his review in *The Trifler* of July 1957 of Pound's *Rock-Drill* which evidently unleashed the real flow of letters from the master over the next three years (a selection being reproduced in the 21st Anniversary *Agenda* of 1980). Pound praised it as the 'best rev/ of Rock-Dr I have seen since Stock's' – and indeed it is a very mature piece of work. He was more in control of *The Trifler* this time. There were two poems by him (one a sonnet), two poems by his mother and two by Peter Russell, and the cover was adorned with the *ling* (sensibility) ideogram. Howard Burns contributed two poems (one also a sonnet) and once again wrote an erudite editorial, on the problems facing the young writer.

Pound's letters were often so telegrammatic that William must have had difficulty decoding them. He was intent on galvanising groups into propagating his ideas, particularly on economics, integral for him with the creation of good literature. Books were prescribed for reading and names and addresses of fellow activists or sympathisers given, including Moelwyn Merchant, Marshall McLuhan, Patricia Graecon ('at my old Address 10 Church Walk, W.8.'), Vanni Scheiwiller, Basil Bunting, Henry Swabey, Gladys Byng, McNair Wilson, Roger Sharrock, William Buckley, Eva Hesse, Hugh Kenner and Jean Descoullayes. He was pleased to think that William was friends with a grandson of Binyon and often wrote of me (usually as 'Binbinides', or some variation thereof) in the expectation that together we might be the nucleus of a group. In his conspiratorial way, he even suggested to William that: 'BinBunius might let you ghost-write under his umbrageous name', forgetting that my name was not actually Binyon and

137

anyhow that it was hardly still one to conjure with. Typical too was his injunction 'Let's see what you and BinBinius can do as manifesto/½ sheet of paper. Principles and/or definitions.' As I was largely unsympathetic, when not simply mystified, by his political and economic ideas, his expectations were misplaced, though I probably adhered to common ground in the slight correspondence I had with him myself.

We were urged to visit General J.F.C. Fuller in Hampshire and actually did together visit the less distant Admiral Domville, an amiable old buffer who did not obtrude his far-right views, as far as I recollect. Rereading William's letters to me, I am surprised to find how much he reflected Pound's notions about the evils of Roosevelt, the role of Jews and so forth. With the optimism of youth, I suppose I thought these absurdities would melt away with persuasion and more knowledge.

Early in 1958 Howard Burns, William and I planned an Italian journey, largely in pursuit of Renaissance architecture. Pound suggested people we ought to meet, including Olivia Agresti, daughter of Rossetti's brother William (and I did indeed make at least one desperate, and vain, phone call in Rome). William's mother, however, proved to be adamant that William should not be of the party – the first intimation I had of how intensely possessive she was of him.

In May 1958 Pound was at last released, and returned to Italy, and in the autumn William, with his mother, got to Italy too, on a three-week visit which included one week at Brunnenburg, the castle in the Italian Tyrol where Pound had come to live with his daughter and son-in-law. William has explained in the *Agenda Anthology* how the idea for the magazine 'grew from this visit'; but the encouragement of his mother was crucial too, showing the positive side of her personality. William has recorded that it was Peter Russell who gave the final impetus and introduced him to the printers Czeslaw and Krystyna Bednarczyk. Their Poets' and

Painters' Press, under the railway arches close to the Festival Hall, was mainly dedicated to Polish publications. They matched William in benevolence, unworldliness, commitment to poetry, loyalty and conservatism. They were also very patient about late payment. They printed *Agenda* till they retired in 1991, using linotype machines that even in 1959 must have been obsolete, but could at least cheaply cannibalise linotype machines discarded by others. As the name implies, these machines set each line of text as a bar (which had to be wholly replaced to make a correction). It was typical of William to like the way linotype printing made an indentation in the paper that could be felt. With a similar feeling for the physicality of things, his first act on picking up a book was generally to smell it.

The first twelve issues of *Agenda*, appearing (approximately) monthly, consisted merely of a folded sheet, like the periodical *Strike* which Pound had sent William in 1955 or *Four Pages*, another Poundian feuilleton, whose name Pound wished William to take over. William demurred, having some inkling of expanding beyond that size, though his first issue did declare itself a 'revival of the publication originally known as *Four Pages*.' It was *Edge*, the Poundian magazine edited in Australia by Noel Stock, which probably provided the closest model for *Agenda*, the title for which translates as 'Things needing to be done': indicating a similar propagandist aim.

Pound was ghost-writer of much of the first six issues, including most of the first editorial. William had the sense to cut or improve on some of the Poundian obscurities and side-swipes in this, though he left in a reference to a Continental group 'run by kindly (but wholly illiterate) old ladies', which he could not have realised was a reference – as my mother assured me – to Margherite Caetani's celebrated *Botteghe Oscure*, a journal which published such writers as Rilke, Brecht, Dylan Thomas and Lampedusa. More significantly, William also added a commendation of MacDiarmid and David Jones.

For the most part, Pound's contributions were what he himself aptly termed 'oddments' when feeding them to *Edge*: supposedly illuminating nuggets of fact or observation. One of the two contributions he initialed was the one-liner 'How can anyone go anti-Semite in a world that contains Danny Kaye?'

Peter Russell contributed the only poem in the first issue, a four-line 'adaptation' of Mandelstam. There was also a short piece by Swabey on the 'loss of the great English heritage of personal freedom' and a longer one headed 'From "Rivarol" 6th November 1958', consisting of a series of quotations (mainly from Pius XII) and other 'oddments' pointing towards Pound's idiosyncratic views on World War II and economics. This was perhaps from Stock.

I certainly protested at the crackpot nature of the last piece; but I should have resigned straightaway from the position of Associate Editor into which I had been coralled, perhaps partly to please Pound. I don't recollect having any significant input – certainly not to the first issue. (In this I was not to be unique among those named on *Agenda* as Assistant Editor or the like). I was no doubt gratified to be able to contribute (completely non-Poundian) articles such as one on 'Planning today' in the second issue. A surviving letter from William of March 24 1959 about another possible contribution from me casts light on my position: 'Nowadays the most vital & urgent matter is the problem of money & its issue. Any political statement which ignores something which has been responsible for 2 World Wars in ½ a century cannot be of first importance', and though he was 'in complete agreement with the principles' of my piece and was not rejecting it, he said he had 'more urgent' items to put in issue 3, such as one 'on Education', which I fear I was unable to send you before press', which he assured me would not 'arouse your disapproval'. My piece was never included.

When more nonsense, as I saw it, about World War II was due to appear, I did resign. This did not significantly affect my friendship with William, but along with more general shortcomings, paradoxically it did bring down Pound's wrath on him: 'O.K. stop *Agenda* with no.4 or 5', he wrote on April 19, 'You will have learnt some of the difficulties of editing. Esp/ having lost BinBunides.

The difficulty of holding ANY group together.
Put yr/self definitely under Stock's orders,
IF he will have you.'
Though he apparently withdrew this command, three letters later he wrote: 'You have missed the point in letter of a couple of months ago. (1) The USE of a 4 page leaflet is to get over ideas unprintable elsewhere ... (2) to form a group. You went into reverse and lost the BINbinides instead of finding a third man.' Poor William! Pound didn't grasp my insignificance for *Agenda* – or that it was precisely the 'unprintable' content that had led me to resign, even though I had written to him on my reasons.

Issues 4 and 5 were indeed largely given over to Noel Stock's further 'unprintable' exposition of the causes of World War II – specifying, above all, Roosevelt and 'organised Jewry'. What is interesting, however, is that thereafter, far from adhering closely to the twofold aims set for it by Pound, *Agenda* moved in the opposite direction – towards the kind of poetry magazine it remained to the end of his life: strongly Poundian and never repudiating his economic and political ideas but abstaining from mention of them in their wilder forms. I am not entirely clear what underlay this change. I understood at the time that Pound himself had told William to eschew politics, but no such instruction figures in the selection of letters published in *Agenda*, though it is true that Pound ceased to send any more 'oddments' after issue no. 6. That, however, may have been due to ill-health.

141

No 9 consisted of poetry alone and issue 10 stated: 'We shall be publishing a greater amount of poetry than previously, which indicates a change of method which can be summarised by restating the principle that creative work is the most valid form of criticism.' This issue was the first with a card cover, thanks to a £10 gift from the actress Virginia Maskell.

William's arrival as an undergraduate at Oxford in October 1960 may have been one factor in the change in *Agenda*. Like Howard Burns, he left Westminster in December 1957, but was delayed for two years, during which time he earned money at Harrods and in the British Museum library. This was because, although accepted by New College, he repeatedly failed to pass O Level maths, required by the university. He eventually qualified by passing the university's own Responsions in the subject, which he discovered he could take more frequently than O Level. This was the last vestige of the medieval oral exam, which had been modernised to equate with O Level. I don't know how often he sat it; but one can't help suspecting that the authorities eventually passed him regardless of performance. It was abolished shortly afterwards.

His mother warmly encouraged his efforts to get to Oxford, where I had arrived in 1959 (having switched from architecture); and his father had left money in trust which paid for New College, as it had for Westminster. William was tutored by John Buxton and by John Bayley – with whom he soon struck up a rapport. Not unlike in character, one was nearly as likely as the other to miss the time of a tutorial. By his second year William was ensconced in a curious old room which we found together, next to the college gateway, with an off-centre window overlooking the cloister and bell-tower. Films were his chief recreation, especially Bergman and Cocteau (with a soft spot for Doris Day too); but at weekends he always had to return to his mother, whose ailments and

142

accidents (some, I suspected, self-contrived) also often required his presence.

Oxford was probably one influence in shifting *Agenda* away from cranky politics, because William was now brought into proximity to rival poetry magazines – and also met other poets. One was the footloose Michael O'Higgins, who early in 1961 introduced him to his erstwhile fellow worker at the Radcliffe Infirmary, Peter Dale (who was now at St Peter's College); another was Michael Alexander (of Trinity College). All three became involved with *Agenda*, O'Higgins as Associate Editor of three issues (from February to October 1962), the other two for the duration, Peter as long-serving co-editor. I suppose the subscribers were also broadening out from what must have been at first a narrow circle of Poundian zealots, though the very first issue – or news of it – elicited a subscription (and order for the *Money Pamphlets*) from none other than Stravinsky, who even offered to write for *Agenda*, if he had time.

By this time Pound seems to have suffered at least an intermittent loss of confidence in his beliefs: 'Wrong, wrong, wrong I've always been wrong', he was remembered as saying in late 1961. His health was also beginning to fail. By the end of 1961 he began to lapse into prolonged silences. *Agenda* must have been affected by all this, if only by a cessation of guidance from the master.

In any event new ground was broken by the double issue for December-January 1960–61. It was entirely devoted to Alan Neame's translation of the poem *Leoun* by Cocteau, who drew a special cover for it: very effective and a considerable coup for William. There followed an issue with another article by Noel Stock, on Poundian economics (covering seven of the eight pages), but that was the last of the 'unprintable' and the last from Stock, save for a short poem in the next issue. Most of this issue instead pointed to the future character of *Agenda*. The editorial was on poetry and

143

music and it included the first contributions from Peter Dale and Michael Alexander: short poems from each and a review by the latter. It was also the first issue with the masthead lettering designed for William by David Jones, an indication of their growing friendship.

The editorial of the following issue confirmed the intention of *Agenda* to be 'mainly concerned with the publication of poetry.' By then I was in Italy, teaching for a year, so correspondence replaced conversation. On December 5, 1962 William told me he had roughed out an editorial partly from a draft by Peter Dale and Wally Kaufman, an American (though in the event there was no editorial). He confessed he was 'distracted' by the heaviest snow in London since 1881 when he wrote on January 2: 'I always get obsessed by snow and like it very much'; but his editorial ruthlessness was displayed in his response to a review he had got John Bayley to write on Peter Levi's poems. This was approved, except for 'the astonishing statement that his "favourite poets of the present date are Stevie Smith and John Betjeman" ... I hope I have not offended him by sending it back for emendation and removal of offending statements.' Quite a high-handed way to treat your tutor! It says something about John Bayley that such treatment did not dent his warmth towards William or *Agenda*, for which he served as Trustee for two decades from 1982, when trust status became desirable to obtain grants.

In the same letter William says that 'Beowulf is occasionally attended to, but, as always, I am failing to work as I should. I am slowly copying the poem into a large book with word for word translation underneath. . . '

On February 25 1963 he sent the now published *Agenda* with a double-underlined request for comments. Though he hardly trumpeted his achievement, this was a historic issue, with the first publication anywhere of Canto CXI and the first publication of David Jones's 'Tutelar of the place', only previously published in America. The issue also contained the review by Bayley, duly modified, and a long review by William of the poems of Dale and others. He ended the letter by noting, no doubt with satisfaction, that 'The cold continues. Water in New College frozen again.'

William received my response to the issue 'with great pleasure ... I'm sure no-one else has read the issue with such care ... Your general comments are of great interest to me as I have been thinking a lot about the matters you mention. I think I shall produce a long article for the first issue of Volume 3 (after schools) in which I shall try to clarify my own ideas about the position of poetry today.' Later he says 'Dale's having absconded is depressing, but he finds he approves more of policy of *Review* ... only serious competitor with *Agenda* in literary magazine field in England.' Peter's desertion was fortunately temporary.

Notable items in other issues of the Oxford years were poems by Ronald Duncan, Peter Wigham, William Carlos Williams, MacDiarmid, Tomlinson, C.H. Sisson, Peter Levi – and an article on Lewis by Howard Burns.

Agenda work made big inroads into William's time, no help in performing well in 'Schools' (the final exams on which Oxford degrees are awarded). He lamented in a letter written half way through these that 'I do not shine in examinations. I find it hard enough to write coherent sentences anyway and when there is no possibility of going over them and rewriting, nonsense is apt to be all that comes. I am too slow ... The worst paper is yet to come, A4, Philology. I have done almost no work for this ... I got up at 5 two mornings to revise and with late nights I was astonished not to be more tired. It shows how much work one could do! President Nasser works 16 hours a day I understand. Anita brought me lunch in my room two of the days...' (Anita Auden was another Oxford friend, whom I originally introduced to William and who was later to do much for *Agenda*.)

His final observation about the exam was: 'I think my answers have been very eccentric, on reflection'. All in all, therefore, he cannot have been too surprised at the Third he was to be awarded.

At this point he had 'No plans for jobs as yet.' It was tutoring that was to provide an income over the next twenty years, especially for Queen's Gate Tutors in the later 60s and early 70s. *Agenda*, however, was always his real job; he never sought a career. There was also never any question of his setting up home separately from his mother; his intense liking of the familiar would alone have militated against such a move and the ancestral books and furniture were shared with his mother. She gave him moral support, but this was the obverse side of her battening on him. She had made no effort to make new friends for herself as the few friends of her husband's generation died off and she had virtually no independent life of her own. As William later confessed, she was intensely hostile to actual or potential girlfriends – and he was too loyal and habit-bound to break free, at least for many years. She also had a drink problem (which William alas was to inherit). It was so well concealed that, naively, I was for many years unaware of it, but I did find her problematic sometimes to converse with and there was an absurd occasion when she suddenly disappeared through the frail wicker seat of the Wordsworth chair, leaving only her legs and head sticking up.

The life they lived was in many ways a frugal one. I think there was still some capital in William's trust, but when he was free to use it on reaching 21, it must soon have been spent on *Agenda*. Fortunately the flat was subject to rent restriction, and in 1971 William was able to get a mortgage to buy the freehold for some £10,000 from the landlord, who wished to be rid of an unprofitable asset. I strongly urged him to do this, as I foresaw an end to rent restriction. He and his mother went to Belgium in 1959 and to Rome in 1961, but I think never ventured abroad again in her lifetime, and, as I remember it, hardly went on holiday at all – both of them anyhow being rather stay-at-homes. William may have taken his ideas from Pound, but in his temperament he was much more akin to David Jones. He liked familiar routines and places and became addicted to *The Archers*. Like Jones, who increasingly kept to his 'dugout', he encouraged friends to come to see him singly or in pairs. He did not relish large gatherings and, if I am not inferring too much from my own experience, seldom, if ever, invited several people together for a meal – though a crew of poets might sometimes come to the flat to read to one another or play literary games. He did, however, maintain warm contact with a large number of writers by correspondence, by phone and in person. All over the flat piles of *Agenda*s accumulated and both a butcher's bike, which William used for deliveries, and an ordinary one were added to the small front hall, untidy to some, if pleasing to him. On the other hand, his small study, with its narrow view of the Thames and array of works by Pound and the other elect, was scrupulously ordered. Likewise, his hand-writing, always vigorous and upright, but often wild in his youth, became a model of neatness and clarity. And though he never developed a proper filing system, he could also be surprisingly businesslike.

Whatever the drawbacks of home life, these years were a golden period for *Agenda*, given recognition by an Arts Council grant from 1966. I can only hint at the riches. The first special issue was on William Carlos Williams in 1963, followed by those on Pound in 1965, on Bunting in 1966, on MacDiarmid in 1968 and Lewis in 1969. A triple issue devoted to David Jones in 1967 notably included his 'Sleeping Lord', begun in the late 1930s but only taken up and completed thanks to William's insistent encouragement. The first issue to be guest-edited was that on Zukofsky by Charles Tomlin-son, in 1964. The first appearance of Geoffrey Hill, R.S.

Thomas and Michael Hamburger, who were to be regular and prized contributors, was in a star-studded anthology issue in May 1965. The strong international character of the journal was shown in a 1968 Double Translation issue ranging from Arabic to Portuguese and again at the end of the decade in an Ungaretti special issue. Through the 1960s (and on till 1996) it was Peter Dale who was the main editorial collaborator on *Agenda* as well as one of its key poets. I had little to do with the magazine, save for the occasional protest at such editorial defects as the absence of consistent numbering on the spines, though I did contribute a few articles. It was only in 1982 when a trust was set up for *Agenda*, to facilitate grants, that I became closely involved again. That, however, is another story.

In retrospect, the close friendship between William and myself was a surprising one, different as we were in cast of mind and radically in some of our views. What was magnetic in him for me was not just his engaging warmth and constancy, but, above all, the personality of someone who embodied the ideal of poetry as central to a civilised life – a truly remarkable person.

William's father

Father and Son

149

MARTIN DODSWORTH

George and William Cookson: Father and Son

For many years *Agenda*'s editorial address was 5 Cranbourne Court, Albert Bridge Road, London, SW11, and many readers will have enjoyed thinking of Chelsea Reach and the fantastic bridge near-by with their 'nineties, and thus Poundian, associations. But Cranbourne Court had another significance for *Agenda* and its editor of which most readers will not have been aware. Even when William Cookson gave me the clue, I did not fully understand its significance. He was writing to me about something, probably the piece of mine that he reprinted in the Donald Davie special number, and mentioned that his father had been the first editor of the journal of the English Association, *English*, which I was then editing. He said that he would like to see the magazine still, and I arranged for it to be sent to him and thought no more of it. It was only later that I found that the original editorial address for *English* had been 8 Cranbourne Court. William's most settled address was almost identical with his father's. Was it the same flat re-numbered? In any case, from that address, in *Agenda*, he had for years pursued interests in poetry, literature and education which only extended those of his father. *Agenda* in no way replicated the concerns of *English*, but it certainly developed them, and I think that it did so largely in tribute to a father who was too little known by his son.

William's father appears in one of his 'Five Poems for K.':

> The caverned face
> of a black stone
> my father found
> beside a grass-choked ditch.
> He said it must have fallen
> from the sky.

150

George Cookson is associated with knowledge in these lines, and a knowledge of the mysterious, the meteorite disregarded in the ditch, a marvel waiting its discoverer. The lines have an emblematic quality; William's career as an editor was largely a matter of discoveries and their expounding, and in this sense he was fulfilling his father's role as it is remembered in his own poem. In a larger sense, fatherhood is about fostering; in nursing his own set of talented writers, William carried on his father's activity within the family and in the world of letters.

One reason why he should have chosen to form himself in his father's likeness, an editor, a poet and an educator, was that George Cookson died when William was only nine. He was a potent absence in his son's life.

George was already an old man when William was born in 1939. He was sixty-eight, and his first thirty years had been lived in the nineteenth century, to which he owed his major allegiance. He was educated at Clifton (where he probably contracted his incurable admiration for the poetry of T.E.Brown – 'A garden is a lovesome thing, God wot') and then went to Lincoln College, Oxford, as an exhibitioner, where he read Classics. He distinguished himself as a sportsman – he captained the University Rugby team in 1891 – but not as a scholar. Probably as a consequence of this, he joined the Egyptian Educational Service in 1895 and spent ten years in Egypt, 'assistant master in the Khedivieh School', Cairo. His first book of poems was published in 1897; it was followed seven years later by *Egyptian and other Verses*. These show some real gift in a late-nineteenth-century descriptive mode. Many of the poems, like 'The Garden in the Desert', end with nicely-judged and tantalizing openness:

And where a Marshal Niel from crown to root
Festoons a palm-stump, and the shade is deep,
Two Syrian nightingales a courtship keep,

151

And to each other all day call and flute,
And in and out the larkspurs, without noise
Soft companies of hawk moths dart and poise.

But there were no more books of poems after the *Egyptian Verses*, though George evidently continued to write – he put another moth-poem into the first number of *English* in 1936.

In 1899 he brought out an anthology 'primarily and especially compiled for use in the Government schools of Egypt' – *English Poetry for Schools*, a book that reflects masculine Victorian poetic taste. He returned to England in 1905 and was on the staff at Dartmouth for six years, where he 'gave special tuition to the Prince of Wales'. Finally he settled as an inspector for the Board of Education, a job from which he retired in 1931. It was a typical late imperial life of duty and devotion (he evidently kept up his Egyptian connections over the years), and superficially very unlike that of his son. William's life as an independent man of letters nevertheless reproduced in different forms both his father's sense of cultural responsibility and his poetic sensibility.

George Cookson retired at the age of sixty and became the first editor of *English* five years later; it was probably the retirement project of a very active man. The English Association was founded in 1906 to promote the study and appreciation of the English language and its literature; *English*, which is now a straightforward academic journal, except in its inclusion of original poems, began as something of a house magazine, with pages of reports of meetings and dinners. The first number led with an editorial on the death of George V and an article by Sir Evelyn Wrench, CMG, LLD, on 'English as a Bond of Union'. This does not sound much like *Agenda*. But the two journals shared an ideal of creativity and centrality. George Cookson, like his son, promoted some poets above others. It is only unfortunate that his taste was of a pronounced conservatism: he encouraged the likes of John Drinkwater, Wilfrid Gibson, E.H.W.Meyerstein and F.L.Lucas, and this was in line with a general distrust of modernism evident in the whole journal. In the second volume of *English* he published an essay by Martin Gilkes, 'Discovery of Ezra Pound' whose hostility focuses on the familiar aspects of 'Homage to Sextus Propertius'. William's devotion to Pound is in contradiction to all this; but it does perpetuate, in its different way, the father's commitment to the cause of culture. William found in Pound a poetry that lived because it was one with belief; his father similarly viewed English literature as an embodiment of the imperial ideals that he had served throughout his life. Indeed, the question arises whether Pound, another great educator, might not in some sense have taken the place for William of his absent father.

If you take down the wartime volumes of *English* from the shelf you can track William's childhood in the changes of editorial address. In 1941 it is 'Plunge', Much Hadham, Herts; in 1942 it is 'Truxford Wood', Elstead, Surrey, where possibly the family stayed when in 1945 the editorial address merged with that of the Association itself in Cromwell Road. Certainly the woods which are so potent a part of William's own poetry feel like Surrey woods with their sandy soil, heather, bracken, pines and birch. If their metric is Poundian, as is their allusiveness and sense of evanescent godhead, then their hauntedness and commitment to dream owe something to the uncertainty of childhood years spent with a father who would soon disappear, and who was probably conscious of the fact that this would be so.

In William's editing *Agenda* from the same block of flats as that from which his father had edited *English*, there is a hint of something which he summed up in one of his own poems, 'Out of the World, Out of Time':

I search for a land beyond death
where old loves, familiar things
are strange and new.

MARIUS KOCIEJOWSKI

'Monsieur, Le Chat est Mort.'

A thinly bearded, rather dapper American whom I'd put in his late seventies came into the shop three months ago, irritated at not having found a copy of the poem he had spent much of the day looking for. Apparently nobody he spoke to had ever heard of it. What it would be to be able to express surprise. Gruffly, despairingly perhaps, he asked for the poem by its title. When, a bit too enthusiastically, I proffered the author's name, in a manner that might have been interpreted by him as a query and not as an answer, he retorted, 'Well, *of course* it is. *Who else?*' Quite honestly, I was much too intrigued by him to take offence. I found him a collection by the said author, a nice one in dustwrapper, containing the work in question. The poem had first appeared on its own, in 1920, in a limited edition of two hundred copies, and as such is exceedingly rare. I did sell a copy once to a man who gave it to the drummer of the last millennium's most famous rock band. I hope it is not being used to prop a window open, for I have heard nothing from that direction of a thumping devotion to literature.

'I haven't got the poem on its own,' I said, 'but it's in here."

The American softened, made the purchase, and then we spoke for a while. I learned then he was related to the author of the poem that, when I first read it in 1971, had such a powerful effect on me, and which still I look upon as one of the cornerstones of twentieth-century literature. 'Well, I'm *his* cousin,' he told me. If the connection would later prove somewhat more remote, the blood argued otherwise, for, as if both had been hewn from the wood of the same tree, the man before me bore a striking resemblance to his distant relative. I think, too, there was something similar in the voice even, a certain rustic crackle. It could well be, of course, that I was too easily prepared to dissolve the differences, that by virtue of having two eyes, a couple of ears, a mouth and a nose, one man is as good as another, especially if they both sport a bit of grizzle.

A resident in London since the War, Thomas Busha – for that was his name – told me he was from one of 'those crazy rectangular states', which struck me as a lovely turn of phrase. I had never met anyone from Montana before, not knowingly, but if I were asked to picture one, this gentleman in his three-piece suit will remain for me a pleasing image of all things connected to that geographical wedge.

Thomas Busha cuts a dandyish figure. I saw him not so long ago wearing a cloak fastened at the neck with a small gold chain. Also, he loves opera, Mozart in particular. He then related a story concerning a creature native to the state of Montana and of how, a few years after its capture, it came to acquire, for him at least, a posthumous literary existence. The story grabbed me, not because of any light it would throw on the history of Modernism, but because I relish the way things meet up in time and space. I wondered if the story had appeared in print before. When Busha replied in the negative, I asked whether he would consent to my interviewing him. 'Well,' he hesitated, and then. with a chuckle, 'why not?' It would be some weeks before that conversation took place but in the meantime, as a form of preparation, he gave me a copy of a rather extraordinary photograph in his possession, which I reproduce here.

What is there to prevent this image turning up on the wall of a steakhouse? It would be, were it not for the story attached to it, an amusing curio, a buffoon's charade devoid of significance. The photograph dates from 1921, probably in the late summer of that year. We know this because the creature in the middle, a Montana bobcat that only recently

156

had been taken captive, would be in Paris, France a few months hence. The gentlemen depicted here are war veterans: the man on the left of the photograph, looking just a little self-conscious in his cowboy clothes, is Thomas Busha's father, Charles Thomas Busha Jr. (1890–1956) who served as captain in World War One and afterwards practised law in Washington, DC, where, very much in line with the democratic principles of his abolitionist forebears, he defended Indian territorial claims. The man on the right is believed to be his law partner, Roy Molumby. The man in the middle, in the aviator's get-up, smiling as though he were the proud father to the creature he cradles, is the pilot Earl Vance, of whom we shall hear more.

Another photograph, too deeply set in its frame to reproduce here, depicts, on the left of it, Charles T. Busha, this time in uniform, and beside him, in the middle, dressed in a racoon fur coat and *képi*, Marshall Foch, head of the

157

Western allies, and to the right of him his aide-de-camp, Capitaine L'Hôpital, 'the very picture of Gallic insouciance', as the current Busha describes him, for he is blowing tobacco smoke in our faces. A cloud of smoke is clearly visible, frozen in time. I have yet to see a better advertisement for cigarettes. The Marshall was, at the behest of the American Legion, on a tour of the United States in the autumn of 1921, and wherever he went, veterans flocked to him in droves. According to one of his biographers, 'the greatest Chief of the greatest Army in the world' confined his addresses to an effulgent expression of gratitude. When Foch came to Montana, he was there presented with the bobcat, which was then shipped back to Paris and installed, perhaps none too happily, in the Jardin des Plantes.

Some weeks later, when I had the pleasure of Busha's company, he spoke to me of his Montana ancestors, of whom there is many a colourful figure. One stands out in particular, his grandmother, Ida Lillian Busha (1858–1949). She was the daughter of Albert Elijah Pound whose brother, Thaddeus Coleman Pound, was the father of Homer Loomis Pound who, together with his wife, Isabel née Weston, produced, in neighbouring Idaho, a son called Ezra who in turn produced the poem *Hugh Selwyn Mauberley*, a copy of which some three months ago Thomas Busha came into the shop looking for, not a little chagrined at having failed to find one.

'My grandmother who I always thought of as being older than God, she was as big as a minute, but could jump over an irrigation ditch. A tiny little thing, she had ten children, my father being the eldest of five boys. She had come to Montana in the early 1870s on a paddle steamer called *The Far West* that came up from St. Louis, Missouri to a place called Fort Benton. She was then put on a wagon train going to the part of the state where she was to teach school. She'd go to that school on horseback with a shotgun across the saddle to defend herself. She had to worry about the rather truculent

158

Indians of the time. She went there from Philadelphia, bringing with her this piano, an enormous concert grand, which is still in the family. When the wagon train got to Mussel Shell River, they set down the piano flat on the prairie, legless, and she played for them down on her knees. Schubert, I think. She was very musical. The piano had its own room on the ranch. It was a part of my growing up. I remember staying with her on the ranch, in a house with chinking between the logs, and sleeping in the Saddle Room, so called because the house had been used once upon a time by a gang of rustlers who, when returning from their adventures, would throw their saddles through the window into the room that would one day bear its name. She would never leave the ranch and she was alert to everything happening on it. She could run us kids ragged. She always wore her skirt down to the ground, was always dressed in a strange way, as a Victorian woman would dress, which probably had something to do with her living a very exiguous and economical life.'

She did, however, take a brief vacation once.

'One thing they were all very keen on in the aftermath of the First World War was aviation which was front and centre. Earl Vance had been an aviator during the war. My father was himself part owner of the airport at Great Falls and Vance had his own aircraft, one of those open cockpit things. Ida said she'd be very glad to try out this business of aviation but only if she could do so in such a way she'd be back at the ranch, in her own bed, so to speak, by evening. So Vance put his mind to it and he decided it would be a simple thing to land his aircraft on her property and take her for a ride. She sat in the cockpit, behind the pilot, as you did in those days, with the wind in your face, and saw the state of Montana from the air and was back in her own bed that evening. Otherwise she never left the ranch, never, never, never.'

She did make one final journey of a kind, though, which Busha recounted to me in his inimitable fashion.

159

'She ended her life with the pixies. She was in her nineties, a bit gaga, I suppose, but it was a curious kind of eccentricity. My aunt told me one day Ida packed a little basket full of things, handkerchiefs, etc. When Aunt Beulah asked her what she was doing that for, she replied, "I'm going to the Crazies." The Crazy Mountains, at the back of this little village, Big Timber, Montana, are a fairly high range, and even in summer there is usually snow on the peaks. The name derives from some Indian legend, concerning a woman who went mad there many years before. Anyway, this was where she was going, to the Crazies, and, sure enough. Iater that day she was sitting at the piano and suddenly fell from the stool and died in the arms of my Uncle Willard who was visiting at the time.'

The picture Thomas Busha gives of Ezra Pound is one that we get elsewhere, of a man declaiming from his armchair, in, to use his words, 'a very disjunct and rambling sort of monologue.'

'I always regarded him as a member of the family rather than as a towering figure in English literature. When I first met Ezra. which was some time in the late forties, at St. Elizabeth's, it was with the thought that he was part of the family. It was an odd sort of thing because my father took no interest at all in the matter. I'm sure his own mother, my grandmother, would have been delighted if she ever had the chance to meet EP because she had some correspondence with him. Frankly, I can't remember the exact dates and particularities. I was young, although a veteran of the second war by that time. I am now 78 years old. When I first met Ezra I was already perfectly aware of his stature, so aware, in fact, that occasionally I was a little bit disturbed that he seemed to regard me as a person who was of interest to him only in terms of my being a student of the law and of politics, things that he also was interested in. Although he often referred to 'Fordie', 'Hem', very occasionally Eliot, he would never single me out for any kind of talk on literary matters. This Major Douglas [the economist whose ideas Pound followed] didn't ring any bells with me. I have often said that Ezra was the most American person I have ever met in my life. That is sometimes met with a certain amount of caution and I don't think everyone is entirely convinced. He would be in a vast, long rectangular room, which had windows on each side and along the lengthy side, and he would make himself a little corner, where usually there would be four or five people that Dorothy asked to appear. Sometimes they would be people of note. It was a period in which Washington was plentifully provided with elderly rich women who found their way somehow to the great poetic figure. Ezra would arrange the furniture in such a way as to isolate himself from the other inmates, many of whom were seriously disturbed. They'd be babbling away and coming up and trying to make talk of some kind and Ezra would be very curt with these people and shoo them away and then come back to his guests.'

It was these verbal snapshots of Pound, which Busha was best able to relate.

'The other thing I want to mention to you concerns a filial side to Ezra. He was much more attached in a sense, more thoughtful of his father than certainly I was of mine. I sometimes found that rather disconcerting. One of those occasions was in Rapallo when Ezra said to me, "I'd like go with you to Campo Santo, to the graveyard." There is a portion of the Italian graveyard, the Protestant side, where both Homer and Isabel, Ezra's parents, are buried. We quickly found this headstone on which there was a death mask. I remember Ezra was somehow moved by the experience of being there and he reached out and put his hand on the forehead of this death mask and for a moment there was something going through his mind. I shouldn't for a moment consider it anything akin to a prayer but nonetheless for me it was an example of his attachment and the

161

care with which he regarded his father. A decade or so later, I was in Rapallo and decided to go on my own to the cemetery. I simply couldn't find this headstone. Finally I went with my two words of Italian to the attendant and said I was looking for a particular headstone that I knew to be in the Protestant cemetery. We went back and he couldn't find it either. We prowled around and finally we found what had happened was that ivy had grown up and completely covered the headstone and so by separating the ivy from the stone we finally revealed the death mask in time; otherwise we would have gone away and concluded it had been removed. I was flabbergasted that it wasn't visible.'

What of the bobcat, though? The story, as related by Pound to Busha, is a sorrowful one although, according to the latter, there was no want of amusement in the speaker's voice. As we know, it was taken to France and it was some point between 1922 and 1925, that Pound, together with his wife, Dorothy, went to the Jardin des Plantes, which was then a zoo, to see the famous creature. They arrived there only to be informed by the keeper, ``Monsieur, le chat est mort.'

The story of the bobcat relates also to my final meeting with William Cookson, editor of *Agenda* magazine, who died tragically on January 2nd 2003, while I was in Prague, on the very day I made a pilgrimage to Kafka's grave. Strangely this prose seems at every turn to lead to a tombstone. I will not say I *knew* Cookson because, in truth, I found him the most difficult of men with whom to communicate. Our relationship was never anything but affable, on the other hand, and it is to him and to *Agenda* that I *owe* the first critical exposure of my own work. I am not without gratitude. Cookson was loyal to what he believed, unswervingly so. Certainly this was the case with Pound on whose behalf he was prepared to defend the indefensible, even the notorious radio speeches, until finally he himself was quite without defences. Stubbornly, absurdly even, he was prepared to rewrite the history of the Second World War in order to accommodate Pound's more bizarre homilies. I couldn't see why he was prepared to put his own reputation on the line, not when Pound had already redeemed himself through his verse. What are those haunting final *Cantos* of his if not an expression of the regret of one who tried 'to make a paradiso terrestre'? Still, I could never join in the mounting criticism of Cookson because I have a natural inclination to side with those who fight losing battles.

A story I have heard is that when people went to visit Pound in Rapallo and then, later in Venice, Olga Rudge would sort out those who were serious from those who were merely curious and would ask the hopeful visitors to recite from memory a single line of Pound's verse. If they passed the test, they would gain admittance. Cookson would have got in many thousands of times over, for he knew the whole of the *Cantos* by heart, such that one could start him off at any point and he could continue. I do not believe for a moment that he set out to memorise them, but rather that his love of Pound's work was so deep, so profound, that they entered his bloodstream. Cookson's death was, perhaps, the death of a species of one. If there was something of a blur in his nature, he was the sharpest, the most concise authority on anything touching upon his beloved mentor. When I last saw him, on the evening of September 17th 2002, I asked him, without ever telling him why, if he could remember a bobcat appearing anywhere in the *Cantos*. I had it in mind to contribute a prose piece, the substance of which I have related above, to his magazine. Who could have guessed it would bear this sad coda? I was rummaging for the information that would help me spring a surprise. It seemed to me highly improbable that Pound would pass up the opportunity to place himself, poetically at least, at a juncture in twentieth-century history, not when a member of his own family, the Great War, Marshall Foch, a Montana bobcat and

163

the Jardin des Plantes occupied a single vortex as it were. I was mistaken. Cookson stood for about a minute, mentally running through the whole of the *Cantos*, which goes some way towards demonstrating the speed at which a mind driven by love can move. 'No,' he replied, 'but there is a lynx in Canto LXXIX.' 'Oh, really?' I said, hoping for a silly moment that perhaps the bobcat had undergone some kind of literary change. The metamorphosis was, of course, of another kind altogether, that of woman into creature: *O Lynx keep watch on my fire.* Cookson seemed annoyed at my ignorance. 'Well, of course there is,' he snapped. It was the last time we ever spoke.

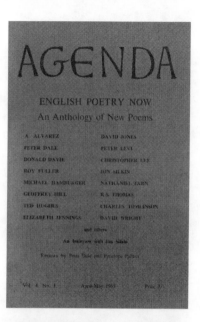

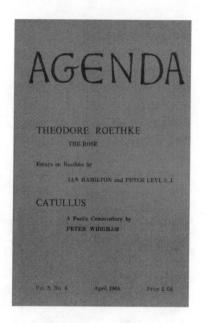

AGENDA

CONTENTS

EZRA POUND
FOUR TRANSLATIONS

IAN HAMILTON
BIRTHDAY POEM

PETER DALE
THREE POEMS

PENELOPE PALMER
RETURN TO MADRID

MICHAEL ALEXANDER
TRANSLATIONS FROM THE
ANGLO-SAXON

WILLIAM COOKSON
ROETHKE'S LAST POEMS

OTHER POEMS AND REVIEWS BY EARLE BIRNEY,
ROBERT BLY, JOHN COURNOS, PETER DALE,
CLIVE JORDAN, WALLACE KAUFMAN AND
CHRISTOPHER LEE.

September 1964   2/6d   Vol. 3 No. 5

A selection of early
work by well-known
poets promoted by
AGENDA

WILLIAM CARLOS WILLIAMS

Iris

a burst of iris so that
come down for
breakfast

we searched through the
rooms for
that

sweetest odor and at
first could not
find its

source then a blue as
of the sea
struck

startling us from among
those trumpeting
petals

Song

beauty is a shell
from the sea
where she rules triumphant
till love has its way with her

scallops and
lion's paws
sculptured to the
tune of retreating waves

undying accents
repeated till
the car and the eye lie
down together in the same bed

THEODORE ROETHKE

The Geranium

When I put her out, once, by the garbage pail,
She looked so limp and bedraggled,
So foolish and trusting, like a sick poodle,
Or a wizened aster in late September,
I brought her back in again
For a new routine –
Vitamins, water, and whatever
Sustenance seemed sensible
At the time: she'd lived
So long on gin, bobbie pins, half-smoked cigars, dead beer,
Her shrivelled petals falling
On the faded carpet, the stale
Steak grease stuck to her fuzzy leaves.
(Dried-out, she creaked like a tulip.)

The things she endured! –
The dumb dames shrieking half the night
Or the two of us, alone, both seedy,
Me breathing booze at her,
She leaning out of her pot toward the window.

Near the end, she seemed almost to hear me –
And that was scary –
So when that snuffling cretin of a maid
Threw her, pot and all, into the trash-can,
I said nothing.

But I sacked the presumptuous hag the next week,
I was that lonely.

TED HUGHES

Cadenza

The violinist's shadow vanishes.

The husk of a grasshopper
Sucks a remote cyclone and rises.

The full, bared throat of a woman walking water,
The loaded estuary of the dead,

And I am the cargo
Of a coffin attended by swallows,

And I am the water
Bearing the coffin that will not be silent.

The clouds are full of surgery and collisions
But the coffin escapes – black diamond,

A ruby brimming blood,
A turquoise beating its shores,

A sea that lifts swallow wings and flings
A summer lake open

Sips and bewilders its reflection
Till the whole sky dives back like a burned land
                                        to its spark –

A bat with a ghost in its mouth
Struck at by lightnings of silence –

Blue with sweat, the violinist
Crashes into the orchestra, which explodes.

Fallen Eve

My mouth is the despair of the God
Formed only for men.

The serpent remains earthen, brutishly veined,
Rooted in crevices, living on flies and men.

The serpent that should have strangled me
And then eaten itself.

I sing, stamping the gruelling drum-beat,
To renew fallen men.

Love is weak to protect as webs.

In April my body begins to frighten me
And my sleep fills with weeping – – –

Again and again the forced grave of men.

Bad News Good!

To act crow, you need not be black.
You only need the appetite,
And the mindless, gloating look
As you pull something's insides out.

The carrion crow that barks and goes
Over the house, disgorges ill-luck
Nowise created by the crows
Gouts of death's abundant black.

A lady here, under crow-possession,
Will pluck out her evil tidings
From your eye's lightest confession,
Then flap off with the evidence bleeding.

Lately she tasted the satisfaction
Of seeing her crow-bodings kill
One brain where she set them in action.
But she did not then sit still.

Since a sitting crow starves and
This real victim was too good
To lose to death. She hopped around
With torn fragments loud in blood.

And still into all sorts of heads
Jabs these grave incriminations –
Then regards with gloating beads
Her sudden eyehole excavations.

What of Iago, idiot, or revenge
There is in her, I do not know –
Lust to rend and to derange
Is the nature of a crow:

Messenger innocence of God's will,
Delivering the black of Hell –
Till every word that wounds be buried
Where it comes closest to kill.

PETER D. DENT

Evening

You don't have to tell me
the flowers are yellow
as your jumper,
reading your book now
beside the electric fire. You
talk among the may quiet petals
of this room, warm
with stories, and
without moving your lips.

TOM SCOTT

Auld-Farrant Gecks

On M.R.A.

Frae toun til toun and fairm til fairm
    In twas and threes and scores,
The morons o the warld re-airm,
    Haean nocht to lose but their mores.

A Writers' Conference.

Douce Embro fowk are in a steir,
    For meetin in a quorum,
A wheen stray dugs hae gaithert here
    And pished on their decorum.

Crime is a business . . .

'Crime's juist a business like ony ither'
Says an auld lag daen time.
Nae dout – but the pynt is whether
Business is no juist anither crime.

Treaty of Union 1707.

'Yae wee island atween us twae,
Union atween us there maun be,'
Said the wowf til the laam as he grabbed his prey –
'The blissit union o you in me'.

Democracie.

O happy, happy breed o men
Born intil Demokracie.
Free to pick your exploiters, then
Free to delude yoursels you're free.

ELIZABETH JENNINGS

Mental Illness

Then this is being mad; there is no more
Imaginings, Ophelias of the mind.
This girl who shouts and slobbers on the floor,
Sending us frightened to the corner, is
To all the world we know now deaf and blind
And we are merely loathsome enemies.

It is the lack of reason makes us fear,
The feeling that ourselves might be like this.
We are afraid to help her or draw near
As if she were infectious and could give
Some taint, some touch of her own fantasies,
Destroying all the things for which we live.

And, worse than this, we hate the madness too
And hate the mad one. Measured off a space
There is a world where things run calm and true –
But not for us. We have to be with her
Because our minds are also out of place
And we have carried more than we can bear.

Personal Easter

Let them bring gifts, let them bring pious eggs.
There are no kings at Easter, only men.
Two nights ago, we drained cups to the dregs
And did not know if we should live again.
The stars move on, we battle with our plagues.
What god will rise now from the frozen stone?

A few flowers sprinkle over ravaged earth.
Birds hover, dive. Why do they fill my mind?
The Holy Ghost has more august a birth
Than this, the tongues of fire could singe and blind.
Oh God, last year I chose my own poor death
Yet you arose me, left Limbo behind.

ROY FULLER

Brother Serene

The peaks are visible from the verandah
– Baboon, G 26, Bright Nipple.
Someone is bashing with the mallet
That hangs by the dented block at our gates.
One more of the epoch's escapees,
Who certainly will knock in vain;
For the novices are already so many
They have polished all excrescences
Off the gods – though typically have neglected
The stove, so that my hands are numb,
Scarcely able to grasp Reminder
As I wait alone for prayers to end
And the hours of meditation to start.
Today it's my office to bear this great staff
And totter between the rows of brothers
Administering first the Tap of warning
Then the Thwack of Reality.
Odd, that however tactful the first
The second always comes as a shock.

A leaf that spent autumn in a crevice
Scutters across the floor as though
On feet: the significant likes to assume
A foolish or trivial vehicle.
Just as enlightenment arrives
As one bickers about a roster of duties
Or the frequency of getting the chipped bowl.
And indeed, the past season, very ill,
Spending weeks in the Preparation Room,
Perhaps for the first time I glimpsed how things
                                        wagged.

Awareness accompanies alarm.
Seeing my robe across mummies' shins,
Mopping my shaven skull, I thought:
No disguise can stop one being human.
And strong little birds, calling at dawn,
Called of their reckless otherness.
In those days I used to look at the swelling,
Stand wrestling with the stricture, feeling
As far from surgeons as from god.
But we have fled from help, albeit
The hands are prompted by profit or fear.

The sky turns slate, the peaks are even whiter,
Then on the vast negative there blinks
A light incongruously golden.
Quickly the verandah is dredged with hailstones
To the sound of thunder and a gong
That calls me to the interior chamber.
Once, I had a name – other than Serene;
And once a body, like a sparrow;
And a life of families, worry and pets.
In fact, despite my hairlessness
And saffron skirts, you'd say, if asked,
That even now I was a man.
The individual nature must
Be evaluated by its secrets.
So I learnt in the world, and because of that
Perhaps gave up the world; and now
May put down my irregular heart
To indigestion as much as fear.

I limp among the squatting Elsewhere,
Passing the grooved or pneumatic napes
Of Vision, Bluebird and Devotion,
Halting at Strongheart. Tap. Thwack.

He will be glad to be reminded:
Even in the ablutions his cloth
Exudes a sanctifying ichor.

What brought me here? The quest for a father?
My own died in my infancy:
Ever after I was an inchoate rebel.
Suppose when he gabbled the ritual
'What is the clew that runs through it all?'

One answered the Abbot: 'Your nasal cyst.'
The lust for authority presupposes
A perpetual lack of respect for it.
Rather as those who receive the spirit
Seems to be quite unspiritual.
Simpletons of nature, they die as they lived,
Crying unselfconsciously of their joy,
Rich hosts to the parasites of blood.
It is error that leads to metaphor:
The heavens, we murmur, looking above
Bright Nipple's pennant of screaming snow
At invisible dust between incandescent
Sea-slugs, sea-urchins, sea-cucumbers,
Whorls of every irrelevant kind.

DONALD DAVIE

The Blank of the Wall

after St.-J. Perse.

The blank of the wall is over against you; which
Is the conjuration into a circle
Of reveries. The image none the less
Emits its cry. An aftertaste of rich
Fats and sauces furs
The teeth your tongue explores
Inside the uneasy head which you have set
Upon the lived with, the familiar
Upholstery of a greasy chair; and yet
You think how clouds move purely on your island
The green dawn growing lucid on the breast
Of the mysterious waters. And it is
The sweats of exiled juices and
There on the hearth the snapping spar,
Split from how cheap a crate, secretes
The resinous strands of all of Canada.
The need is lived with, that this answers to.

WALLACE KAUFMAN

A Stifled Theft

He fenced his garden just beyond my reach
as if he knew me before I saw his flowers –
knew to the inch what length my arm would stretch
and then worked many Sunday hours
with shovel trowel and iron bars;
and all to build a fence whose one design
was to make my rib-cage meet hard iron –
my fingers just one inch from rose-of-sharon.
I meant to give those flowers with my love
to one as bright as them, as much alive.
In that foreknowledge he seemed to have
could he have known my stolen gifts
would ask for love she did not give.

You There, I Here

These mountains, a ragged tree,
black goats and shepherds –
I see what you would see.

You would have stared in joy
this afternoon
at a white-clad gypsy boy.

So I too stopped to look
and heard you
opening his beauty like a book.

Love is more thieving than wise:
you gave your heart,
I also took your eyes.

IAN HAMILTON

Birthday Poem

Tight in your hands
Your Empire Exhibition shaving mug.
You keep it now
As a spittoon, its bloated doves
Its 1938
Stained by the droppings of your blood.

Tonight
Half-suffocated, cancerous,
Deceived,
You bite against its gilded china mouth
And wait for an attack.

LOUIS ZUKOFSKY

From 'A' 12

He who knows nothing
Loves nothing
Who loves nothing
Understands nothing.
Who understands
Loves and sees,
Believes what he knows,
The horse has large eyes
Man's virtue his feeling,
His heart treasures his tongue, certain
That a *yes* means no *no*,
What else is happiness. . . ?

C. H. SISSON

Easter

One good crucifixion and he rose from the dead
He knew better than to wait for an age
To nibble his intellect
Or depress his love.

Out in the desert the sun beats and the cactus
Prickles more fiercely than any in his wilderness
And his forty days
Were merely monastic.

What he did on the cross was no more
Than others have done for less reason
And the resurrection
You could take for granted.

What is astonishing is that he came here at all
Where no-one ever came voluntarily before.

PETER LEVI, S.J.

For Peter Hacker

These quiet autumns hide despair,
old rhetoric, my mental state,
day after day through misty air
the dry echoes reverberate.
Now climber on his cliff, too scared to climb,
I search from rock to rock, misted in time.

Gardens and roads when I was three
first lured my wandering sense to spin
these crystals of maturity
to expose imagination in.
Water brought dusk, autumn released in rain
the dropping leafage with its dying stain.

Then in the pages of school-books
I found stories about my life;
the masters gave me curious looks,
I fiddled with a small pen-knife;
all savage pleasures, and that pain and shame
vanished in moon and mist when autumn came.

The antique writers, the dead style,
horrific symbols, bleak comments
seemed altered in a little while
to a nervous kind of ornaments,
or roughened shells or craggy rock faces
worn into shape by cold autumnal seas.

All those philosophies have gone,
since pleasure, doubt, the sense of death
teach schoolmasters their own lesson
in voices tangible as breath,
and adolescents, studying when I write
note the dead foliage and the dying light.

Now an intense reflective rage
by seasonal rebirth and loss
rips away words, page after page,
ringing eros on thanatos;
I study bare landscape, question the dead,
listen to cold rain falling in my head.

CHARLES TOMLINSON

Brilliant Silence

Smooth light: all bronze
and polished like a bell
that, biding utterance
hangs heavy with
the fullness that it does not tell.

Yet do not stay too near
the heart of fire, but watch
the way it takes the trees and they
in looming clear, resist it.

Sun-burst: the dam
goes down in silence, feeds
the thirst of shadows, and
brilliance, quiet, distances
attest a counterpointing land.

Portrait in Stone

(For H.G.)

Face in stone and
Stone in face:
Compacted in this still embrace
Neither displaces either.

The eye that married them,
Grown wiser with the deed,
A twofold matrimony thus
Makes mind and eye unanimous.

The labyrinth of strokes
Has left the rockheart sheer,
That eye and mind may taste the calm
(Want and discord found it there)

And, with their satisfaction, know
The strength that bred this radiance
And brimmed the surface of the stone
To rule a city with a glance.

MICHAEL O'HIGGINS

Corncrake

Why does the corncrake
                    disturb
my tranquility,
                    sending ragged riffs
out of the secret places
                    of deep meadows
into the echoing sweep
                    of the sky
in the threaded heat of the day
and the long silence
                    of dead evenings,
hiding in the tumbling corn
                    or running over
the green-haired clay
                    in a dense forest
of grass saplings?
When the plumed clouds
                    have gauntleted
the dying sun
    I have heard him in his loneliness
drumming up the ears
                    of patient wheat,
discordant with the choirs
                    of tired birds
and in the night
                    even as I made love
he has called to me
                    holding my attention
so that I lost a lover
                    for a woman can be jealous
even of a corncrake.

PETER RUSSELL

Visions and Ruins

Extracts from a Long Poem

IV

In the small furnished-room of the Soul
You will find comfort, my friend,
Not by rigours, asceticism, flagellation or gloom –
Sit in the room with the old gramophone
And a dozen well-worn records. You will hear
The Music of the Spheres, the rejoicing of Angels and
the voice of Gods.
Do not lie on the silk divan beneath the gilded mirrors
While slaves are toiling outside to keep you comfortably dead,
Lost in the empty palace you can never fill.
Lie on your bed in the small furnished-room,
Gaze in the mirror over the basin and see what you see.
Apes will see no apostles, quicksilver will not transmute
Death into life, doom to a candid smile.
Look in the glass, see what you see.
You are what you see, what you do, what you will.
Be what you will – Angels and Gods will gaze back
Into your triumphing eyes . . .

Your sins are forgiven when you see your Self in the mirror.

Tristia

First English translation of Osip Mandelstam

I have learned the whole art of leave-taking
In bare-headed night-lamentations.
The oxen chew: anticipation lingers
And I honour the ceremony of that cock-crying night
When raising their burden of sorrow for a departing traveller
Eyes that were red with weeping gazed into the distance
And the wailing of women mingled with the song of the
    muses.

In that word 'leave-taking' who can tell
What kind of separation is in store for us,
What it is the crying of cocks promises
When fire burns on the acropolis:
And in the first red dawn of some new life
When lazily the ox is chewing in the shade,
Why does the cock, the new life's own town-crier
On the city wall beat madly with his wings?

I love the way the thread is spun –
The shuttle runs to and fro, the spindle hums –
Look now – already like swansdown
Barefooted Delia flies to meet you!
O the meagre pattern of our life –
Even our happiest words are threadbare!
Everything has been of old and will be again:
For us, only the moment of recognition is sweet.

So let it be: the little gleaming image
Lies on the spotless earthen dish.
Like the stretched-out skin of a squirrel
Stooping over the wax the young girl gazes.
It is not for us to guess about Grecian Erebus:
What's bronze for man for woman is only wax.
Our destiny befalls us only in battles –
They see the future as they die.

1918.

DONALD HALL

In the Kitchen of the Old House

In the kitchen of the old house, late,
I was making some coffee
and I day-dreamed sleepily of old friends.
Then the dream turned. I waited.
I walked alone all day in the town
where I was born. It was cold,
a Saturday in January
when nothing happens. The streets
changed as the sky grew dark around me.
The lamps in the small houses
had tassels on them, and the black cars
at the curb were old and square.
A ragman passed with his horse, their breaths
blooming like white peonies,
when I turned into a darker street
and I recognized the house
from snapshots. I felt as separate
as if the city and the house
were closed inside a globe which I shook
to make it snow. No sooner
did I think of snow, but snow started
to fill the heavy darkness
around me. It reflected the glare
of the streetlight as it fell
melting on the warmth of the sidewalk
and frozen on frozen grass.
Then I heard out of the dark the sound
of steps on the bare cement
in a familiar rhythm. Under
the streetlight, bent to the snow,

196

hatless, younger than I, so young that
I was not born, my father
    walked home to his bride and his supper.
A shout gathered inside me
    like a cold wind, to break the rhythm,
to keep him from entering
    that heavy door but I stood under
a tree, closed in by the snow,
    and did not shout, to tell what happened
in twenty years, in winter,
    when his early death grew inside him
like snow piling on the grass.
    He opened the door and met the young
woman who waited for him.

GEOFFREY HILL

Soliloquies

1. THE STONE MAN, 1878
        for Charles Causley

Recall, now, the omens of childhood:
The nettle-clump and rank elder tree;
The stones waiting in the mason's yard:

Half-recognised kingdom of the dead:
A deeper landscape lit by distant
Flashings from their journey. At nightfall

My father scuffed clay into the house.
He set his boots on the bleak iron
Of the hearth; ate, drank, unbuckled, slept.

I leaned to the lamp; the pallid moths
Clipped its glass, made an autumnal sound.
Words clawed my mind as though they had smelt

Revelation's flesh . . . So, with an ease
That is dreadful, I summon all back.
The sun bellows over its parched swarms.

2. OLD POET WITH DISTANT ADMIRERS

What I lost was not a part of this.
The dark-blistered foxgloves, wet berries
Glinting from shadow, small ferns and stones,

Seem fragments, in the observing mind,
Of its ritual power. Old age
Singles them out as though by first-light,

As though a still-life, preserving some
Portion of the soul's feast, went with me
Everywhere, to be hung in strange rooms,

Loneliness being what it is. If
I knew the exact coin for tribute,
Defeat might be bought, processional

Silence gesture its tokens of earth
At my mouth: as in the great death-songs
Of Propertius (although he died young).

JOHN MONTAGUE

Hill Field

All that bone bright winter's day
He completed my angle of sight
Patterning the hill field
With snaky furrows,
The tractor chimney smoking
Like his pipe, under the felt hat.

Ten years ago, it was a team
With bulky harness and sucking step
That changed our hill:
Grasping the cold metal
The tremble of the earth
Seemed to flow into one's hands.

Still the dark birds shape
Away as he approaches
To sink with a hovering
Fury of open beaks –
Starling, magpie, crow ride
A gunmetal sheen of gaping earth.

R. S. THOMAS

Two Versions of a Theme

I

You couldn't, I thought, ask for
A seedier crowd than these Welsh
People, men and women, in their
Cheap shoes and expensive
Hats, blowing their noses, shuffling
Their cold feet, listening between lulls
In the gossip to the minister
Praying, while the stiff corpse lay
In its coffin beyond the reach of
Such cant. I would have turned
Furiously from those lurid
Noses and blear eyes to my
Car, but that a low sound
Arrested me, a hymn tang-
Led in that misshapen
But human wood, that directly
Freed itself and became art,
Palpable beauty hovering over the
Bent heads, waiting to be
Owned by them, had they looked up.

II

So, having said it, what have you said?
Made intelligible noises;
Beaten about a small bush
With the bird flown,

You went to a funeral, the same old thing,
And were disgusted:
Bleary eyes, and bald heads, and the prayers
A collection of cant.

You were turning away – they began singing,
Effortless beauty,
Spiring as most art has spired
From soiled fountains.

You forgot the crowd, the flowerless manhood
In its rank garden;
Seeing only the way the hymn
Endeared itself

To more distant mourners, the Welsh hills.
For a long moment
The music became the poem, that became you,
It is quenched now.

MICHAEL HAMBURGER

For No One

So we meet again, little girl
Whose blue eyes taught me
How to say nothing, to look
And be merged in looking.
I saw you there and I listened,
But you cannot hear me,
Nor do I know where you are.
No need, in that place
Where to look is enough,
Where to meet is a marriage
Nowhere, for ever,
Nothing can be undone.

Here, I should have passed by, unrecognizing,
You a woman now, still young but not beautiful,
With a bad complexion. But Beatrice was your name,
Recalled to me without words though your eyes were not
                                        even blue

And now you chattered gaily about yourself,
About living from hand to mouth, luxuriously.
Because you were Beatrice, nothing had changed between us;
Because nothing had changed between us, I knew your
                                        name.

JON SILKIN

Burying

It is not in the face.
That force has broken off
Which pressed through the ducts the liquids
Nourishing your life.

And absolutely as
You had not before been, with a
    Marked stiffening that

Composed your short frame,
The flesh settling noiselessly onto
    The compact bone

A bricklayer tooled that space
You drew the entire process of your growth in
    And died in, gradually.

With no bodily pain,
But with grief, akin with the aged; your face
    A mass of sea weed.

And after you had died,
Thickly pallid. I could not think
    There was no breath left.

I paid a few pounds for
something to case your flesh, it seemed required
    By trade you should have

Chewed pulp with fibre
Crushed into shape by the corrugation of men's will.
    A child would not have

Perceived the poorness in that.
Your preferred nothing, with a likeness of absorbed
    Wills acting separately.

Such as the buriers have.

The psalm, as a shade
Of flower, touched merely
    Where you were.

I think that if I could
Have paid more for you,
There would have been more persons
Standing above that hole.
Much good might that do still
Although the mouth has gently
Chewed your flesh into
The ineradicable
Humus, the thriving muck
Which feeds the things we feed with;
For you were not honoured
Except with a thin box,
And the soil, which fastens
Each living thing to itself
Without ceremony or hat
Or anything casual.

KEN SMITH

Beyond

Beyond grass is a country
that shifts
without shadow, a country
of dead sticks where no water
preys on the soil.
Only rocks are firm;
only its stars are fixed.
The seeds' hunger
for water
is crying with no sound.
The stones that lie down
in white silences
are rootless.
No moss can stain them. Beneath
are no creatures the light burns.
They fall open, shrivelled by the wind,
broken by sun. No roots
intercede between them and sand
and no grass holds them down.

That land is all glittering, heaving
like slow seas
beyond grass, beyond sureness;
scrub country, thorns also and thistles,
starved twigs that gather the sand in their joints.
There are no tracks.
The lips ask for water.
Flesh becomes bones
or moves through this silence
where no pity is

It sifts to no end.
There are no places to hide the dead.
The small prints of the feet are soon lost.

POEMS TO AND
FOR WILLIAM
COOKSON

Painting by William Cookson

Poems to and for William Cookson

LEO AYLEN

Stone Circle and Burial Mound

and the dead, unreachable, especially by archaeologists

Burial mound and standing stones;
Vastness of green stretches away
Into a distance of frozen mist.
Dream! Listen for ghost. Could a scrap of bone's
Mutter through slumber tease us to play
Games learnt from their skeleton forest

Where giants and dwarves loom like shadows
Sliding between the stones, and laughter
From royal spectres echoes on the hills
In answer to the dead kings' burial barrows?
Are the words clear? They're spoken softer
Than ladybird rustle on daisy petals.

Here is a home, but not for us.
We're given glimpes, a whisper, a scent . . .
Will it lodge under memory,
Forgotten, unnoticed, until some loss,
Some strange pain, knockes a tiny dent,
A crack, in consciousness, and we

Are sucked back out of time's entrance
Becoming for this immeasurable minute
The burial mound, and the dead within it,
As the standing stones begin their dance?

ANNE BERESFORD

'Each Soul Brings Its Own Heaven'

for William

That land beyond death
is not so easy to find, my friend.
It's a land which draws the adventurous
fills them with dread and longing.
A land where houses are all awry
and dark streets leading to emptiness.

Old loves, familiar things
do not come here.
Those who visit bring back no photographs.

But you must journey further
into a forest with trees larger than life,
the sun dazzling in Spring,
a mass of bluebells underfoot.

At last, as you embrace the light
the dream of years will wake you
to an ancient knowledge
in a fountain of stars.

HEATHER BUCK

The Dead Bequeath to the Living

i.m. William Cookson

In my world the dead are out of range
yet within my thoughts I give them space
because they still enrich with what they gave.

The way they widened our horizons
beyond the crowded city streets
to remote and deeper springs of life
where thoughts have soil for growth.

In every age are those who excavate
the myths and legends that we recognise,
hanging the images they find
upon the walls and corridors of time.

PETER DALE

Second Reading
i. m. William Cookson

Time travel. Our favourite defunctive bard
that neither of us, young, thought worth a light –
where we agreed so well, Good for a laugh.

I'm thereabouts again so late in life
since months ago you happened to remark
how recently you'd warmed to the odd line.

Still clear, our jokes, the barred and gemlike flame.
I trudge between, in hopes of coming by
the lines you'd found, to share and understand.

It's even harder going now you're dead.
Our jokes, the fustian clag, and in three minds:
two dead and one still crawling to The End.

Just one more chance, old friend, to meet on words,
the last together, nailing lines of verse.

(First published in *The London Magazine*)

JOHN FULLER
Different Places

The world is always beginning somewhere,
Springing again to life in rooms
Lost for a time in darkness.

Look: the pad of your finger presses
The affirming plastic, placed in the corner
Of its white wall like a postage stamp

And the room is suddenly sheepishly lit,
Encouraging talk and smiling, like
A theatre during the interval.

Decision, motion, intention: all
These we are reminded of
By the room's connected distances.

But then to enter and enjoy
Must be to leave the somewhere else
That you inevitably were

To its equivalence of darkness,
For despite our wishes, we are never
In more than one place at a time.

. . .

Proposal: to turn unthinking habit
Into the first superb performance
Of something you have long rehearsed,

To make a lively parade of waking
Wherever we happen to find ourselves
And to know that now is always different.

And so to bless hot water stirring
In the veins of the house, the practical talking
Of a child who has forgotten his nightmares

And other distant sounds: the thud
Of a neighbour's door, the bronchial revving
From the street of someone's early start,

And nearer: the breath still passing
Above or below the palate, a tide
That laps the hull of destination

In the almost audible warmth of the skull,
The one place where you always are,
The steady engine-room of the heart.

MICHAEL HAMBURGER

Memorial

Raincloud, hailcloud, snowcloud behind them,
So fast the north-easterly drives
That no sky can cohere:
Against a black horizon
For a minute, stark
In full rays broken through
The beech-tree long barkless
Stands as never when leaved,
All golden its wrecked limbs.

RICHARD HAMBURGER

Nightfall

(for William)

New moon's brightness seems to seep
out beyond its circumscription.
A slender filament that dazzles
in a thinned ink sky.

Zig-zag of charcoal cloud
heralds those shapes to come –
black masses of heart's burdens.

Patterns on a scroll unfold
in time, the peace to watch.

The light source shrinks to a spark.
Then nothing – until they have passed.

JAMES HARPUR

John

(from 'Joseph of Arimathea')

We left in early morning darkness
And found the foot-hills in the glow
Of dawn that spread the path before us.
We rested every hour or so
To pray or drink or eat some bread.
He did not say a word to us
And we were too preoccupied
Tackling the stony paths ahead
To ask what we were doing there.
By evening we had reached the top
A little plateau with three cairns.
Far to the west, blue haze of sea
Grey haze of mountains to the east
And at the bottom of that drop
Boulders had turned to shiny pebbles
And spiky trees were clumps of grass.
We felt like prophets, birds or angels
Rising among the snow and rocks
Breathing the wind, as sharp as ice,
Majestic as the world around us.

The sun was growing white and dim
the twilight hesitated then
Descended like a sacred presence –
He suddenly withdrew from us
And walked towards the mountain's rim.
I thought, just then, more snow had fallen –
There was a glare, the air was brighter
Then it coarsened imperceptibly

Into a mist, but much more fine;
And still it kept on getting brighter
And it was almost crystalline,
A sparkling canopy or sea spray –
It was as if we were inside
A waterfall without the sound.
We saw him standing by the edge
His skin and clothes were of the sun
And he was like a spirit fountain –
Light radiated from his flesh
And floated in the atmosphere
In drifts of scintillating petals
Rising above this holy mountain;
We felt we were inhaling light
Gulping, like fish, the glittering air
And marvelling, and marvelling

Enfolded in a timelessness
And almost unsurprised to see
Figures appearing out of nowhere
An angel either side of him
Three shafts of flickering white flame
Contained within three human shapes
The three of them quite motionless
Yet seeming to communicate.
It seemed like hours that we stared,
Before the light became just air,
The coruscating motes diminished,
The angels faded and were gone.
Alone again he came towards us
And Peter started babbling on
While James and I burst into tears
Sobbing and laughing soundlessly
Until we felt him touch our shoulders.
Calmer, and drained, aglow and glad,

We saw the world in shades of grey –
The snow was scruffier, the boulders,
The stones, the sky were dingy, sad.
The darkness that had been delayed
Descended suddenly.

It seems like only yesterday
That ecstasy of joyfulness
The realization who he was.
I never thought we would be worthy
To be his witnesses, to see
Those shining figures side by side
Their stretched-out arms raised up like crosses;
Three figures standing side by side
Their flesh become a spirit light –
We knew, from then, there was no death
Just transmutation into light.

ALAN JENKINS
Ex-Poet

(i. m. William Cookson: who kept faith)

Twenty-five years back (about one third
Of a late-twentieth-century life, pre-cloning
And perhaps one-third through his life –
Though what did that mean then?), ecstatic,
He took a famous novel at its lying word
And brought his girlfriend here. In a rented attic
They ate, slept, read, drank, fought
And made up; sometimes he'd rise at dawn and write,
What was more dreamt than thought
In lines that hardly ever needed honing,
The miracle she was, his love, his muse,
The knowledge he would not betray or lose,
The vision that accompanied him here:
How life can break free of loneliness and fear
To be this richer, riskier thing, like theirs
Who searched for the beautiful and true.

Twenty-odd years later (two-thirds through),
He has come back
To the green flames of cypresses, and palms
Like birds whose tattered, brown-edged feathers
Rustle in the midday sun; to shuttered squares
With fountains dripping moss, and coffee, black
And bitter as the thought of freckled arms
That held him, of her inner weathers - in the generous shade
Of patched and peeling plane-trees; to the light
He loved then, light that burned his northern eyes
And showed him beauty (or, how all things ache
To be expressed), the truth that what was made
And made well, no-one could unmake.
The girl's long gone. What he wrote were lies.

ROLAND JOHN

Landfall

The lake placid: how many times have
I watched it pitch out there? Isolated,
a perfection in its slow moving glacis.

Forbidding? But that's not it,
the layers slip, unwind, we've so few
days left, where not even words

will ever invent. Stray feelings
lapped insensitive and falling in
to the long night's insensate drift.

All unspoken yet between us,
neither knowing; becoming perhaps
our last observation before the shore?

MIMI KHALVATI

Blessing

for Hafez

Between the living and the dead,
may your memory be green;
in the book beside my bed,
may your signature be seen.

May your memory be green
for every lover, every spring;
may your signature be seen
inscribed on every living thing.

For every lover, every spring,
breathing clouds against the frost
inscribed on every living thing,
sees how every breath is lost;

breathing clouds against the frost,
because breath is always warm,
sees how every breath is lost
in the one beloved form.

Because breath is always warm,
Hafez, yours ignites the dark.
In the one beloved form,
it is still a living spark.

Hafez, yours ignites the dark
in the book beside my bed.
It is still a living spark
between the living and the dead.

224

LOTTIE KRAMER

Lying in State

In Westminster Hall
The great hammer-beam roof
Survives the death-watch beetle.
A Lying in State.

Our lives continue
Little holiday outings,
Take the boat down the Thames
To the white elegance of Greenwich.
The river a big empty mouth
Broadening each minute,
Learning a new language:
The loss of trade.

Lining the route
Warehouses stand large
And hollow like unused
Victorian hospitals,
No longer bulging
With cargoes from the sea,
To cranes bending down.
Gratefully. The green slime
Of the river bank creeps
On shore where we read
Funeral names:
'Free Trade Wharf,
Metropolitan Wharf,
Oliver's Wharf'.
Another Lying in State.

Alone

(Herman Hesse)

Many roads and paths
Are leading across the earth.
But all have the same end.

You can ride and travel,
Two of you or three,
But the last step
You have to go alone.

No knowledge,
Nor ableness is as good
As tackling all difficulties
Quite alone.

EDDIE LINDEN

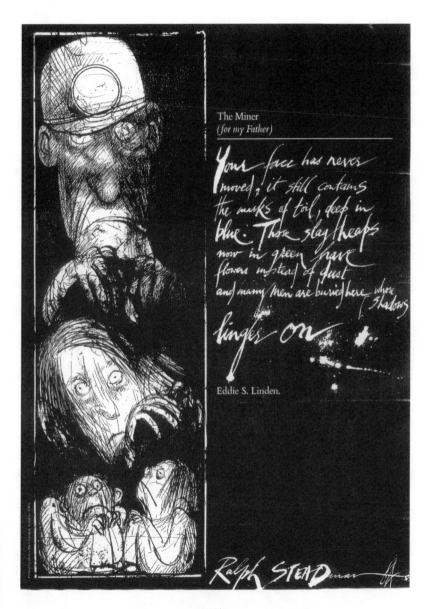

The Miner
(*for my Father*)

Your face has never
moved, it still contains
the marks of toil, deep in
blue. Those slag heaps
now in green have
flowers instead of dust
and many men are buried here, whose
shadows

lingers on

Eddie S. Linden.

Ralph STEADman

DINAH LIVINGSTONE

(From the sequence: *Presence*)
Beyond

Is there a presence beyond the cloud of unknowing?
Can it be pierced by a strong spear of love,
which passes like a plane through murk to the sun above?
No. Not this. Not that is where I'm going.
Is there someone speaking at the heart of being,
wording the world and everything alive,
uncreated author of all we are and have?
No. That is not what I'm hearing, seeing.
Brightness beyond dark, silence beyond speech, absence
of interruption hold the moment still,
the instant of pure energy to contemplate
what is always flowing, all at once,
make sense and love, yes, urgently to feel
warm with this life, right here where I sit.

PATRICIA McCARTHY

Your Death

(For William Cookson)

There were signs. Sound lost, your words,
rasped out, causing a stasis in the night,
had suddenly, unknown to us, been transferred

to the throat of the jungle-coloured bird –
offering surprise sestinas from a roof
the next shocked morning. It never occurred

to us that those dark angels you wrestled with
would win over your grasp of the bright;
yourself too intrinsic a part now of the myths

you ached always to re-read and to recite.
Then, as if playing a trick with truth,
the terrible certitudes we did our best to fight:

the coat you wore when we saw you last
shaped by your ghost shoulders on the back
of an unused chair; your voice oddly in the past

on the answer-phone still - like some quack
having with your name a tasteless joke
you would never have played; the stack

upon stack of poems piled like bricks to house
your Muse; the gas fire relentlessly flickering
reds, greens, yellows and blues to arouse

the child in you whom you retained, unfaltering
in vision. Small wonder we willed
portents to resume: such as the star honouring

you to be added to the sky; the moon
to be held – your last chance of a woman –
in your telescope; the snow you sent as a boon,

it seemed, in flurries, to cover you with an amen
before death scrawled its calumny over
pond and bench behind gates impossible to open.

Could we be back with you in Battersea Park
walking along an owl's reedy cry, or standing
together on Albert Bridge, in a light-hearted dark

as if in the painted treasure ship from your dreams –
we would not need the river rushing to redeem
with its polyphony while we wrap you in our esteem.

The Walk Not Taken

I wish I had walked with you once more
across lands teased out by your lording mind

to the open, winding through worked woods
in the search for oracles where druids stood.

It was the trees you listened to most,
to ancient oaks soughing like cellos

over lightning scores of thunder-gods.
You would have ensured the paths we trod

led to concert halls in your past
where pianos stroked by your mother's touch

from each dark and ivory note sang
the Vivaldi and Bach you learnt by rote.

It was the trees at your window that lipped you
into alphabets with Ogham lettering

of dryads and nymphs and unnamed goddesses
to draw you from shy recesses,

trees that opened leaves like hands spread
for you to trace, between unread lines,

all the tangling masses of maidenhair.
In the green felt ground-light muffling the air

you would have delayed the winters stripping,
to crotchets, the branches partnered by winds.

I wish I had walked just that one day
arm in arm with you. And not have balked

the major and minor keys of rains.
We could have transferred tides never pulled

by moons to a crinkling rust-gold ocean.
While boughs breathed their steady tempo

I should, somehow, have delayed you there
to conduct wing and claw, then dream up

impromptus to be sight-read, turning those
loved more than yourself into virtuosos

rather than elegists. I wish I had walked
through the trees you listened to most –

instead of, with my ear to trunks you knew,
now lisening and listening out for you.

SAM MILNE

Winter

In memory of William Cookson, 1939–2003
(eftir Hesiod, Warks and Days)

The north wind blaws: the earth and the forests roar.
Trees fa; beasts shiver. Bide at hame,
draa close ti the fire. And if ye're ti ging oot,
put on your thick coat – and dinna forget your cap!
One desire anlie: ti eat and ti drink.
Daan is caulder whan the north wind gousters;
a freezing fog frae the hard grun rises –
in time will mak for guid hairvests!
The birlin rivers – heelie-gousterin – aye rin–
and haars ti the luft are lifted, hurled.
Near gloamin ti rain it turns:
                              and sometimes a bluster,
        and the cluds aye shooken.

233

ROBERT NYE

Walking in Cloud

Walking in cloud a man becomes
Half cloud himself, and half despair
That he must wear a shroud of air.

Song Talk

Some say the nightingale improves his song
By adding new notes to it, year by year,
Correcting any bits he first gets wrong
Until the whole is simple and sincere.

But others say that bird sings from the heart
And does not need to add or change a thing
Because he is inspired from the start
To know what song a nightingale should sing.

I say it does not matter which is right
So long as the bird truly tells his tale;
Nor do you need to understand the night
To sing your heart out like a nightingale.

Vigils

Bees (some believe) on Christmas Eve
   Wake from their winter sleep
To hum a honey song of praise
   And night-long vigil keep.

Only the pure of heart they say
   Hear bees or angels sing
These Christmas hymns. I listened once
   And never heard a thing.

Still, I don't disbelieve. Who knows
   What songs the wise heart hears
If it is pure, or not impure,
   And kept awake by tears?

DESMOND 'O'GRADY

In Memoriam

If death when it comes will insist, then let it be sudden too;
But sudden as the unheard shot that bursts in the soldier's
crown,
Or the blind child that kills through the shocked mother's
womb,
Or the hired sword that martyrs the priest on his altar stone.

Let it be sudden provided it takes like the sailor on board
In the maw of the storm, or the poet-man dead in the middle
of the word.

Otherwise, death should be something already known well
when it comes;
Something as close as our women and respected as our
elders
For the detached familiarity of its patient presence;
something with drums
And a sober march about its finality; certainly not the
stranger's

Blade by mistake in the back, or the spitefully unsaid word
Of warning; for that is the noble reduced to the merely
absurd.

PENELOPE PALMER

Street Bar in Madrid

I sit under acacia trees
Loving them, that the people passing
Are all blessed.

I touch the rim of my glass
And the rim of your glass, drinking with you.
You make me light

To this swaying
Of trees falling flowers
Sometimes, on my hair.

In the dappled light
Under acacia trees, dropping flowers,
I precede myself

Into the trees, the glancing light,
The white flower that drifts
Now, to your hand.

To My Mother

Ulanova
In this picture she is dancing
And the children of the ballet school
Lined up behind, to watch.

And on the next page
The faces of the watching children,
Most beautiful of any children
For in them there is nothing of themselves,

Is all gone out
In dedication to the dancer.
How their eyes are big and dark,
Each mouth slightly apart

In wonder,
And necks and shoulders crane
To the line of the dance.
How each face is full of grace

And the terrible fragility
Of her finger-tip,
The bend of her arm,
And her fine-working brain.

(Do not breathe now,
For this is more than flesh
Can do, or any heart
Form to a poem.)

And seeing these faces now
With her so clear within them,
How, mother, you come into view
For I always knew

Behind all
That makes us human and inhuman,
Your spirit was a dancer.
And when I think of you

Without the world's part,
Always a white figure
With a poised grace
Dances before me,

(For how your eyes
Will sometimes tell, and I
Have seen you watch a dance
With such an empathy

There was no breath between
You and the dancer,
Freed into joy
In but a point of space).

Say I saw you
With the look on my face
Of one of these chlldren,
Bond beyond flesh.

Harvest

Wanting to rest and wake refreshed with you
I've stepped into some nineteenth century part:
The far romantic, the tubercular fool.
Far closer than the gaming and the hunt
Draws this quiet ardour and ambiguity
To keep me this quiet night. It bears the tune
That plays behind your tender irony;
The counterpoints of hope and an early home.
We meet as though we'd been good lovers long,
Our summer harvested against the night,
Complete, content with a cheek, an arm:
How did this ancient knowledge come? And the light
Which privately informs our least caress,
The ease and question in our silences?

Note: Penelope was a valuable friend and relation of William from his student days until Penelope sadly died in 1981. Penelope's collection *The Lamp* was published by *Agenda Editions*. Grateful thanks to her mother, Diana Pelham-Burn, for her generous gift to this issue.

MARY de RACHEWILTZ

For William Cookson

*(remembering the 1958 visit with his mother to Ezra Pound
and years later his reading of the Cantos)*

Sweetly William read her poems
in a world that was all green –
now gone, with him and Rachel
and everyone that was young.
Parched lips pray for rain and eyes
can see but sparrows pecking.
Here all angles are oblique
and lead from apocalypse
ad inferos, the spiral
stairs reflect a turn of mind
ascending high, descending
deep into the bluish-white
antimony where women
of rank with time on their hands
smooth the rough emerald path
into a crystalline heaven.

(Brunnenburg, March 2003)

ROBERT RICHARDSON

Sensibility

i.m. William Cookson

i
These encounters with content
which also merge into

a poem's aspects of the world
link up to thoughts of feelings

and by the words that fit them
become in a way unfurled.

ii
When a poem is not filled
then it is back to this place

that's moved in most of the time,
the dream of a moment is stilled

is absent, nothing seems new;
but it's somewhere to live in

and all that might be hoped for
is probably passing through.

STEPHEN ROMER

TO ONE WHO KEPT FAITH

'There is a distressing lack of communications between isolated outposts. Some of these are no doubt frivolous, some eccentric – outposts cannot be central' – EP

Cranbourne Court

A call from a coinbox next the bridge,
and the coatless young man
whose name is legion, a nobody
at a loss, and a stranger to London,
splashed by buses sloshing by
finds the impetus to cross the bridge
without stopping, or throwing himself over,
locates the block, and tremblingly the bell . . .
and is received
into a vastness and a volume
and the sweetstale smell that is home.
Led down a threadbare corridor, not knowing
where to start, the coveted objects
in alphabetical order, the old with the new,
when a voice comes drawling back to him
If there's anything you'd like to review . . .
Soon he's drowning in an armchair
and the ceremoniousness of tea
dispels at length the vestiges
of his psychological hour. Of his host
he remembers chiefly
a radical mildness of demeanour
and a conversation punctuated
by the rattle of faxes coming through
to Isolated Outpost, Battersea.

Less the Young Turk, than the Old Survivor,
straggler in the desert, up hill, down dale,
from a crenellated outpost in the Tyrol,
in Italy, in Suffolk, or in Lewisham,
with a berth for the new, and even, bless him,
for the not-so-new-anymore...

* * *

As numberless 'authors'
swan around
manouvering
with tilted goblets
there's a final glimpse
of our hero exiting
freighted with plastic bags
of the unsold bumper number,
tribute after tribute,
a stooping lynchpin
of the little world of letters
qui file a l'anglaise
and without applause.

So raise high the roofbeam
for the genial peddlar
of the small magazine
the footslogging
fundraising
festival-going
sandwich man
in for the duration
not just the issues
to publish self and friends
but forty years on

from the young man at Oxon,
the long haul of fealty,
and taking on the young,
through much right-headedness
and a little wrong,
let's hear it for Cookson
as he waits in the rain
for the night bus
to carry him home.

NANCY SANDARS

Running Down

The days of the weeks of the months of the years
of paradise never run down with the cosmic clock.
Time is a toy, but don't touch the doings
or you might get a shock.
Time is a toy, and we inside,
here we must bide,
where we are we must stay,
for the toys running down and the key was lost
long ago on Creation Day.

MICHAEL TOLKIEN

Displacement

You've been ransacking ways
to make another string of words
appear to dance on air.

What you wrote from the heart:
would it be honed yet sing
in cadences like warblers
composing while they feed?

Out there storm clouds flex
and fold up. Prototypes crumpled
and binned in thin air.

Suppose you delighted listeners
with your anguish, would they
tempt you to sing and sing
again, and suffer more?

New-fledged crows fly
into a stiff wind, parry
each lunge of air.

You're in a smoke-stained room
watching rain. What riposte
will the chimney thrush fling
into your empty hearth?

Patchwork

Another year's tilting away.
A last triangle of sunlight
has folded back the lawn's
far corner, picking out
a bindweed's shrunken white
lantern. Sign of warmth
to a wavering Red Admiral.
Such embroidered blazing
as it opens wide, and finds
no comfort. The only one
to warm me this season,
and never too late. Call it
'Rare Admiral', harbinger
of inner fire and outer
scarcity. Wrapped round you
like a shawl, it won't fray.

CHRISTOPHER TRUMAN

Absence

With no reaching cry
or sodium song,
as if surveying
                    a territory

a seagull
turns on the afternoon breeze

circling lower
before moving on

                    not a wave, breaker
under piercing attack –

the ocean littoral
a lonely summer.

On each briar rose, a bare
shore sunlight. I know
it is fine in the salt garden
where you no longer walk.

Galaxy Fire

The stars are harder, brighter
in the dry sea of the desert,
over tundra, piloting
clearer air.

They do not veer
or give, intimidating

as the cold at night,
their dimension nearer:
when we are lost

they are distance
all the way back,
the fire burning in you

and the hope
in the vision, the journey.

CLIVE WILMER

The Ladder

... this any *place where God lets down the ladder*
— Ruskin

"Don't let go yet. What was it made you cry
Just then? Keep holding on to me. You cried
Like a new baby launched upon the world,
A singer at her pitch of ecstasy,
A trapped animal howling against pain."

I cried?
                "As if from a shut room inside.
Not like your own: like someone else's cry
                Sounding within you."
If it was me that cried,
Or if through me the two of us, it was
That as we grappled here we seemed to touch
Some nerve of inwardness. Let me turn preacher.
I have, in former discourse, been inclined
To speak of love as though it were a thing
Outward and visible: the which thing is
In truth a fallacy. Consider Jacob,
Who wrestled with an angel and prevailed.
Where was that angel? Or those other ones
He witnessed in a nameless desert place
Somewhere between Beersheba and Haran?
The scriptures use the figure of a ladder
Propped between land and sky to body forth
The dream he had, head pillowed on a stone,
Of angel hosts ascending and descending.
But now, from the new exegetes, we learn
Of a stark outcrop glacially planed,

251

A table-land, with terracing for stairs;
Or – since it was, he said, the House of God –
Of a stepped temple, a symbolic mount
Like a vast altar, from whose surface priests,
With cries to distant gods, offered up smoke,
Throwing it forth, as charred bones fell away,
A frail and ghostly bridge from earth to heaven.

"We have travelled a long way
From the dark chamber of your inwardness.
What could have caused that resonance today?"

I don't know. It was nothing. I can't say.

The Ruin

Cattle browse in the meadow the sprung arch,
shot of its tracery, frames

Form looking out of ruin, a different view
shaped by the form's persistence
                            Miracle,
no other word for it, the enduring face
of Andrei Rublyov's *Saviour*, gazing out
from what, after several centuries as a doorstep,
the context gone, is plainly still a board:
not Christ the judge, this one – a hurt survivor
with knowledge it is hard to look away from
of what is suffered here
                          And come again
as Radnoti's last poems from the dark
and warmth of a mass grave, which they had shared
with swathes of greatcoat and corrupting flesh,
till brought to light
                       So the old bagwoman,
raddled, incontinent, hoists her reeking skirts
and, her lips pursed for crooning, rasps aloud:
Paradise, boys, come on, you can have it now.

Plenty

Apples,
   as if they were blossoms,
     left to drop.

Overnight Snow

There are star-crystals shining white on the blank earth.
It is a visitation from on high,
Where there is nothing but exploding worlds
And radiant fragments of infinity.

KIERON WINN

A Victorian Heaven

In the dark-stained Heaven this window shows above
The Cross of Mercy, Pity, Peace and Love,
Stiff-frocked saints each pay the Lamb his dues.
Many good people, shifting in hard pews,
Surely dreaded Heaven would be like this,
No running, no growing, no drunkenness,
Without a place for difference, or the taint
Of blood high in the cheek. Would every saint
Glance askance, hungering, incomplete
At the riotous flames of Hell and love their heat
And hate a frigid Heaven spare and sparse
As these wrought attitudes in brittle glass?

A Night of Snow

Angels in freefall, ceaselessly descending.
Like all experience, the snowflakes come
As though from ink-black space and melt in the grasping.

What schemes, what engines, what beat of sparrow's wing
Brings it to all, swift, sad, alive and dead?
All there is left to do tonight is look.

It is falling like forgiveness, whitening sins
In their intricate, fretted forms. Come morning, witness
Bright fields and lanes, unprinted, never so new.

ESSAYS

William's Mother

Rachel Cookson (Pelham-Burn) was the youngest of the five
children of the Venerable William Pelham-Burn, Archdeacon of
Norwich (1857–1901 and of his wife, Margaret. She was a very
gifted pianist.

JOHN KINSELLA

A Loss of Poetics

To write poetry you don't have to like it. I've been increasingly recognising that language and its correlatives in music and art are not the pure coordinates or sole arbiters of poetry. There are two issues evolving out of these comments that seem pivotal to me. The first pertains to the suggestion that poetry might happen either out of necessity, or, paradoxically, incidentally. The second, that poetry does not rely on an aesthetic response to the tensions involved in reconciling interiority and articulation of the external world. These two simple principles are becoming the turning points for a personal re-evaluation of what constitutes the poem for me as a reader, or more precisely 'experiencer', and what it means for me as a maker of poems.

On the surface, I am inclining towards poem as gesture or utterance arising out of the pre-cognitive, or maybe out of the half-realised. I have often used the expressions 'error zones' and 'anchor points' to describe the tautological discomforts that drive the written or spoken poem for me – the error zones being ambiguities that arise out of apparent errors in syntax and form, out of parataxis and enjambement, a disturbing of the rules of prosody, juxtaposed or interacting with 'realisms', points of concrete and external referentiality which clarify and focus perspective – anchor points. This is the hybridising of the unified self and the disrupted or displaced lyrical I.

So in writing poetry I have tried to merge a reference to a specific moment in time, recording with subject-object certainty, and a sense of linearity, with a series of, say, tense or syllabic or syntactical disruptions. The wandoo tree covered in pink and grey galahs morphs into an exploration of something metonymically associated with tree or bird that

259

might then evoke a series of historical or etymological associations and so on. In other words, it's a poetry of digressions and associations based largely – though by no means exclusively – in one language, having a point of reference common to the whole work in the epistemology of the language itself. And even should the work digress into other languages, the process of orality becomes the unifying signifier-signified construct. That is how it has been, but it's no longer that way.

Two words best sum up the shift in my poetics: mimetics and mnemonics. Poetry, in form and in language, in how it is said and why it is being said (which is desirably, at best, at least partially inexplicable on the surface level of 'meaning'), is a process of imitation and reproduction. The word itself derives from the Greek 'mimesis', and in many ways my mimetics is really an adapted and 'personalised' mimesis. Maybe the medical meaning of mimesis is even more relevant: symptoms appearing *without* the actual disease. We might compare the process to watching a mime play, and recalling it later as being rich with language, with voices. We can hear the movements of the players. The same happens for me in the creation of a poem.

The poem forms as a series of sounds and images and associations that seemingly have no specific register in language – that is, words don't necessarily correlate to what is being seen or heard, nor is explanation offered. But when it comes to placing them on the page, creating an artefact, or to speaking it aloud – that is, reciting it – language finds its dynamic equivalent, and the poem that was sounds and images becomes an imitation, a mimicry of the original language-less poem.

Sometimes this emerges as the short imagistic poem, distilled, such as the Finch poems:

Finches

Salt Paddocks

Down below the dam
there is nothing but salt,
a slow encroachment.

Fighting back, my cousins
have surrounded it
with a ring of trees.

At its centre
lives a colony of finches,
buried in tamarisks.

Finch Colony

The leaves, like wire, are so tangled
we dare not venture too far into their heart
where flashes of song and dull colour
betray a whole family of finches.

We hold our breath
and become statues.

Is this fear of disturbing their peace
or of a delicate raid from unknown spaces.

Finch Flight

To join the finch
in his tenuous kingdom

amongst tamarisks,
the hot snow of salt

You must gather
trajectory and direction,
sharp summer flights

Exile yourself
from the wind's hand.

Finch Death

The dead finch lies on salt,
tight-winged and stretched.

The others shimmer
loosely in heat

the salt's white mystery
coveting tin cans, skull of sheep.

Slowly, death rides this hot glacier
further and further away.

At others it flows in a more cinematic way, and with less pause
or hesitation. It's like too much information trying to distil
itself but shifting rapidly from one (often metonymic) connection to another. This is not simply a problem of the
synapses, brought about by the excesses of my youth, but a
life-issue associated with insomnia, hyperactivity, and a
mobile mood register. Poetry becomes tied up with the
chemical balance and imbalance of the body.

One of the problems I live with and which has certainly
been compelling my mimicries and their attendant inverted

mnemonic transliterations (I write to unremember, not to remember – it's a matter of rearranging the flood of information into art, not into confession or nostalgic reconnection), is the constant interruption of past moments of my life into the present. I can be sitting in a park in St. Louis, thinking about an Elizabeth Peyton image, and I'm instantly in King's Park in Perth, with my wooden sailboat, scratching at the rust around the mount for the mast. I can taste the rust, smell the sail that has been soaked and dried dozens of times over in heat that will eventually lead, one day when I am older, to the removal of skin cancers. I can see the twenty-eight parrots exploding emerald and sapphire and yellow in the eucalypts. There are interpolations – a banksia blossom from another time and another place, a heightened emotional moment. There's no biography to this in the strictest sense, the incidents are too fragmentary. But the tactility of the moment is preserved.

A few years ago I wrote an autobiographical or anti-autobiographical work, *Auto*. The experiences are fragmentary, the narrative shifts around. Issues of duration become pivotal when a brief moment extends into pages, and massive events (on a personal and historic level) are glossed over in a sentence. Time is not as it should be. But then sometimes the words move as they were chronologically enacted. As author, I retell my own story from a variety of points of view, never stable. What is truth – as remembered by whom? My mother's version of events will most often be different; my brother's closer, but still different. And so it goes.

You bypass circadian and diurnal rhythms. The cave is open to light, the Fremantle Doctor fills it with fresh sea air in the late afternoon. You stay in lit places at night. You close your room off to the light in the day. Jet lag kicks in and out. It's midnight and cold out on the hundred acre. The fuel is metal cold as it spills over your hands, the funnel slipping. The heavy soil is sticking to the tines and a fox is barking up towards the Needlings. You grow groggy. The tractor's lights glow silver and orange. Another two hours at least, the figures of eight that cut out the corners harder and harder to do – the light inadequate, the body hard to steer. Your lift back down to the city arriving at first light. A serepax to link the events. Night seeding & notions of property.

Dizzy with figure-eighting
the corners of his fields, the drills
filled with seed & super

and closed over under
the tattooed rash of night,
foxes' muffling barks

& fighting to cover tracks
with a starpicket the axis
of a compass whose North

is wire-guided & lethal: silver
tennis balls exploding in their spiralled
swing on totem-tennis poles

for here stillness shivers & moves
like frost moves the shattered
flesh of quartz

over the wasted plots. A clear
dawn is soluble anyway
& the tractor gnaws,

its queasy stomach
turning slowly & coldly
with winter:

        dispossessed
the farmer moans – a sudden downpour
shaves his precious topsoil.

The ghosts clamour about the microwave
& television set, the stove broods
in this sauna of politeness.

City people are expecting billy tea
& damper & the sheep to bleat
in unison. Nous regrettons parler.

There wasn't a kangaroo to be seen.
Night-seeding, the tractor's floodlights
are blood-red & ovarian –

nurturing the cloddish soil, & always
the farmer working the wheel, hands
gnarled & frostbitten & large.

Katherine can't sleep. Think of something nice, you say.
Think of Walsingham, of the Shrine of Our Lady. Of the
Stations of the Cross. Of the Catholics and Anglicans
taking tea together. Can't sleep. Go to sleep. John
Kerrigan has invited us to lunch out at the cottage. A
vegan feast. Daddy falls to sleep after he's been awake all
night. He falls asleep on the couch listening to the stereo
and watching the television. He watches the television
when he's asleep. Can't sleep. Go to sleep. I can't go to
sleep because I'm worried I'll be tired in the morning. I
don't want to think, thinking keeps me awake.

Dear S

Is it possible to have a series of dreams? Well, in keeping with a theme, I dreamt last night that you came to a meeting in a large colonial house (with necessary wrap-around verandahs) to discuss the compilation of a new international anthology. The publishers were trying to convince you to do some television appearances to give the anthology a nudge. Why the dream was set in Australia I'm not sure but our family property – 'Wheatlands' – was the setting. It had a sad atmosphere of decay as the property has been broken up over the years and in many ways it is my writing it that keeps it conceptually 'together', and retains the family ties. Fortunately, its proudest moments – the reclamation of land ruined by salinity ('the hot snow of salt' I wrote in 'Finches') – has been safeguarded. It's like a wildlife reserve and a great achievement, if somewhat ironic given that the family originally cleared it, drove off the indigenous peoples, and destroyed it in the first place. But times have changed, and there is a distinct effort to make amends. Not an excuse, but something important all the same. Anyway, in this dream, when there was a break I managed to catch your eye and you came over for a chat. I asked if you'd read Simone Weil, a thinker I really admire. I had a copy of *Gravity and Grace* in my hand. You began to weave an incredible poem that tied the colonial situation in Ireland with the colonial situation in Australia, weaving the different landscapes in and out of each other. 'Every separation is a link, every separation is a link...' repeated itself like a prayer or mantra. Suddenly my sight began to blur and I couldn't see you, only hear your voice... and I woke. Well, a strange dream, eh? Best, JK

My head is going fast inside. Go to sleep. Think of the walk to the Slipper Chapel, the fighter jets cutting in over the coast, the ear-tags of cows destined for slaughter as the mist lifts from the field and the thistles dry and the world begins to glow.

What I did in *Auto*, was to imitate or mimic systematically the experiences of my life as I remembered or re-remembered them. These experiences were presented in different shapes, with different prosodies. A system of mimetics tied them together, but the imitations constantly shifted. As a reversal of Dante's guiding principle of using prose commentaries cutting across poetry texts, though, I make tangential commentary and illustrate with a verse by the object of my subjectivity!:

Last year I bought my wife a new flute – to replace the one I'd hocked and lost at the beginning of our marriage. As a teenager I'd hated body fluids and dirt and loss of control. I then devoted a dozen years to overcoming these phobias. That's one way of looking at it. Andrew Burke turned up with Tracy at my flat in South Perth near the river. I was pretty far gone. I said something about fucking Tracy and Andrew was disgusted. When I did, or maybe I already had, I burnt the curried vegetables and shaved the hair from around her pubis. She'd written a poem called 'Hair' which I'd published in *Salt* long before I knew her. It went:

The length
of my body is an odd
nudity, what is it
doing there, how
did the hair
get pared down

to just
these patches
we cultivate
like fetishes
meant to excite
when we want
to play animal
or we control
to stress and make
the difference between sexes
as if otherwise
we couldn't find
ourselves.
I can't force
what once was
to grow now
in a strange season.
I'm caught
between
the dreams of befores
that paralyses
and the need
of my own nakedness
which is there,
which is there.

Back to the park. The poem forms between the moment I
actually occupy and will occupy, with the short-term past and
the imitated (but highly 'real' to me) past that interrupts my
thoughts with painful and disturbing clarity. I know that
every revisiting of this that's foisted on me, though I recall
them as being identical, is mediated by the place and context
of where they occur. As with the text read in a different place,
or the poem you've read a dozen times, meaning never
remains stable or consistent. It shifts.

Maybe this is why I see the draft as the most relevant part of the poem, why a poem for me is never completed. It's part of an ongoing conversation in which a dialogics forms between the text and the unwritten 'seeing' of what that text might become as conditions of production and reception change.

The mnemonics also has a personal angle. It won't fit the poetry definitions volume. These are associations that assist memory. They're tools of remembering and remembrance. For me, they become tools to lose the moment so I won't have to revisit it compulsively. Now, I've just said that poetry gives no closure to me, that it's an ongoing series of drafts, a revisiting, a reanimating or mimicry of tensions between the past and present and future, of the real and imagined, of the perceived and conceptualised. All of these. But now I am suggesting that I don't want any of it. And I don't.

I DO NOT WANT TO WRITE OR READ POETRY. I am addicted, compelled. I cannot stop. This is mental illness of a sort, and not inspiration (or delusion of this), but compulsion. What we've tracked so far is the subtext of the poem, the reason it might come into being. Moving along, the process of transcribing or translating or transliterating this compulsion into a form (visual or oral – or never uttered but seen or heard in the head), is a very different process. This is where un-mnemonics become pivotal for me. I encode my work in traditional ways – often using traditional rhythms which I disrupt with colloquialisms and dialect, using set forms from a variety of cultural spaces (conscious of the appropriative issues therein) – but also encode it with unmnemonics that cause a disintegration of sense upon rereading, especially as context shifts and changes.

Those points of ambiguity become increasingly larger, and suddenly the anchor points don't hold. The repetitions and patterning of words, that assist us in our ability to recall them, become unstable – an apparent volta is seemingly not where it should have been, a noun is really a verb, and so on.

269

The stock epithet isn't quite the same each time. When I read aloud I do so mainly from memory, with the page of the book as a rough guide. No two readings of mine have ever been the same – not only in tone and performance qualities/ styles, but in actual textual consistency. I try to be inconsistent. Only slightly. A changed word, a reshaped line.

I can close my eyes and see the poem on the page because I have that kind of memory, but I can also see the drafts that led to that version, and the versions of the poems I should write. They are key points of memory in the poem – specific words that have a texture, a strong form and function association, or that are emotional triggers. Some fit an idiomatic pattern that comes with being brought up in a specific space. The mnemonics are where I try to disrupt, to subvert the poem.

Mnemonic systems can work by abstracted repetitions or patterns of association as much as by, say, a string of music, or a series of visual or verbal prompts. For me, it's a question of disturbing juxtapositions that come out of having witnessed animal cruelty or death, or some natural phenomenon that is inexplicable: glowing fields, ball lighting, will-o-the-wisps. Patterns build up in my subconscious, repeat themselves in recreating the poem I have mentally formed onto the page, or in recitation from memory. A chair, a table, a tree might trigger locations and patterns of words, help in the recreation of a poem resembling what I have 'thought'.

Location Triggers

The pillared porch, Corinthian
because it's easiest from books,
plastered, upholding world's ceiling
that goes through to the next story
always colder in winter, maybe cooler in summer,
airflow and loveseat, swinging

where foliage redresses trees
in gendered avenues, sweeping uphill
as around flat fields, the grey rot
of corn stalks, Japanese beetle
driving towards modification, it's said,
avoiding upper rooms where heat unsettles
small windows, vicarious
and remembering a purple rising light,
hillfolds and outcrops bettered
by kites and glider, their freedom
paramount over scrub and small animals
they'd destroy, farmers alarmed
by drop-ins, all land there
like thermals and updrafts, but suddenly
undercut, we resist calling it revenge,
colluding with indifferent Nature,
visa and permit, green card
as crops spread: they won't let me
into their pastoral entirely,
invited to ride the header,
to harvest cobs and interiors
that exchange chemical appearance,
protectionist policies and markets
fill supermarket aisles, fill
hunting and trapping magazines,
fur around collars, covering
cold ears, addressing steers
on Texan clichés, clinging like ideas
of Kansas. We take back leaf-litter
stirring in warmer years, lack of snowdrifts,
birds chopping and changing
or not there at all: correlations so easy,
suppressed to keep mystery
intact... or fenceless plurals
full of Wallace Stevens,

growing randomly and imitating
gardens, as if you'd fly straight
from Columbus to Paris, or get diverted
to New Orleans, or Bâton Rouge;
I track these infinitudes,
connect nouns from an uncle's paddocks
in places threatened by closure,
by tariffs, sucked into global
silos and temptations,
cantons and guilds and red barns
lit by nuclear light,
as fission is comradeship,
alliance, the blind leading the blind,
and grain swelling on lightless nights,
Biblical texts written with a human hair
on rice, as faith makes cars run
and the fringes shutdown:
deny all access.

Having spent a lot of my adult life living in various countries
other than that of my birth, and being doomed (against my
wishes ultimately) to be a perpetual wanderer, memory and
the associations of words with a specific place tend to be
disrupted. Maybe that's why I also persistently write over the
place I come from. That's where most of the flashbacks take
me. But it's no longer the story of that place I'm telling, that
place has changed and become something else, I am telling
in poetry the story of hybridisation, of dislocation, loss and
disruption. My poetry is full of death, and maybe this is why.
It shifts register dramatically. Maybe this is why. I don't feel
comfortable in any 'school' or 'camp'. Again, maybe this is
why. Poetry, for me, is an eclogic structure: a dialogue
between disparate parts of myself, most often centred in the
rural, and between conflicting cultural inputs. Characters
are speaking through me – sometimes characters close to

myself, but they are all mimicking someone from the real world. They are not real. It's all a simulacrum.

I see romanticism in revival. There are obvious culturo-historic reasons for this, and the threat of war (we have been in a state of world war for a number of years now) always brings on a search for a sublime, especially in a world where nature is increasingly being destroyed or disturbed, or can be undone in extreme ways, instantly. The end of language poetry and the rise of new-lyricists such as Lee Ann Brown, Lisa Jarnot, Lisa Robertson, and Jennifer Moxley, with their strong consciousness of the tensions between deployments of tradition and the fetishisations of linguistic innovation (especially regarding 'class' alienation), illustrates a shift in receptivity not only to environmental and social concerns (also pivotal to language poetry), but to a concern about the ecology of language and meaning. Consider Lee Ann Brown's poem 'No Melpomene':

No Melpomene

Re: Lone poem, pen nomme
Pommel pope poop
Olé, Olé, Ol' Pop Pomp

Pelé mope
Mono men pole, lop me
One pen open poem

Peel 'em:
La Pomme, pome, pommelo

Moon pone molé

There is no lyrical self, mediated or otherwise, located textually here, but there is a subjectivity in the texture and

273

immediacy of address. This lyricism locates itself in the implication of song, the implication of self, without being dictated by the unified self. These are poets who do not wish to lose referentiality, or to deny it entirely. Here's the end of Shelley's over-quoted *Defence of Poetry*:

It is impossible to read the compositions of the most celebrated writers of the present day without being startled with the electric life which burns within their words. They measure the circumference and sound the depths of human nature with a comprehensive and all-penetrating spirit, and they are themselves perhaps the most sincerely astonished at its manifestations; for it is less their spirit than the spirit of the age. Poets are the hierophants of an unapprehended inspiration; the mirrors of the gigantic shadows which futurity casts upon the present; the words which express what they understand not; the trumpets which sing to battle, and feel not what they inspire; the influence which is moved not, but moves. Poets are the unacknowledged legislators of the world.

The above-mentioned poets and other innovators, steeped in the historicity of their poetries, the environments their languages arises from, might be forced into this mould. I say *forced*, because their individual intentions and agendas couldn't be bent in this way. It's the convenience of the overview. There is an emphatic belief that poetry can make a difference. The mere production of it suggests this. Despair hasn't closed the door to utterance, though, of course, it might in the future. Their significance is in the recognition that the moment of self is undeniable within or outside a political intentionality. Their poetry is a poetry of purpose, they have something to say: it is semantic and linguistic legislation, even if it's a civil or linguistic disobedience.

I would like to consider myself simpatico with them as poets, though more recently my despair has driven me away from cause and effect, and certainly beyond the ironies of engaging with the sublime. Prayer is still poetry for me, and poetry prayer, but nature can't even work as a mimetic construct. The paper I use, the books I read mean suffering for this 'nature'. My existence as a print poet becomes a process of bad legislation, and consequently denial. I wrote a poem when I first became a vegan called 'Of':

Of emulsifiers and preservatives
extracted from boiled-down animal,
of houses with walls of horse hair
and thongs of leather to restrain
the tortured awning,
of feet covered in dead cow,
kangaroo, crocodile . . .
the business of pig-skin briefcases,
of those whose guilt lay in fish,
of those sucking the nectars
of sacred beasts,
of the differences between clean and dirty flesh,
of those who seek truth in the burnt offering,
of 'perfect and upright' Job, slaughterer
who sought to appease over and over,
of *Julius Civilus With A Dead Cock*
arrogantly accepting what is
over and over, back and forth, to and fro.

I don't enjoy polemical poetry, but then I wonder if all poetry isn't polemical the moment it is written or sung or spoken. There's another kind of politics when it stays in your head, even if fully realised, but more relevantly, a less explicable politics when it remains half formed. Literally, for me, poems are a series of mime enactments in which characters are never

275

given names. They are dumb eclogues. It's the stone, the leaf, and the made object. Okay, that's easy. Not original. But it's a truth for me. I wonder what it is I am articulating outside my own chemical disconnections and odd internal wiring. As an anarchist, am I legislating, laying down a series of commands for others to follow? If so, I should stop, stop now. But here's my quandary: I don't want to stop the stone, the leaf. My interpretation of a bird's flight, a baby crying, creates a series of associations that struggle to separate themselves from the thing as thing-in-itself. Past memories burn back. I can't dispose of the connections. I don't want to be part of a poetic experience, but I am. If there is a 'modern sublime', then maybe therein lies part of the necessity of this contradiction.

Can we reclaim, revamp, and reprise the sublime? Consider it a viable literary tool or mode of expressing a reverence and awe born out of terror for nature? To give an alternative name and face to beauty? Yes, if Burke's 'ocean' with its terror is sublime not only because of tidal waves but because of heavy metal saturation, butchery of its life, oil spills. The sublime of the polluted, the sublime of the greenhouse effect. It's an angry irony. The sublime never worked as more than an idea. An exchange with God or nature that can be transmuted into artistic expression is simply a version of mimicry.

The sublime becomes the space-travel or star-gazing experience in an environment disrupted and destroyed. As a subtext of deep ecology, the sublime may work as an inspiration, but the layers of contaminants and the paucity of wildlife and forests work against it. The mountains become engagements with different kinds of contaminants. There was rubbish for Coleridge and Shelley, they were tourists – they made rubbish and were tourists themselves. Nature has overwhelmed me in its infinite complexity in places like Bluff Knoll, or The Gap, both in Western Australia, but simultaneously I feel its loss and destruction.

276

The sublime is a textual displacement, and divergence, in a cautionary tale of not what will happen, but what is happening and has happened. Time shifts. The duration doesn't match. We inject caution in the reading of who we are. That it might not translate into the way we treat each other. But it does. The transcendent that cannot be pinned down in words, despite the movement of the self towards its possibility, the veneration the path to an unrealisable actuation. Beauty is isolated, and we grapple towards it. The majesty of the sublime remains, necessarily, unobtainable.

I would argue that the sublime has been rendered as trope, as construct that is obtainable in so far as beauty has been forced into subjectivity by modernism, and becomes the ironic footnote in a world perceived in its wholeness as having been made increasingly ugly. The sublime, outside text, rests in the lens of the Hubble, and a cracked mirror is corrected so it can be maintained. The need is there, but it is textually subservient. Maybe it returns to John Dennis, to the 'sublime object', simply an issue of style. The separation of the sublime and the beautiful is a tension in modern poetry. The beautiful is a fetishised advertising construct that, even in private moments, we are required to question. The sublime suffers the same fate. In isolation they exist per the moment as well, but constructed in the poem a consciousness of language and its history renders 'purity' impossible.

Here's an extract from Edmund Burke's essay 'Sublime and Beautiful':

THE passion caused by the great and sublime in nature is astonishment, and astonishment is that state of the soul in which all its motions are suspended, with some degree of horror. The mind is so entirely filled with its object that it cannot entertain any other, nor reason on that object which fills it. Astonishment is the effect of the sublime in its highest degree; its inferior effects are admiration, reverence, and respect. No passion so effectually robs the mind of all its powers of acting and reasoning as terror; and whatever is terrible with regard to sight, is sublime.

It is impossible to look on anything dangerous as trifling or contemptible, so that even serpents are capable of raising ideas of the sublime. The sublimity of the ocean is due to the fact that it is an object of no little terror. How closely allied are terror and sublimity we may judge from the Greek language, which has but one word for 'fear' and for 'wonder,' another for 'terrible' or 'respectable,' while a third means either 'to reverence' or 'to fear.'

And:

The last extreme of littleness is sublime also, because division, as well as addition, is infinite.

Infinity fills the mind with that sort of delightful horror, which is the truest test of the sublime; and succession and uniformity of parts, which constitute the artificial infinite, give the effect of sublimity in architecture. But in regard to the sublime in building, greatness of dimension is also requisite, though designs, which are vast only by their dimensions, are always the sign of a common and low imagination. No work of art can be great but as it deceives.

Another kind of infinity also causes pleasure, as the young of animals are pleasant because they give the promise of something more, and unfinished sketches are often more pleasing than the completed work.

The loss of the sublime is in the idea of a universe – expanding but finite in content; but it remains in the idea of the 'unfinished work'. A resistance to closure can be an act of

278

sublimity. I write only drafts, and that's a sublimity? It fits the category of mimetic sublimity. It relies not on nature, but a human construct, or an interpretation of a damaged nature. The ocean is still a place of terror, but we are led to believe it is being controlled. Science works to harness it. It resists, and the sublimity is retained in this. Or a meteorite hitting the planet. The beauty I find in the white wastes of salinity that have destroyed the farm. So it's there, just reconfigured. This from Lisa Jarnot's 1996 p(r)oems, 'Sea Lyrics:

> I won't go to the waterfront anymore, I am basking on a beach far from the army, I am pointing to a thousand speckled birds, I am watching the salads roll down to the shore, I am on the grounds of Mission High School with the murderers, I am near the edge of all the bungalows, I am reaching toward the pineapples to reach, I am dreaming the dreams I hardly know and know I have tattoos, I am in the ambulance at dawn, I am in this town beneath where you have jumped from bridges row by row, from the midtown light, I am in the dreams Lucretius, I have helped you to assemble all the mammals on the lawn.

Parataxis, rolled text, and pollution of beauty make the sea as sublime terrible before the sea is actually considered. There's a displacement of the sublime by the terror of the incidental, the matter-of-fact. Sublime still, but brought down to ground. The awe has been defamiliarised.

The ur-text of the sublime is now believed to come from the middle of the first century A.D., Longinus's *On the Sublime*. Here's an extract from Chapter 1:

> 3. As I am writing to you, good friend, who are well versed in literary studies, I feel almost absolved from the necessity of premising at any length that sublimity is a certain distinction and excellence in expression, and

that it is from no other source than this that the greatest poets and writers have derived their eminence and gained an immortality of renown. 4. The effect of elevated language upon an audience is not persuasion but transport. At every time and in every way imposing speech, with the spell it throws over us, prevails over that which aims at persuasion gratification. Our persuasions we can usually control, but the influences of the sublime bring power and irresistible might to bear, and reign supreme over every hearer.

And an extract from Chapter 9:

Now the first of the conditions mentioned, namely elevation of mind, holds the foremost rank among them all. We must, therefore, in this case also, although we have to do rather with an endowment than with an acquirement, nurture our souls (as far as that is possible) to thoughts sublime, and make them always pregnant, so to say, with noble inspiration. 2. In what way, you may ask, is this to be done? Elsewhere I have written as follows: 'Sublimity is the echo of a great soul.' Hence also a bare idea, by itself and without a spoken word, sometimes excites admiration just because of the greatness of soul implied. Thus the silence of Ajax in the Underworld is great and more sublime than words (Odyssey XI. 543 ff., at Perseus) 3. First, then, it is absolutely necessary to indicate the source of this elevation, namely, that the truly eloquent must be free from low and ignoble thoughts. For it is not possible that men with mean and servile ideas and aims prevailing throughout their lives should produce anything that is admirable and worthy of immortality.
(Trans W. Rhys Roberts)
It is easy to see how the latter is undermined with every

modern irony. Aesthetically, it's the mean and ignoble I search for in language. The Warholian piece of trash, the art that is Cicciolina rather than the Venus or David. These are the contemporary registers of popular culture, of the new sublime. These elements of the 'filthy' sublime, as maybe we could call them, become codes and triggers in my personal mimetics, another form of mnemonic mapping. My effort at confronting the irreconcilability of the classical and modern, though the conditions of oppression, environmental destruction, and cultural destruction share much in common, is 'Bluff Knoll Sublimity', a poem more about language as object and a construct of sublimity, than about the sublime in nature:

Bluff Knoll Sublimity

for Tracy

I

The dash to the peak anaesthetizes
you to the danger of slipping as the clouds
in their myriad guises wallow about
the summit. The rocks & ground-cover
footnotes to the sublime. The moods
of the mountain are not human
though pathetic fallacy is the surest
climber, always willing
to conquer the snake-breath
of the wind cutting over
the polished rockface,
needling its way through taut
vocal cords of scrub.

II

It's the who you've left behind
that becomes the concern as distance
is vertical and therefore less inclined
to impress itself as separation; it's as if you're
just hovering in the patriarchy
of a mountain, surveying
the tourists – specks on the path
below. Weather shifts are part of this
and the cut of sun at lower altitudes
is as forgiving as the stripped
plains, refreshingly green at this time
of year. You have to climb it because it's
the highest peak in this flat state,
and the 'you have to' is all you
can take with you as statement
against comfort and complacency:
it's the vulnerability that counts up here.

III

You realize that going there to write a poem
is not going there at all, that it's simply
a matter of embellishment, adding
decorations like altitude,
validating a so so idea
with the nitty gritty of conquest.
Within the mountain another
body evolves – an alternate
centre of gravity holding
you close to its face.
From the peak you discover
that power is a thick, disorientating

282

cloud impaled by obsession, that
on seeing Mont Blanc – THE POEM –
and not Mont Blanc – THE MOUNTAIN –
the surrounding plains
with their finely etched topography
can be brought into focus.

As the horrors of the twentieth century are exacerbated and
perpetuated, I am guided by Adorno in the belief that I
cannot but work towards silence. What I am performing is a
mime, enacted to a tune in my unconscious, while sublimity
raises its polluted head and becomes the acceptable, the
desirable awe.

GABRIELLE J. REED

Chosen young essayist. Age 29, educated in France and St. Paul's Girls' School, London. Read Classics at Trinity College, Cambridge, specialising in Textual Criticism, Linguistics and Hellenestic Poetry. Classics teacher at St. Leonards-Mayfield School since 1999.

The Magic of Ovid

He did not bequeath us the tragic love story of Dido and Aeneas, nor versify learned discourse on natural philosophy; his delight was to entertain his audience and rejoice in the pleasures of romantic and erotic love, and yet he has left Western literature some of its most poignant moments.

Ovid is best known as a love elegist in the illustrious tradition of Propertius, Tibullus and Gallus. Who could forget his advice on how to get the girl of your dreams or how to mend a broken heart if it all goes wrong? Such levity of subject matter surely doesn't demand serious scholarly consideration. It did however prompt the emperor Augustus to send him into exile. How do we reconcile this aspect of his work with his discourse on the many sacred holy days in Rome's calendar, or the often calamitous tales of human and animal metamorphoses?

The key lies in the opening couplets of his *Amores*:

> *arma gravi numero violentaque bella parabam*
> *edere, materia conveniente modis*
> *pars erat inferior versus: risisse Cupido*
> *dicitur atque unum suripuisse pedem.*

Amores I 1, 1–4

Following the precedent of the Hellenistic poets beginning with Callimachus and continuing through Propertius and others, he offers his apology for not embarking on a grandiose epic, but for treating instead the much lighter theme of love. (Such an attitude might surprise us, given the immense corpus of love poetry which exists nowadays, but any serious poet then aspired only to compose epic or didactic verse.) Other poets in their apologies claimed to have been dissuaded from epic by an admonition from the solemn god of poetry himself, Phoebus Apollo. Ovid however claims that the mischievous Cupid has played a practical joke on him and stolen a metrical foot from his verses, thus simultaneously reducing both metre and subject matter. This witty parody of the genre is reinforced in the very first word, *arma*, the most famous opening word of Roman poetry which echoes through the centuries:

arma virumque cano, Troiae qui primus ab oris

Virgil *Aeneid 1. 1*

Ovid's listeners would have known their Virgil by heart and they would have appreciated the allusion in this witty reworking of an epic opening.

He has set out to challenge the poetic conventions of the time and yet superficially pays them lip service. In his autobiography written in exile, he calls himself a *tenerorum lusor amorum Tristia IV 10, 1*, a player of young loves, as he contemplates the achievements of his life.

Propertius' girlfriend Cynthia was a real woman with whom he shared all the hopes and despairs of love, but Ovid has not documented a banal relationship with his own girl Corinna, probably a figment of his imagination. In Amores 1.5, he describes a daytime encounter with Corinna. The opening verses set the scene: a sultry afternoon, the shutters

285

half closed. Suddenly Corinna enters and four lines describe her and compare her to mythological beauties. But Ovid wastes no time, and in two words has torn off her tunic, *tunicam deripui* 13! A further six lines of sensuous description of her naked charms are abruptly curtailed, *singula quid referam?* 23, and the act of love making itself merely alluded to, *cetera quis nescit?* 25. He ends on a note of self-satisfied complacency: *proveniant medii sic mihi saepe dies* 26. Propertius would have agonised over the possibility of losing his girl; for Ovid the art is in the seduction and prospect of success, the act itself is universal and personal.

In the *Ars Amatoria*, he mockingly adopts the persona of the didactic poet. The concept of poet as teacher is older than Homer and can be traced back to Hesiod's *Works and Days*. The master himself, Virgil, composed the *Georgics*, a learned rather than practical manual of instruction in the art of keeping a country estate. The outdoor pursuits of hunting and bird catching were favourite topics for didactic verse, but Ovid humorously substitutes girls as the objects of the chase, and suggests the ways and means of securing your desired prize and the most effective techniques. Race meetings at the Circus Maximus were a preferred occasion for indulging in this game. Frivolous as it was, the *Ars Amatoria* coupled with a mistake, *duo crimina, carmen et error*, nevertheless resulted in his banishment from Rome during Augustus' crusade to purge the city of amorality and return to the family values of his ancestors.

The idea of transformation from human to animal or inanimate is one which had preoccupied philosophers from classical Greece onwards. Ovid's *magnum opus*, which afforded him countless opportunities for recounting scurrilous or risqué love affairs, is a testament to his technical skill and ingenuity. Composed as a mock epic, *perpetuum carmen* 1. 1,4, the *Metamorphoses* tell the stories of over 200 transformations in the natural world. The task of maintaining unity of composition without surrendering to monotony is monumental. The use of hexameters lends a stately tone as do all the tools of a rhetorician: set speeches, similes, catalogues. The range of stories told spans history, *primaque ab origine mundi/ad mea tempora* 1 1, 3–4, and the links between them may be narrative, thematic, coincidental or other. Thus in book 10 Orpheus consoles himself over the death of Eurydice by singing of other lost loves. The variety of tone employed is distinctive, from the pathos of Daedalus' loss (*inter opus monitusque genae maduere seniles/et patriae tremuere manus. dedit oscula nato/ non iterum repetenda suo* 8. 210–212; *at pater infelix, nec iam pater, 'Icare' dixit,/'care' dixit, 'ubi es?'* 8. 231–232), to the parody of Apollo's desperate plea to Daphne (*nympha, precor, Penei mane! non insequor hostis;/ nympha mane! sic agna lupum, sic cerva leonem,/sic aquilam penna fugiunt trepidante columba/hostes quaeque suos: amor est mihi cause sequendi!* 1. 537–540). The touching simplicity of Daedalus' distress contrasts sharply with the contrived words of the libidinous Apollo. Ovid had found an almost perfect vehicle for showing off his poetic genius.

Alongside technical skill and variety of subject (which the Hellenistic poets called ποικιλια), poets prided themselves on their display of learning. In his *Fasti* Ovid is harking back to Callimachus' *Aetia* which sought to trace the cause or origins of various aspects of ritual and custom within society, and seeking to recreate it within the framework of the Roman calendar. Here again is scope for variety of tone and subject: the eccentricities of Roman religious practice were many and obscure. Yet amongst the opportunities for praising Augustus and making displays of serious learning, the urge to lighten with the touch of humour remains. During the festival of Anna Perenna, the personification of endless years, couples would camp outside and drink as many cups of wine as years they wished to live, and stagger home inebriated. Ovid has captured a vignette of everyday life:

287

occurit nuper (visa est mihi digna relatu)/pompa: senem potum pota trahebat anus 3. 541–542.

Although his exile was a source of great sorrow to him (his *Tristia* bear witness to this), Ovid was a poet essentially in love with life. Quintilian the teacher and rhetorician described him as *nimium amator ingenii sui,* too fond of his own genius. His passion for life is observed in the immediacy and intimacy of his detail. However it is the fusion of technical skill, variety of theme, learning and allusion with biting and often self deprecating wit, that make Ovid as exciting and unexpected today as he was to his own time.

GLYN MAXWELL

Ariadne to Theseus

[after Ovid, Heroides X]

As blank as the white page before there falls
The print of loss, so were the sheets I rose
To find this morning, and the roar of shells
    Was all my voice,
    Theseus –

Sleep vaulted the horizon, and the moon
Was sorry to be seen. On the cold shore
I echoed every rock that told me *Gone* –
    My tangled hair,
    Theseus,

Would not have let you from its labyrinth.
And the first letter of this far lament
Was *A* on a blank page, a sail's length
    No more. The wind,
    Theseus,

Lit up my eyes like candles, and like flame
I stood, I was blown back, I stood again.
The waves crept back and left behind your name
    Spelt on the sand,
    Theseus,

And in the mountain ridges of the sheets
Of our lost kingdom where I reign alone.
Nobody journeys here, I scale the heights
    And the horizon,
    Theseus,

Is all I see: a line that forms a ring
Forever and forever utters O.
What horrors prowl that circle? There's no string
    For me to follow,
    Theseus,

Out of such a place. Only to go
From all the world, as you from all of mine,
I dream of. A kept vow, a broken vow,
    Each is a chain,
    Theseus,

And in the grinding of the green salt sea
You hear me roam my island like the beast
You left for dead. I love you. Now the sky
    Darkens the east,
    Theseus,

Darkens the shore, shortens the little page
I beat upon, and how I meet the end
Is all that's left untold, a ragged edge
    For the undersigned
    Ariadne.

W S MILNE

Homer Updated

Christopher Logue, *All Day Permanent Red: War Music continued* (Faber and Faber, £8.99); Judith Kazantzis, *In Cyclops' Cave: The Odyssey Book IX 105–566* translated (Greville Press Pamphlets, The Greville Press, 6 Mellors Court, The Butts, Warwick CV34 4ST, £2.25).

When we read Homer, even in translation, we go back to our roots, both historical and linguistic. Where would we be without *theos, logos, bios* and *psyche*, for example? Or, indeed, in my own case, as a loyal Scot, *presbyteros*? It is this ever-fresh source of western literature which every translation of Homer acknowledges (or, at least, ought to). It is the first garden of our thought which every so often needs to be revisited for replanting, restocking and watering. Each new, worthy translation is a life-saving grafting. Both Christopher Logue (in his major way) and Judith Kazantzis (in her minor) bring this proper feeling of homage to their tasks – Logue's in progress and, one surmises, Kazantkis' *in conclūsum*:

Dust like dry ice around their feet
As Hector draws away
Onto and up the rise above the well, three spearcasts now
Above the Skéan Road
Beside him, Ábassee, Chylabborak, T'lespiax. . .

(Logue)

All day across the strait we saw the smoke of fires
and far off sheep cried out the hours.

The second dawn we rowed across, and found disaster,
we found the cave of a man monster,

291

a keeper of sheep, crag high and huge and ogreish
with one eye out for human flesh. . .

(Kazantzis)

As Homer's two epics themselves resulted from the inter-
action of great near eastern cultures such as the Hittite,
Phoenician, Syrian and Babylonian (we couldn't have
Homer without the *Epic of Gilgamesh*, for example) so it is that
the great Greek revival begun in the late fifteenth century
continues apace today, right across Europe and the USA.
Logue, Kazantzis and all recent translators of Homer (one
thinks of Philippe Jaccottet in France, Robert Fitzgerald and
Richmond Lattimore in the USA, Martin Hammond in
England, and William Neill in Scotland – the last working on
Homer in both Scots and Gaelic) are acknowledging in their
contemporary fashion the pioneering work of Erasmus and
William Tyndale. Intrepid religious reformers came first: the
poets (Chapman, Pope and Cowper, for example) followed
thereafter. (It is worth remembering that Dante knew
Homer only in Latin.)

Let us start with two questions, and answer them as best we
can. Firstly, in general terms, what is it that makes a good
translation? George Chapman said it was to observe the 'true
sense and height' of the original; St. Jerome 'keeping the
sense but altering the form'; and Schleiermacher that 'no
one could easily change a span of horses and replace it with
another ... Everyone produces original work in his mother
tongue only'. Walter Benjamin thought that the translator
should 'allow his language to be powerfully affected by the
foreign tongue'. Logue and Kazantzis, each in their own ways
and in different ranges, observe these qualities pragmatic-
ally, keeping to the boundaries of what is possible in clear
English diction and strong narrative drive:

The ridge.
King Agamemnon views Troy's skyline.

Windmills. Palms.

'It will be ours by dark'
(Logue)

There lies a land of giants, miles from anywhere,
the Cyclopes, who neither pray

nor plough, yet own a paradise of bleating flocks.
One cursed night, caught by the tricks

of a dense fog, our blind ships crashed aground,
through unseen waves, onto an island. . .

(Kazantzis)

Both authors avoid the pitfalls of becoming interpreters only.
They are not, after all, official translators employed by
the European Commission! They are creative, autonomous
writers capturing the multivalence of the world, its linguistic
and therefore human potentialities:

Sparks from the bronze. Lit splinters from the poles.
'I am hit.'
'Take my arm.'
'I am dying.'

'Shake my hand.'
'Do not go.'
'Goodbye little fellow with the gloomy face.'
As Greece, as Troy, fought on and on . . .

(Logue)

Think how an iron blade when plunged by the smith
to temper it and get it tough

gives a great hiss. That's just how Cyclops' eye
Hissed. He screams horribly...
                              (Kazantzis)

Our second, more specific question, is: 'What do we expect
from a first-rate translation of *Homer*?' As William Hazlitt wrote,
the primacy of action is foremost in Homer and again this is
evident in most pages of *All Day Permanent Red* and in *In
Cyclops' Cave.* Honour (*timê*) should be predominant, the
tenderness and pity, the evanescence of human life, Virtue or
Greatness (*aretê*), and the Reward of Fame (*kleos*), the
portrayal of the whole human being starting from inner
reflection, the all-important Delphic necessity of 'knowing
thyself':

Bow your head. Beg for your life. Death without burial.
And there – as if
    Inside a moonlit sandstorm God allowed
    The columns of Palmýra's speech –
The Greeks encouraging their host:
    'I am here. I will help.
Stand still and fight. At any moment they will break.'
Though they do not.
                              (Logue)

Fool again, I thought, I'm not so stupid. And I racked
my brains in our peril, and looked,

with all my wits for a way to outsmart him. At
last I saw how to run the gauntlet...
                              (Kazantzis)

Dying without fame (*akleos*) is considered a disaster, hence the tragic impact of Achilles telling Odysseus that he would rather be alive and the most obscure human on earth than dead and famous in the afterworld. We cannot expect much from the afterlife: it is at best only shadowy and dark, and herein, as much else in Homer, lies the awakening realization that humankind must rely on its own passion and its own insight if it is to discover the mysterious works of nature, divine as the latter's source may be or not:

Hay and manure, some pools of blood.
They look towards the centre of the ridge. It's dust, like trees.
Aeneas says:
'Delay. The day depends on you.'
Hector: 'On God.'
'Lock onto them. Exhaust them. Hope they charge.'

Oh, but they do!
(Logue)

'Cyclops my name is No One . . .'

he fell back onto the dung, snoring and slobbering,
and milk and lumps of flesh ran bubbling

from his gaping mouth . . .
(Kazantzis)

Without these opposing moral forces a translation of Homer would be nothing, and both these books prove the authors to have done their homework, particularly managing to strike the balance between pathos and rational insight:

The sea.
The city on its eminence.
The snow.
And where King Agamemnon drew his sword
And all Greece drew soon after seven today,
Flat, broad, declining stripwards, and
Double the width of Troy,
The ridge...

Host must fight host,
And to amuse the Lord our God
Man slaughter man...

(Logue)

At this time he lifts his hands to starry Heaven
and prays out loud to his raven-
haired god. 'Great Poseidon, who embraces
the earth, hear my deep curses.

If you admit me as your own, then give me notice
that Laertes' son, the Sacker of Cities,

Odysseus, who lives in Ithaka, never will find
his home again...'

As Jasper Griffin has said, 'Homer makes it clear that the enemy is just like us, and his death is terrible'. Both sides are subject to the inalienable force of fate (Schopenhauer's 'the complete certainty of unalterable necessity'), the acknowledgment that life is pain, and that we are caught up between mortality and eternity:

Πηλεὶς δ'ᾤμωζεν, ἰδών εἰς οὐρανον εὐρύν.

296

(Peleus' son was wailing and lamenting, looking up to the broad heaven).

Οὔμεν γάρ τῖ ποὖ ετιν ὀΐζυρώτερον ἄνδρος
Πάντων, ὅσσα δε γάϊαν ἐπι πείει τε χαϊ ἔρπει.

(Of all that breathes and creeps on earth there is no more wretched being than man).

Ate 'has tender feet'. She needs them, 'for she walks not on hard ground, but only on the heads of men...'

It is not just a question then of capturing the poetical effects, but of understanding as deeply as possible the intellectual power of the epical drive – the force of the gods and of humankind. Logue and Kazantzis have a grip on these aspects of Homer but sometimes one feels that Logue opts for the local effect to the detriment of the overall tenor of resolution. One recognizes, of course, that the poets are working on different texts, but there seems to be more of Homer's natural good humour, urbane taste and civilized balance in Kazantzis' work than in Logue's. Logue's work-in-progress does however capture other significant facets of Homer lost on most English translators of the *Iliad* at least: the competitive Hellenic world of games, battles, speeches and trials, the whole philosophy of *agon*. In this world, men respect but do not live in terror of the gods. There is nothing redemptive about pain and misery *per se* – only in an objective consideration thereof. It is this very quality we discover in 'the beloved heart' (φίλον ητορ) of Homer's poetry – that the tears we weep are tears of sympathy, both for ourselves and for our enemies. Partisanship has nothing to do with it. Such shortsightedness was anathema to Homer in his feudal society, and his critical attitude towards it foreshadows the great rational, dialectical society Greece was to become:

Silence and light.

The earth
And its attendant moon
(Neither of great importance
But beautiful and dignified)
Making their way around the sun.

Logue also captures the melodic line of Homer beautifully,
and the whole arena of prehoplite fighting, monarchical
assemblies and chivalric masses (much beloved of Milton),
the taste of iron in the blood, the shudder of cold in the
spears, all of Homer's 'wind-fed' words:

Impacted battle. Dust above a herd.
Hands wielding broken spearpoles rise through ice-hot
twilight
Flecked with points.
And where you end and where the dust begins
Or if it is the dust or men that move
And whether they are Greek or Trojan, well
Only this much is certain . . .

He sees the Islands of the West.
He who? Why, God of course.
Who sighs before He looks
Back to the ridge that is, save for a million footprints,
Empty now.

In Logue's continuing *War Music* the earth trembles, and the
poetry celebrates 'le coeur endurant'. However, Judith
Kazantzis holds on to the other side of Homer wherein we
can see the curbs which restrain 'the grudge nurtured within
the breast' (φύμόν ἐνι στήθεσσι φίλον δαμάςαντες
ἀνάγχῇ):

298

... We lay and we slept out there
till dawn dimmed star after star

and, rosy-fingered, lit the eastern sky. I bided
no longer but at once ordered

all to the benches. Away we rowed from the island
of Cyclops, that blood-soaked ground,

carrying our dead for always in our grieving minds,
glad and free to rove on the sea winds.

Horace may have been mortified 'when the great Homer
sleeps' – it is just as galling surely when fine translators do.
Happily, that is not the case here, and one can sit down and
enjoy both works fully alert and awake to the glories of both
English and Greek literary traditions, their craft, grace and
poise. I can think of nothing better than to read these
versions of Homer on a Mediterranean holiday, preferably
on an island in the Aegean.

WILLIAM BEDFORD

Robert Lowell's *Collected Poems*
(Faber & Faber, £40 hardback)

This is a magnificent work of scholarship and friendship. All the major collections are included, usually in Lowell's final versions, and extensive annotations explain not only the backgrounds of individual poems but the reasoning behind such sensible editorial decisions as the exclusion of *Notebook* (1969). *Land of Unlikeness* (1944) is printed in full in the 'Appendices,' along with magazine versions of several poems where Lowell's revisions have raised significant issues. 'Waking Early Sunday Morning' is obviously the most famous of these, and Frank Bidart uses the arguments raised by this poem for an interesting discussion of the whole problem of 'revision' in Lowell's creative practice. The decisions Bidart and David Gewanter make – difficult decisions with a poet who rewrote as obsessively as Lowell – seem to me entirely right, and I am particularly grateful to have the longer versions of 'Beyond the Alps' and the wonderful 'Waking Early Sunday Morning.'

As an editor Frank Bidart is particularly well placed to make these decisions. He joined Lowell's writing class at Harvard in 1966, and was actively involved with Lowell's work from *Notebook: 1967–68* onwards. It is this involvement and friendship which seems to inform the whole volume, and I can't imagine a better edition for the non-academic reader. It is also beautifully produced and a delight to read, not a small point in a thousand-page volume.

* * *

I first read Lowell in the spring of 1959 when *Life Studies* was published in Britain. An American friend soon lent me *Lord*

Weary's Castle (1946) and *The Mills of the Kavanaughs,* (1951) and Lowell has been a constant companion for most of my adult life. What is fascinating about reading the *Collected Poems* is the way that the poems have escaped their original readings. This is an inevitable process, but especially important with Lowell: throughout his career he was seen as one kind of poet, and yet time shows us a different kind of poet altogether: a conscious maker, rather than an obsessive autobiographer.

Reading *Lord Weary's Castle* is quite a shock. Public poetry of the kind Yeats and Lowell took for granted has gone out of fashion. Deconstructionists and 'death of history' theorists have no time for the authorial 'authority' which Lowell's work assumes, and the 'confessional' mode which Lowell supposedly introduced has long degenerated into the anecdotal. New generations of poets have ignored Lowell since his death in 1977, preferring at their best the very different examples of Wallace Stevens and Elizabeth Bishop.

Certainly, public events are the occasions for many of the poems in *Lord Weary's Castle*. 'The Quaker Graveyard in Nantucket' is the most successful of these, the poem being among Lowell's greatest. But the greatness is closer to Milton's 'Lycidas' than a mere *homage*. Lowell's artifice, his maker's ambition, takes a public event and a marvellous passage from Thoreau's *Cape Cod* to produce something wholly original. The achievement is entirely to do with language: it is the stumble of consonants, the clash of nouns and verbs, which creates the unforgettable music.

What we find throughout *Lord Weary's Castle* is the clotted violence of a unique imagination. The subject matter, the objective correlatives, to use the Eliot term much favoured by Lowell and his friends at the time, really function as objective correlatives, not, or not primarily, as biographical inspiration. As Lowell is noted as saying in Ian Hamilton's biography, by 1946 the Catholic Church had 'served its purpose.' Much the same may be said of all the experiences and family histories

301

behind the poems of *Lord Weary's Castle*. Personal experience may provoke, but what remains, and stands out much more clearly with the passing of time, is the mastery of language.

Lord Weary's Castle seems to me one of Lowell's best volumes, with an amazing range of achievements from the extraordinarily baroque 'The Exile's Return,' 'Colloquy in Black Rock' and 'Christmas in Black Rock' to the eloquent 'Mr Edwards and the Spider' and the brilliant narratives of 'Between the Porch and the Altar.' With the translations and the family biographies, it is a volume which heralds the future.

Unfortunately, Lowell's mastery of language and forms was capable of leading him astray, and *The Mills of the Kavanaughs* seems an example of his misjudgement. As his friend Randall Jarrell commented in a review, he had no gift for the longer narrative poem, and the model of Browning was not helpful. The poem is full of explosive images, but the incoherence of the narrative makes it difficult and unrewarding to follow. Having said that, there is something strangely compelling about these poems: their very obscurities fascinate, details from a Catholic world long abandoned by Vatican 11, a tortured imagination which holds us precisely by the power of its violence. I think Lowell always had this power. I have never really understood what the line 'The Lord survives the rainbow of His will' is supposed to mean, but the poetry resonates down through the years.

Lowell may have realised his own failure, and was silent for several years. It was the influence of the San Francisco Beats which provided him with the way forward. He sought to break with the formalism he had inherited from Modernism, or the very American version of Modernism that had come to him from Allen Tate and John Crowe Ransom. Giving public readings, Lowell realised that he needed to edit his early poems to make them clear to a live audience. The formal experimenting led to *Life Studies*, and an apparently new approach to his own experience.

At the time of course all of this seemed very simple. The anecdotal loosely-structured family poems attracted most of the attention precisely because they were something new in poetry. Where these poems retain some power, it is invariably because the experiences behind them have force – most obviously and predictably in the poems about the poet's mother and father – but that power is just as evident in the prose versions of the material; it is nothing to do with the tension generated by form. The most powerful of these 'life studies' explore Lowell's own experience of mental illness and prison, 'Waking in the Blue' and 'Memories of West Street and Lepke' being two of his greatest poems.

Once the autobiographical essay '91 Revere Street' was included in new editions, it was possible to see how Lowell had rearranged the original anecdotes to produce the effect of 'chopped up prose.' This is not to deny the force of the poems which succeed – artists use whatever means they can find – but it is to recognise something characteristic about Lowell: he works best when the violence of his own experience comes into conflict with the tensions generated by form. What is obvious now is that the truly great poems in *Life Studies* look back to *Lord Weary's Castle* – the wonderful 'Beyond the Alps' – and forward to *For the Union Dead and Near the Ocean* – 'Man and Wife,' 'To Speak of Woe That Is in Marriage' and 'Skunk Hour.' It is the rhyme in these marvellous poems which sounds the hypnotic music, the discipline of the line which contains the unbearable anguish of the experience. 'Skunk Hour,' with its reference back to Milton – 'I myself am hell' – reminds us immediately of the force of artifice which makes 'The Quaker Graveyard in Nantucket' one of the greatest poems of the last century. 'Skunk Hour' in its very different way seems to me as moving and significant.

Ian Hamilton has noted that we learn far more about Lowell from *For the Union Dead* (1964) than we do from *Life*

Studies. What the 'confessional' label has confused is the nature of Lowell's practice. Whether the subject of his poems has been the characters of history or his own life, what actually happens is that the details become the objective correlatives for his art, for his making. Biographical details, as in 'Skunk Hour,' become symbols, just as Catholicism provided symbols in *Lord Weary's Castle* and 'Beyond the Alps.' There is a kind of omnivorousness to Lowell's creative life. Towards the end, he said that he had enjoyed writing about his life more than living it, and reading the Collected Poems there is a sense of a powerful machine eating experience and turning it all, whatever it is, into material: whether the figures stepping out of history and myth or the cleaning lady he happens to meet in the hall. The massive sonnet sequences – where you truly get the sense of a machine eating-up experience – have obscured the fact that this was Lowell's practice from the start of his career, where there are just as many poems about his family as in *Life Studies.*

For the Union Dead makes the point negatively. It is a flat, tired volume, despite being full of personal anecdote. There is a sense of exhaustion. 'Water,' 'The Old Flame,' 'Middle Age,' they all have some power, the force generated by felt experience, but it is not the power of the best of the *Life Studies* poems. 'Night Sweat' takes the same personal experiences for its material, and rises above the sourness of the rest of the volume precisely because of the formal properties, the rhyme which makes the anguish sing. 'Night Sweat' is the penultimate poem in the collection, hinting at Lowell's own awareness – he spoke of the sour lemony tone of the volume as a whole – and preparing us for the great title poem, 'For the Union Dead.' This again is one of Lowell's very greatest poems, a very public poem which addresses the 'state of the union' from the details of Lowell's own childhood Boston. The child watching the fish in the Boston

Aquarium becomes the man studying history and the citizen struggling with moral dilemmas and making judgements in symbols:

> The Aquarium is gone. Everywhere,
> giant-finned cars nose forward like fish;
> a savage servility
> slides by on grease.

I suppose the perfection of Lowell's method as artificer, turning personal experience and history into great poetry, must be 'Waking Early Sunday Morning,' the opening poem of *Near the Ocean* (1967). So much has been written about this masterpiece that it is difficult to disentangle it from its historical circumstances and our own personal experience of living with the poem. It is as important to me as Mailer's *Armies of the Night*, and captures an entire period of history with effortless grace.

But Bidart is right to publish the much more private magazine version. In contrasting the two versions and studying the drafts as Alan Williamson did in the *Agenda* Lowell edition and his subsequent *Pity the Monsters*, we can see Lowell's omnivorous imagination at work. The version in *Near the Ocean* is the more straightforwardly public poem. The *New York Review of Books* version is more inward, more privately tortured. Both are masterpieces, showing us Lowell's method in action, allowing us to see into the creative mind. The formal choices here, in 'Waking Early Sunday Morning,' 'Fourth of July in Maine' and 'Near the Ocean' – Marvell's elegant eight-line stanzas – work to make the unbearable sing in a way reflected upon within 'Waking Early Sunday Morning':

> they sing of peace, and preach despair;
> yet they gave darkness some control,
> and left a loophole for the soul.

305

Reading *Near the Ocean,* you know you are in the company of the poet of both *Lord Weary's Castle* and *Life Studies:* the successes of *Near the Ocean* are earned in the formal experiments, the formal struggles, between those volumes. Having the *Collected Poems* merely helps us see the course of that struggle, the way in which Lowell's private violence seeks formal devices to transform his material: the material in a sense being irrelevant. With the passing of time, what interests us is what the poet does with his material, not the original experiences. This may sound like a case for the aesthetic over the ethical, and the final stages of Lowell's career certainly provoked heated argument about his casual use of his own and other people's lives, but after thirty years, much of the heat has gone from the argument, and we are left with the poems.

Having said that, thirty years certainly makes clear the failure of *For Lizzie and Harriet* (1973) and *The Dolphin* (1973), and the surprising success of *History* (1973). These three volumes were carved out of the various versions of *Notebook,* and again Frank Bidart is especially well placed to justify what the editors have done with the *Collected.* With hindsight, *Notebook* did muddle the private and the public in an uncreative, confusing way. Separating out the poems into three volumes allowed them to be judged as poetry. The easy thing to say is that *For Lizzie and Harriet* relies too much on private experience which remains private and self-indulgent. *The Dolphin* has flashes of great beauty but the collection is basically a narrative which relies for its force upon the reader being given enough information to understand the individual poems: and for entirely private reasons, Lowell withholds much of the information we need. He distorts his own story to protect the innocent. It isn't a way of writing which was ever going to please anybody, or produce a creative transformation.

I said *History* was a surprising success, but again after thirty

306

years it is possible to see why the volume works. Put simply, Lowell does here what he did in *Lord Weary's Castle* and the isolated great poems of later volumes: he harnessed his own violence to the details of his material, in this case the whole of *History*. It works because we are interested in Lowell, and indeed because he is interesting, or his imagination is interesting. The terrible, violent, pessimistic imagination which created 'The Quaker Graveyard in Nantucket' and 'Skunk Hour' is at work here on the horrors of history, and the pleasures we enjoy are the aesthetic pleasures of all great poetry. If we knew their lives, no doubt exactly the same could be said of Sophocles or Shakespeare or any great artist. Here, it is not history which is interesting – though it obviously is – but the *History* which the poet makes of it.

Day by Day is a sad end to Lowell's creative life, a flat, tired, repetitious, anecdotal volume, with none of the fire which enlivened some of the anecdotal poems of *Life Studies*. It is a rather salutory experience to go straight from the end of *Day by Day* to the 'Appendices' and the early violence of *Land of Unlikeness*. It is also somewhat ironic. The most famous poem in *Day by Day* is undoubtedly 'Epilogue,' where Lowell wrote beautifully about his working method:

Yet why not say what happened?
Pray for the grace of accuracy
Vermeer gave to the sun's illumination
stealing like the tide across a map
to his girl solid with yearning.
We are poor passing facts,
warned by that to give
each figure in the photograph
his living name.

I say ironic, because however beautiful these lines, this is not what Lowell's career shows us him doing. His work is full

307

of the 'poor passing facts' which make up a life, but he does not use them for confession. He uses them to create poetry. It is Lowell's aesthetic response to the 'poor passing facts,' whether of his marriages or the Vietnam protests, which will guarantee the life of his work. The *Collected Poems* is a monument to that creative life, a superb edition and one of the finest collecteds Faber have produced.

W S MILNE

Elizabeth Cook, *Achilles*
(Methuen, £12.99 hardback)

At the beginning of Elizabeth Cook's *Achilles* we are presented with a fine description of two rivers asserting their 'separateness' as two enemies opposed. It is this opposition, paradoxically, which forces glory upon us hymning the authenticity of struggle and aspiration. It is in this type of division that the relationship between man and woman, for example, or life and death, or peace and war, begins and ends. The clash between Achilles and Hector, to take one representative emblem, is the enmity between two such destinies or polarities. When they fight there is a melding of distinctions and dichotomies in the very flux of the actions and counter-actions of battle. In this sense *Achilles* is a prose-poem (the prose is markedly musical) concerned with relationships and their destruction, the physical immediacy, the hunger and longing ('layer upon layer of longing'), the reciprocity of love, especially sexual love, even in its andro-gynous forms, and that which binds and severs. It is the blood-lust of life which Achilles misses as an etiolated spirit in the underworld, an abstract and intellective reality far removed from the joys and splendours of the body once lived in – jealous, avaricious of the living, breathing, 'bent with longing for a sup of that steaming blood'. There is no comparing the glory of the living Achilles with the dead Achilles, 'As if life and colour have been sucked from the world. As if his own heart has suddenly emptied'.

In the afterlife there is only 'A sense of green, where there is none', a rather ironic use of the word 'sense,' as all of its force is now impacted upon intuition and not on lived sensuous apprehension. There is a definite hint of vicarious-ness in its use, a leaching-off life at a remove. Death here in this circumstance, this dispensation, is seen as 'Pluto's rich labyrinth' (rich for Pluto possibly, but scarcely anyone else – 'no-one here knows anything' it is stated bleakly), 'the black that is uppermost', 'a shore not lapped by sea', a place 'where the waters untwist and drop their cargo' and where 'men have lost track'. Although some of the dead may possess 'a clean heart' of innocence, they all still hanker after 'the blood-tank' of experience, a paradox which reminded me of Blake's vision in *Songs of Innocence and Experience*. Even in this predicament, as in life, Achilles rises above the 'common herd' in his emphasis on courage. The 'message' (if that is not too blunt a word) is 'To choose ... fearlessly, your lungs drinking the air ... It makes the gods ashamed'. It is this courageous 'leap of faith' which determines authentic self-being, and puts the stamp on 'what we earn by our nature' (what Hopkins called 'instress', the arriving-at one's own individuality through the forging of a distinctive style in life or in art).

Towards the end of *Achilles*, Achilles, the man of action, is supplanted by the poet Keats, the heroic man of the Imagination, holding his own with the Man of Character or deeds. (The tri-partite structure of the book – 'Two Rivers', 'Gone', and 'Relay' – offers a resolution of sorts, in a dialectical fashion, of the thesis, the man of action, *Achilles*, pitched against the antithesis, the man of imagination, John Keats, meeting in the synthesis, *Achilles*, the work where thought and action meld.) Such a choice (and it is not viewed in any way as Kierkegaardian, or Christian at all, more Hobbesian in its stress on the life of 'man, short-lived and ignorant') enables the brave individual to surmount tawdriness, to win glory over 'the blank' of life and death. The qualities thereby praised, or lauded, in sharp sentences and precise images are those of self-possession, solitariness and self-delight (in the Yeatsian sense of 'Caught in that sensual music all neglect/Monuments of unageing intellect'), 'the flame of life' itself, 'the fine fuse' of poetry, the Heraclitean flux of fire, water, air and earth, all the elements commingled and celebrated.

The scene-shifting strategies of the book surprise a reader at first, until it is understood that these metamorphoses are the binding structures of the mind's imaginings and nature's plenitudes – always changing, always shifting, always moving on away from us. From out of the 'scalding water' of life arises the 'filament of fire' which is the imagination triumphant, 'fresh-materialed ... controlling consciousness ... a chain of fire', as though man's heart could 'ever be healed'.

This rich philosophy (if this is not too ratiocinative a term) instantiated in language both verbally tight and texturally expansive, like elastic almost, serpentine yet at rest, 'the open ground' of the page, as it seems to me, is used as a poet uses it, not as a novelist, for enacting the silences, the pauses that are as crucial as the dust and turmoil of speech and battles, 'like a lover taking in every inch of his beloved', a full attentive consciousness and not something half-baked.

Love is not reified in Cook's world, but is tragically evoked as all we can rely on, – 'her back still sings with the memory of him', she says lyrically of Panthiseleia remembering Achilles, glutted with life, the flesh wiser than the mind, 'eyes blazing into eyes as each takes in the form and splendour of the other', the apotheosis of love's recognition and destructiveness.

The qualities which further stream from this emphasis on the sensorium are those of faithfulness, loyalty and courage, attitudes rarely praised today, and this enables the author to endorse the admonition to 'follow the brightness of one face before it is eaten by dark', to fend off death's terror with affirmative love.

Such an achievement smiles grandiloquently in the face of 'eyes ... raw with weeping', and elegiacally counters the wasteful war of the Trojans and the Greeks and the short life of John Keats, belittling all the furies that gnaw.

In this way death and pain can be relinquished partly because 'Before there was the name there was the shadow', Achilles' and Keats's destinies realized in their heroic (or, if you like, Homeric) actions and imaginative achievements.

As Geoffrey Hill has written in another context, 'It is the way with contraries, that each is bound to the other by implication', and in the case of *Achilles* the glories of the mind are established on 'the ground', the wisdom of the body rather than the wraiths of the intellect.

In this important work we feel (either as readers or spectators) that it is the press of impersonal forces upon the individual and the individual's ability to rise above them which establishes authenticity of being, and gives us a clue as to what is best and healing in human nature, both in its public and private domains. Although the starkness of Elizabeth Cook's language at times conveys the bareness of the human landscape, it also, in its rhythmical grandeur, tells us it is good and noble to commit oneself to a cause (or vision) greater than oneself. In dying for that cause (or vision) one may surmount not only one's time but also times to come, and thereby cheat death a little – 'You have brushed your sight against new leaves', mocking all the pomp and glory of human reputation and vanity. Having cleared a strophic, antiphonal space for all that is delightful and best in life, like Keats in his poetry and letters, one can lay 'one's mind open like a bird', 'to rinse your mind clean' of 'the stinking freight' of the world:

The two men hold each other and weep: for those they have lost, for those who will lose them, for all the men gone down in the slow years of this wasteful war.

The two rivers have flowed in contrary directions, but at last they meet, if only temporarily, and are at rest in one place. The dust and turmoil have settled at last for a while, but at great cost:

'. . . since I never more
Shalt see my lov'd soil, my friend's hands shall to the
    Stygian shore
Convey these tresses.' Thus he put in his friend's hands
    the hair.

Achilles is a work not only to be read, but one which also must
be seen and heard.

LYTTON SMITH

Chosen young reviewer, age 20, grew up in Galleywood, Essex and had just completed a B.A. in English at University College, London. In August, he is moving to New York City to study an M.F.A. in Creative Writing (poetry) at Columbia University, New York.

Glyn Maxwell, *The Nerve*
Picador £7.99

In the title poem of Glyn Maxwell's debut collection, *Tale of the Mayor's Son*, the narrator considers how he might unfold his narrative:

> I could say what was sold in the bazaar,
> I could be clearer on the time of day,
>
> I could define Elizabeth.

As important as the events of the tale is the question of how to tell that tale. A not dissimilar focus informs the more mature *The Nerve*. In poems considering necessitated and voluntary immigration, the community of the family, growing up and growing old, and the problem of loss, Maxwell strives to discover the innate, elemental qualities of sights and events in order that they can be most perfectly related.

The tautologous title of the opening poem, 'The Sea Comes in Like Nothing but the Sea', is the first potential method of succeeding in this. The limitation of the method is instantly acknowledged – the sea 'comes in like nothing but the sea,/but still a mind.' The relationship between the thing related and the relating term is shown to be less simple than the poem's title suggests. The sea, rather than the poet, 'reorders' words, deviating from the expected state where

314

>   All that should sound
>
> is water reaching into the rough space
> the mind has cleared.

In a similar deviation, 'the god,' rather than the created, exists in doubt, needing to ask 'a breathing life of us,/to prove we were still there.' Glib acceptance is prevented by this opening poem, which urges instead a quest for the underlying – for 'the nerve'. This is the title of the next poem which, with the opening poem and the following 'Haunted Hayride', forms a triad of poems concerned with the transitory: the sea ebbs and flows like belief; 'a single nerve' follows 'a breeze being gone' and the moment when 'you cross a line;' time and distance recede and return, 'into the past, and from it.'

This descriptive restlessness prepares for the strange events of 'The Man Who Held His Funeral', which the observer can only relate in ambiguous terms – the man as 'rugged and silken, like a country singer/both these things'; his car business as 'solid, sold'. These metonymically similar words draw attention to how effortlessly descriptive transition can alter something: in 'An Earthly Cause', two people see a shape which 'could have been a body: for a while/it was.' It is as if, to adopt imagery from the closing poem, *The Nerve* were a snow globe, and every time the flakes seem destined to settle, Maxwell again sends the world into potentially enlightening disorder. His experience of leaving England for America has provided a frame of reference which aids the examination of things from fresh angles, as the same experience did for James Lasdun in *Landscape with Chainsaw* (2001). Interesting parallels might be drawn between the two collections but it is the divergences that most illuminate. In *Landscape with Chainsaw*, core words and phrases recur in altered contexts as the narrator hesitantly negotiates new relationships with an unfamiliar landscape.

315

Lasdun's main interest is in exploring the social and historical memories that affect personal interaction with a new land. Maxwell, on the other hand, concentrates on how a new land, geographical or abstract, might be perceived, understood, and then related by those observing.

Naming is thus a central preoccupation of *The Nerve*. In the touching family portrait 'One of the Splendours', the narrator muses 'it's time to learn some names' but acknowledges, seemingly without regret, 'we won't though. I know us.' The apparent issue is familiarization – the acceptance by articulation of new faunae and aquine life – but the implicit question is how fundamental a name is to accurate expression. 'We'd done without since coming here,' reasons the narrator: even though he knows 'it's time' he confesses that

> we like to see
>
> stuff strain at us from nothing.

Interestingly, because of the stanza break, the reader sees blank space initially, a 'nothing' which could either reassure or be problematic. The passing of time frustrates the narrator's attempt to linger in blissful ignorance: 'stuff' will

> be there, not have been there and appear now –
> then yellow at the wall in the few days
> following, and fail not knowing how'.

The potentially comforting consonance of 'll' in fact prefigures a failure that puzzles not only the unknown 'stuff' but also the unknowing narrator.

As these lines demonstrate, *The Nerve* is a technically accomplished collection. Hinted rhyme, such as 'following' and 'fail', is effectively utilised, especially in the half-rhymes of 'Refugees from Massachusetts,' which hope towards para-rhyme and verge on disintegration. Importantly, given how the collection attends to the essence of 'stuff', technical perspicacity is very much fused with theme. Just as rhyme parallels the changing expectations of the refugees, repetition reinforces the precariousness of success and failure, fugue and reality:

> There is a wood
> They come to in a downpour, or have dreams
> They come to in a downpour.

This echoes how Ernest Hemingway, in 'Cat in the Rain', used repetition to re-create the sea disappearing down the beach 'in a long line in the rain to come back up and break again in a long line in the rain.' Both writers have in common a fascination with what Hemingway phrased 'what things were' – the thing itself. All writers consider this question, but what Maxwell particularly shares with Hemingway, aside from an impressive depth of exploration, is an awareness that blankness, manifested as white space or as silence, has a vital role in successful relation.

Appropriately, therefore, the 'blank page' is a central image in the collection's *pièce de resistance*, the lovely 'Island Painting, St. Lucia'. This poem depicts two artists attempting to paint a landscape under the watchful eye of a tutor. The question posed by the narrating artist is 'how much of this can be?' Achieving only 'recurring errors' in his attempts with the brush, the narrator appreciates the 'relieving cool of a blank page' but still re-attempts, convinced of the possibility of 'the one true colour.' 'Island Painting, St Lucia' presents not just interaction between the relation and the thing related, here 'the ever-painted island', but also between blankness and expression. 'The relieving cool' of the blank page is the 'one picture true to light' and also a

317

canvas transformed by a representation fated to 'end/how all movies end, all wrong.' In this failure is the seed of success – the determination of 'we can do this better' recalls Herman Melville's belief that 'he who has not failed somewhere, that man cannot be great.'

The Nerve's disparate topics, which range from American history and adjusting to modern America, through childhood and growing up, to poetry and experience, are all connected through manifestations of *tabula rasa* and attempts to mark them – 'there was nothing but snow about;' 'an all-American young girl // took shape;' 'an empty room [...] with a typed sheet.' Maxwell repeatedly and from various perspectives considers the journey from blank page to completed page, renewing the blank page in 'The Snow Village'. In the exact quatrains of this final poem, the page becomes a 'snow village' and the snow erases a traveller's footprints. The connection between travel and poetry is not new – Oðin, liberator of the mead of poetry, was both traveller and patron of poets – but the use of the connection to analyse the interaction of blankness and description is engaging. The traveller's 'step becomes unknowable/and the whiteness knowledge' because of the snow – experience and relation become almost synonymous.

Such a conclusion draws attention to the collection's nature as physical artefact, how Maxwell's echoing sounds and carefully depicted scenes have filled fifty-eight once-blank pages. From the title page whose only 'certain/sign of life' is the two bold words 'The Nerve', blank space is expertly manipulated, just as in 'A Child's Love Song' 'thumb and finger make a ring/to see the future through.' Maxwell thus demonstrates how successful expression must take account of the 'uses of silence,' as Mark Slouka has suggested. Indeed, within *The Nerve*'s 'snow village,' we discover a poet 'who'll teach/the simple things for ages,' not only in this collection but also through marks to be made on places currently blank.

318

Poems from poets who have special
issues of *AGENDA* dedicated to them

Orpheus in Darkness

Where have you gone, Eurydice, oh, my love
of life? Where have you fled? In the dark
the music casts no light; my hands lie dumb.
The pipes are broken and cracked the harp.
Eurydice, what music can be strung
on dry sticks? I'll find my voice. I'll bring you,
wherever you are held, a song of love.
It will marmorealise all Dis
to set you free. Orpheus, the singer,
swears you this.

The Last Nursery Rhyme

Close your ears,
        sleepy head.
I am tucking you up
        in your last bed
with these tears
        and this dreadful story
that if you wake
        you will remember
the hands that snugged you here
        and he won't be far away.
You little pretender
        lie doggo. I'll play.

Cameo

A young girl in sling-backs
scurries along the river walk
in the lank shadows of sunset
towards the bridge and bus-stop,
cutting it fine, her evening out.

On a far hill an old woman
looks down on the dry valley
watching a girl dawdle the path
tallied off by willows, a river's
ribbon of licorice skimmed with glints.

The cod-flakes of cloud parting.
Did she see them? A bird's cry
like the yard broom scraped over concrete.
Like hers as it may be. Miss Dashing.
Hasn't heard a thing. That heron.

She shows a leg to board the bus
whose destination seems a number.
Sleeping a catch off, fixed as a post,
sunning – or could it be a chink
of silver birch through curtains of willow?

SEAMUS HEANEY

Two Admonitions
from Antigone

I

Remember Danae, walled up in the dark,
Princess banished on a prophet's word,
Barred and bolted in a tower of brass.

Yet molten Zeus, a battering ray of light,
(O nebulous shock! O blossom-stripping shower!)
Ungirdled and dishevelled her with gold.

Implacable Fate always fulfils its ends.
Not military power nor the power of money,
Not battlements of stone nor black-hulled fleets

Can fend off Fate or keep its force at bay.
Blood under maenads' nails, on the mountain path,
Cries on the wind, weeping heard in the palace:

Whoever has been spared the worst is blessed.

II

Wise conduct is the key to happiness.
Always rule by the gods and reverence them.
Those who overbear will be brought to grief.
Fate will flail them on its winnowing floor
And in due season teach them to be wise.

GEOFFREY HILL

Wild Clematis in Winter

i.m. William Cookson

Old traveller's joy appears like naked thorn blossom
as we speed citywards through blurrish detail –
wild clematis' springing false bloom of seed pods,
the earth lying shotten, the sun shrouded off-white,
wet ferns ripped bare, flat as fishes' backbones,
with the embankment grass frost-hacked and hackled,
wastage, seepage, showing up everywhere,
in this blanched apparition.

JOHN MONTAGUE

Horizons

I

Dimness of a coast,
a necklace of islands
strewn offshore;
through the mist I glimpse
Hy Brasil, the Eternal West.

II

Our houses, our loves;
sheets of water glint
on a white sandy shore,
dissolving with the tide,
renewed again
with the waxing of the moon.

A Hit at Hardy

Old Thomas Hardy,
I be ashamed of thee;
Writing of true love only
When she sleeps, 'neath the tree.

Your costive love hobbled
Decades of English lyric;
Gave our shared Muse
A phial of physic

Larkin learnt from you
How not to love,
And when it was over,
To hardly forgive:

Between proud Yeats
And your so humble craft
There is an arrogance;
– yours, alas!

In your parched
Lyric, only dead love exists,
But in Willy Yeats
There is sweet permanence.

When in your remorseful
Lyrics, love is rerun,
You speak, alive, alone
Above her skeleton.

Through the rotting coffin
Boards, she cannot hear
The words she longed for,
In her young and pulsing years.

In memory of Kathleen Raine

(Issue at the moment out of print)

A TRIBUTE TO
K A T H L E E N
RAINE

On a Deserted Shore

*

Forty New Poems

*

An Interview

*

Essays by
Christine Jordis, Brian Keeble,
Grevel Lindop, Jean MacVean,
W.S. Milne, John Montague,
Judith Robinson-Valéry,
Peter Russell and Tom Scott

A FEATURE ON W.H. AUDEN
Essays by Grey Gowrie, Glyn Maxwell and Peter Mudford

*

HEATHER BUCK on T.S. Eliot's *FOUR QUARTETS*

*

Poems by Anne Beresford, Alan Brownjohn, Peter Dale,
Michael Hamburger, W.S. Milne, Neil Powell and others.

*

Reviews of James Fenton, Marius Kociejowski
and E.P. Thompson
N.K. Sandars on Tom Lowenstein's *Sacred Whale*

Kathleen Raine on the Prose of Ted Hughes

Vol. 31 No.4 - Vol. 32 No.1   Price £8 ($16)

Note: If there is suffficient interest from subscribers, it is possible that *Agenda* might re-print this special issue on Kathleen Raine.

328

CHARLES TOMLINSON

In January

After dark weeks of rain, the world
   Seems shut round on itself, itselves:
There is a secrecy, a veiling back that you
   Will never penetrate although you hear
A hundred voices tell it, far and near –
   Rain on the roof, wind in the leafless tree –
Or catch the sound that two streams make
   In moving across the territory
They divide between them before meeting.
   The slant rain, the receding light,
The closing-in of fields gone grey
   Beneath shadowless trees, refuse the blame
We would attach to them by robbing with a name
   The completeness of the nameless presence here:
'Miserable' – we try to make it fit,
   But weather washes our lament away
With a susurration that does not even scorn
   Our refusal of the encounter: our grain
Of misery waiting to sprout and spread
   Is not of the kin of twilight or the steady rain.

Cotswold Journey
2001

A day before the war and driving east,
 We catch the rasp of ignited engines –
Planes practising combat above this shire
 Of Norman masonry, limestone walls.
In their quiet, they seemed so permanent
 Under the changing light. But the tower
We stand beneath is hacked by sound
 Out of the centuries it has inhabited
With such certainty. After the flash
 We stand once more on stable ground
Under chevroned arches, climb the stair
 Up to the dovecot where the priest
Once fetched the victims down that he would eat.
 The form remains, the victims have all gone
From nesting places squared in stone,
 Boxes of empty darkness now. The planes streak on
Returning out of the unsteady brightness,
 The blue that rain could smear away
But does not. Sun turns into silhouettes
 The gargoyles clinging to sheer surfaces
That rise above us. Sun travels beside us
 As we penetrate deeper in, lose track
Of the plane-ways that leave no vapour trails
 To decorate their passage through
In abstract fury. Courteous walls
 Rise out of stone-crowned summits,
Prelude and then surround a dwelling space
 With church and inn – for us the solace
Of a now twilit afternoon. We explore
 Before we eat, the inn-yard and the street beyond,
Where Saxon masons, raising arch and jamb,
 Cut leaves of acanthus whose weathered surfaces

Hold onto fragile form. The night
　　Slowly extinguishes their edges but bequeaths
To the mind the lasting glimmer still
　　Of stone come to life. The inn
Recalls us through the village street
　　And I remember how a friend once said,
Speaking with a Yorkshireman's conciseness,
　　'A native gift for townscape, a parochialism
But of a Tuscan kind.' Our return
　　Is silent although we travel by
Lanes tracing the outlines of the airbase
　　And, there, all we manage to decipher
Is the gleam of wired restriction, barbs
　　That bar us out from sterile acres
Awaiting the future in a moonless quiet.
　　Rain, with the clink of the lifted latch
On our arrival, bursts from the darkness where
　　East and west, preparing to unseam
The sleeping world below that height,
　　Downpour drops its curtain on the past
And the cry of the muezzin infiltrates first light.

JAN FARQUHARSON
NO DAMNED TEARS
A SEQUENCE

Dear Mr. Farquharson,

Thank you for submitting The Purgatory of
Heaven — I find the sequence moving —
it's rare to come across the true voice of feeling
among the many submissions that arrive here.

I wish to publish the sequence entire
in our next anthology issue —

Yours sincerely,

William Cookson

Photograph by Polly Farquharson

Jan Farquharson was born in 1934. Having read languages at Oxford, he worked briefly as a journalist in Paris, then settled in London, dividing his time between writing and work as a drama lecturer. He wrote and directed plays for large student casts which were performed in a number of venues, including the Edinburgh Fringe.

Meanwhile he wrote two novels, some poetry – published in *Encounter, Stand* and *The Spectator* – and won a national award for poetry speaking.

In 1985 he moved to Devon and became a community playwright. He also wrote and co-directed a bilingual play in collaboration with a French theatre company, put on pantomimes in Brazil and California, and won the Bristol Festival of One Act Plays competition in 1991.

In his last decade he increasingly concentrated on poetry and was a member of the Devon River Poets. He won the Orbis prize in 1997 and was published in various anthologies and journals, including *Agenda, Psychopoetica* and *Tears in the Fence.*

He enjoyed two marriages and had three children.

He sent this sequence of poems to *Agenda* while he was still alive, though dying of cancer. They are such moving sonnets that William Cookson and Patricia McCarthy decided to hold them over until they could be printed in full, as a sequence. Hence they appear here posthumously.

Sooth

He sprouts tears often. They fall like grains of truth,
maturing in him slowly, steadily.
Diseased, flat on his back, he wipes his eye.
The ward is quiet. His mind allows him sooth.
Cream walls and curving curtains are a stage
for long recall and grateful reverie.
A paper towel dispenser gleams nearby.
Death reawakens life from youth to age.

The men and women he's known and half-dismissed!
So has he always done 'just as he please'?
He loves them now, sees all their charms
though he betrayed them in the rush and twist
of life when bounding health was his disease.
And most of all the woman in his arms.

Diagnosis

Five months of growling pain, then diagnosis.
So, not a nasty – not the beast with claws
and teeth that holds you in its beaky jaws,
not the big C but – *diverticulosis!*
What's Diverticula to him or her?
A pet of ageing flesh, of no allure,
a no-way fatal kind of paramour?
They hunch in silence thinking 'What's the cure?'

Three websites say one should contain the pain.
'Then can you please contain it, doctor? – Do!'
His wife smells something; says, 'They can't explain.
There must be something else going on here too.'
Then in the hospital they learn it's cancer.
What are the chances of this desperate chancer?

Light

She moves through sunbeams of the daytime ward
with a grave face, the flowers in her arms.
There's calm in how she looks, of landscaped forms,
of stateliness, and in the way she's poured
the water into vases, freed a bud
and snipped the leaves, and jugged each stem
of the tall blooms gently, jiggling them
upright in autumn light's ceramic flood.

Then suddenly she's in a pout, her weight
on his. He feels her lips pucker. A cry,
muffled by tears: 'I don't want you to die!'
'I know' he answers. 'But you'll be all right.'
'I know,' she weeps, 'Oh but you won't be there!'
And then it's over. They feel light as air.

Intensive Care

From Spain and London blurry shapes take form
and there – his son, son's partner and his own sweet wife.
They've come to view his salvaged listing life.
Tubes to his nose and down his throat deform
his son's scrub kiss and handclench, then it's good
to meet the long straight fingers of the girl
that twine in his, and feel his comfortable
old love push past the epidural tube.

Welcome! He's almost dumb. The weight of drug
and anaesthetic lies on his poor tongue.
But they know how to say there's nothing wrong.
All's right, all's right – they hug and kiss and hug.
And now he sees this love was his long past,
which all his life he had reserved till last.

Quarry

'I opened this one by mistake,' she said,
holding the letter. DANGER: DO NOT MOVE!
The red-rock quarry of guilt he'd worked with love
gaped open at his feet again. A bed
of drift leaves, rubble and sticks and creepers barred
his way. BEWARE THE OVERHANG. Dizziness.
'Just throw it away,' he said. Months since he'd shared
his secret with her. The affair was finished business.

'She writes as if she'll meet you again in heaven.'
'She's cuckoo then,' he says. 'You must have written,'
she says, 'just once at least.' No flowers today.
Her lip's a bulge of bitterness. Forgiven,
he can still wrong her through the post. Bitten
by guilt two ways he says, 'Just throw it away!'

Caring

Look at these hospital bays' important beds,
their angled lamps and lockers – three to a wall –
their sumptuous monkeybars and TV sets
guarded by gangways, curtain-rails and all
the cogs of watch and communal kindness,
expense, consideration, appointed skill . . .
No touch of love's great flame here or its blindness,
no answer to the cries inside the skull.

No wonder we accept the risks of love
when things are running smooth and dull; for either
it burns or brightens. But what we should approve
is that we're patients, carers of one another
and need benevolent kindness that can move
within the apparatus of our love.

Pain

Anvil of body, striking hammer of life –
its feelings, thoughts and moods get caught between.
I want, I only want, want now – morphine!
'I am in pain,' he whimpers to his wife.
'Poor sweet,' she murmurs keeping up the tune –
his are the heavy notes, hers the more light.
She's thinking *half* his pain, he of the night
and how he'll live it through all on his own.

The 'Get well soon' cards hanging at his head,
the clamour of the nurses having fun,
his bedsores, aches and pills ... Oblivion
come quickly or he'll rise up in his bed
and curse his god that he was ever born!
Surprise – love visits him next shining morn.

Home

Now that he's home at last from Cancertown,
thank god, ward feelings fade. But when she pops
out shopping or to fetch his pills life stops –
there's a dull ache in the house of her being gone.
The pictures hang dead; flowers fade; crocks climb
precariously on shelves; the scattered books
just hold their own in space, though falling looks
as if it could attack them any time . . .

Fragility of his life. The springiness
of hers! He is dependent on the chirps
she gives the cat, gives him, the 'Hi's, the slurps
she makes with tea, the bony nakedness
of feet outstretched on chairs. – He wants her there,
inside the glow she makes. Her buoyant care.

After the Oncologist

They drove to see the floods down by the quay,
the water seething in the bridge's throat,
trees torn up by the roots – grimly afloat –
and chests of drawers bouncing to the sea . . .
Too late. Nothing. The swans were in a line,
the water lapping round them, floods all spent.
For fierce convulsion they must be content
with washing wind-puffed on a washing-line.

Yet something to reflect nature gone wrong
was what he'd wanted, knowing disease was sapping
life from his bowels and bones, storming and slapping
at tissues which he'd thought till then were strong
but hadn't now a chance in hell to hold.
Not now – not after what they'd just been told.

Nunc dimittis

Sun steeps the windows of this uptown spot,
converting midday to a languid space
where sofas and frilled lamps lift up the face
of luxury. Crumpets and coffee, piping hot,
served by the owner, tell them, *This is class!*
And then, towards lunch, a drift of cheerful noise
brings mothers, buggies, children clasping toys,
clogging the gangway with subdued sweet fuss.

'They're from the flats,' she tells him, 'up above.'
He wonders what he feels about young doom
and post-lactating mothers in their bloom.
Oh restless ocean-search for peace and love!
Truth is he's known it well and been a wave.
He's tired. And now he'll soon be in his grave.

His Daughter

Because he'd left her out – really or not,
it's hard to say – this time she told him: 'Yeah,
I had a funny feeling with *Intensive Care*
I didn't count as family.' The plot
of thirty years' divorce and separation!
'You're in another poem – not written yet,'
he answered quickly. They were both upset
to think the love between them was on ration.

Reading her *Nunc dimittis* then he wept,
and she was moved to put her cheek on his,
reminding him of love before all trauma –
before the past. Their last things now . . . He kept
forgiving her, she him – simplicities
that left both in the loop, prepared and calmer.

To go or not

'Let's go to Westonbirt,' he offered. Trees
were lives ... An arboretum in the west
with café, wheelchair, all facilities,
something to dream of. Trees were lives ... The crest
of groupings etched on sky, the trunks and spars
that lifted, limbs that stretched, and heads of leaf
that wavered thought-like on high. Trees without scars
suggested beings detached and free from grief.
To dream this way with her ...

                    'It takes three hours.
Do you feel up to it?' she said. He hitched
himself in bed – the pain jumped up and jived.
The trip, he felt, could be beyond his powers ...
And what he dreamed with her could be unstitched
by going – the opposite of how they'd lived.

The House

Storms break about the house this morning. First,
the fist of wind, a thumping curse, then rain
in curving sheets that slat the windowpane,
dispersing in a gummy, blubby burst –
water galore! and knockout sounds and sound
of threshing underlaid by *basso forte*
chimney pots, and wires' whistle and sporty
piping as they whip and lash around.

She says he's been like this most of his life.
Stormy with guilts. 'And would it have been better
with someone else?' she asks. 'Oh no – wetter,'
he answers, 'windier and with more strife.
You stood against the storms. You were a douse
to frenzy and lashing sorrow. Like this house.'

The Curtain

'I'll take away the sun,' she said. 'That's sad,'
he thought. The beautiful morning halved his doom.
And as she pulled the curtain on the gradually wheeling rays that filled the room
he thought of everything he must resign –
frost and the shine of sunlight on the sea,
how macrocarpa blocks the coppice-line,
how there's a stillness in a wind-stripped tree . . .

The million things the bedroom curtain must
exclude as surely as the sun remains
to light the curtain on the other side;
while she herself, this side, he'll keep and trust,
as all-embracing as the sun's great skeins
of light and earth's sharp shine. Their salve and thrust.

General Anthology

I've read all the books but one
Only remains sacred:this
Volume of wonders, open
Always before my eyes.

(From the Collected Poems of Kathleen Raine, Golgonooza Press, 2000)

PETER ABBS

The Last Journey of Odysseus

There is one last journey to be made. Expect no accolade.
Not the smallest scrap of recognition.
Take this oar. Well-fashioned, warped by the tidal

Tug of waters, it has witnessed your encounters with gods
And daemons, labyrinthine tracks,
Cunning stratagems. Yet it would be insensitive to flaunt

The numbers you have slain in the flush and gore of battle,
Dubious conquests, wrecks, trials
In your arduous journey back. These inland people

Know nothing of the sea. Nothing of ageing Telemachus.
Nothing of dead Penelope.
On the mainland it is folly to brag of islands or archipelagoes

Or tout for pity. Here you must unpick the epic of your life.
Observe the distant constellation
Of the stars, the growing emptiness within, lengthening

Shadow on the stone. Cut back your showman's eloquence
Till silence becomes you.
Then take this oar, plant it deep in the earth's rhizome

And let it stand high, a memorial sign – the tall vertical
Cutting the mean horizontal,
Under the cloud's turmoil, fall of light, call of the owl.

MICHAEL ALEXANDER

An Alexandrian Quartet

I

The Anthologists' Stichomythia

Virgil. Ovid. Homer. Lucan. Statius.
Anon. Anon. Anon.

Li Po. Tu Fu.

Leopardi.
Thomas Hardy.

Plath.
The Wife of Bath . . . .

Come on!
And me. And you.

II

Native Woodnotes

Geoffrey of Monmouth was a liar,
Geoffrey Chaucer beat up a friar,
Sir Thomas Malory was jailed for rape,
Sir Thomas More put Pope above King.

Christopher Marlowe was smoked in an inn,
Rare Ben Jonson killed a man,
John Milton justified divorce,
Regicide and missing church. Of such I sing.

III

The Alternative Tradition: A Student Remembers

We heard about the death of Grendel's Mother.
We heard a lot about the Wife of Bath.
We covered the end of *Gaveston's Friend*,
And *Caliban*, by Shakespeare's Sister's brother.

IV

The Historian of Literature Speaks to the British Press

'Of all the English who have played the lyre well
From Abbot Aldhelm almost to Benjamin Zephaniah I tell.
All English Literature is here. It has taken me forty years.'

'Are there enough Welsh writers, immigrants, and queers?'

PAUL BAMBERGER

The Old Man in the Worn-out Coat

The old man in the worn-out coat walks the dunes of the outer bank.
Storm is his signature.
The dunes are his solace.
Mystery wakes after a long sea-sleep.
At sunrise,
as we in town sleep our half sleep
dreaming of answers
cursing the nation for not keeping up
in the name of great pursuits harm being done,
he walks the dunes.
Mystery can come no closer.
Walks as the men and women of the town wake
to stand another day at their machines
lost to the largeness of another day.
Walks as whistle fades door slams.
Walks as clock strikes.
The old man in the worn-out coat walks the dunes of the outer bank
while at the edge of town a jackal stops to tongue blood from a paw.
Behind each stove a dog waits its meal.
An old man in a far place walks
as moonlight through acacia tree gives way to morning.
But for us,
we who live in town
we who have come too far to be dogs sniffing at the wind,
there is nothing not to be gained
for us there is the *word*
more than what it suggests
there is the young man penning his name to the dotted line
that we may go about each day knowing continuity can be found even in stony places.
The old man walks the outer bank
keeping to himself

as a whisper at the edge of madness keeps to itself.
But at the end of each day
when the old man cries out his sea-wise words
where the sea break breaks back against the sea
you must choose your music you must find your key.

JOHN BURNSIDE

The Definitive Journey

(an imitation, after Juan Ramón Jiménez)

So I will go;
but the birds
will continue singing,

and the garden
I leave behind
will continue to flourish:

the green of a tree,
the lit gap of standing water.

The days of that future world
will be blue and still,

the church bell
will ring for hours,
as it rings this evening;

and all those who loved me once
will be dead and gone,

lost in the current of time
and the faces of strangers.

The town will renew its life
with each passing season:

the early loves,
the lifelong feuds,
the feast days;

but no one will see my ghost
on those long afternoons,

though my spirit
will turn from its book,
in the last days of summer,

to listen for rain in the leaves
and the voices of children

Five Paths

In the morning I crunched ash,
Scattered from my father's fire,
Into five sacred paths.

The first led alongside vegetables,
Buried secrets
Like the carrots' orange.

The second crept through mantles,
High gold rods searing,
Shading with robes, my hiding places.

The third spread outwards,
Handstand ceremonies on open grass,
Curved around the regal Pear.

The fourth leapt and crouched
Between scattered stones,
Under the canopy of scramble roses.

The fifth was overgrown.
The quiet way to the Silver Birch.
A pale lamppost, shadowing snow:

An evening gateway to other worlds.

Two Tree Garden

The garden is placed around the two:
The refuge of the Beech.
Our thrown out rope to the other side.
Password called for swinging.
Long time ago echoes: of singing,
Gnawing at nuts, spitting out shells.
Safe from the approach of the one who tells.
Crouched under the leaf green tent pitched in the sky
Throwing out love, warm sunlight, kisses.

The other tree's branches, heavier low
Thicker cavernous hides, sunk into leaf filled bowls
Of wet mulch – black leaves.
The scared child waiting for the one who sees.
Crouched against the outline of a shadow
Darkening the entrance, lowering the branches.
Spongy, spidery, wet recesses.

Between them grass, laid out like the sea –
Green water turf lapping at trees
Tide soon to come in engulfing memory.

Run to the Beech and cry.

PETER CARPENTER

Cuckoo

Monday

and Nanna Cuckoo
presided over the line, drying
weather or not, occupying
the kitchen: a vast tent
of sounds, belonging

'*Cuckoo*'

her calling card
with knuckled rap at the veiled pane
of the backdoor.
Hawk nose, hour-glass calves
bandaged

(*Cuckoo*)

turban-style
raincoat on indoors
'just in case'; playing to win
at chess, cracking down flush or run
at whist, lifting pieces

(*Cuckoo*)

at dominoes, making me howl
'not fair, not fair.' She was cold meat, mashed
potatoes, huge scrapings
of chairlegs, tea thick with sugar.
Then her death:

(*Cuckoo*)

the niff from tins
of humbrol paints, glue,
thinners for my Airfix kits;
and the way she looked one Boxing Day
from our car back to

our house, told father
that she knew a family who lived there too,
called him Bill, not Pete.
We didn't see his tears. He practised
his golfswing

in the back garden
whistling replica *air flo* balls away up
into the hedge off
a doormat shredding from the impact
of each shot

until the light started to go;
foraged in privet and hawthorn
for 'stock', some crushed, some
lost for good, hacking
around with a three iron

into leaf-showers
sawdust dry, trying
not to hear
a voice fluttering, telling him over
and over it was only her going

Cuckoo

    Cuckoo

Cuckoo

Killer

i.m. Kenneth Curtis, teacher

Prefects in Carew whispered 'thumbscrews',
made you the 'killer' of repute for first-year ingenues.
The same man who threw us *Persuasion,*
interrogated Blake, spoke of the 'language of men',
gave me *Death of a Son* to read last lesson
in his rain-drummed hut. It was something else Ken,
you know how words come, unbidden,
a quarter of a century on, how they can settle in

the right order. Wordsworthian negotiator
of fairway any rough! Pacer past chalk pit or
drought-fissure! You understood life's grammar
of diminishing returns. It's close on five to four,
and you're striding for home, natural teacher,
up Hessle Grove, no bigger now than this hand.

MATTHEW CHAPMAN

Native Title

Parched earth is not its own reward,
here a day's work
might yield a nest of beer cans
in a dry river bed;
the sun beats at a scream.

I think of a lawyer
with red earth on his soles
and a sheath-full of land claims
strapped to his back.
He carries talismanic objects
in hands that know a day's labour
of pen and paper.

The swag of land and business
which he unrolls
before the people's hopes
resolve to a tented court
sombre under the stars of the southern sky
hearing the evidence of stone and feather.

Surf Fishing

He knows weighted tension,
Can calibrate a bite and snag,
And know one from the other.
His feet, painful in cold surf,
Are planted firmly on wet sand;
A tensile arm is raised,
To let bait and line
Be caught between fat fingers,
Firm hands.

His line like one sinew,
Stretched inside his palm,
Plays him slowly
Between hook and tide.
In a moment this sea
Might overwhelm him,
Or make him dance a circle
On the beach,
With no catch to interrupt
The steps.

There are no fish
To take him from the task
Of watching the sea
And moving with it.
Standing in the splintered shade
Of a beaten pine
This man knows
That his best catch
Is a moment of Ocean
Held in his hand
Between float and weight and hook.

MERCEDES CIARASÓ

Renewal

The wall was crumbling.
Slowly
over the years
gravity worked on loose stones
pursuing its parsimonious way.
The seasons helped –
frost, wind and rain
beat on the wall.
Ivy too, seen at first
as welcome ornament,
played its destructive part
prising wider each crack
pulling out stones
holding them poised in the air
ready to drop.

For years the wall held on.

Till one wild night
the wind flung all its fury
against the tottering structure
and the whole thing collapsed
into a heap of rubble.

New vistas opened up on either side.

Angel

That day
the angel of tranquillity
was with us.
Great golden wings
were spread above.
And in their tender shadow
the glory of the humble things
of daily life shone forth.

Each cup became a chalice
each chair a chariot
and on the radio they played
the music of the spheres.

ELIZABETH COOK

Real Life

An old woman, dressed probably in black,
sits outside in the sun. Feet
shoved into flat slippers, her thick legs
placed wide apart. Her lap is wide.
And on her lap a large round tray,
or possibly a sieve.
And she rests her well-used hands upon the sides,
and the tray or the sieve or the bowl rises and falls
gently with each breath.
Now I could easily pass whole days
going over the grains on this full tray;
my body no more that a light
balsa-wood frame
for remembering, marvelling.

Dawn Field

I want to remember this:
all the grass bound and covered with cobwebs;
small baskets, cat's-cradles, dew-wet, white in sunlight;
like linen on hedgerows, or an encampment –
like the Field of the Cloth of Gold in silver.
A whole field ready, laid out with snares.

Raid

(Iliad x)

Of course it is true: there were horses,
swift and keen as the Black Sea
winds that stirred them to swiftness
and keenness; manes white
as the snows on Rhodope. Whiter.
Of course it is true that Diomed and Odysseus
needed to take them from Thracian
Rhesus, knot reins together
so they'd move as one team,
then, whacking them, loose them
into the hot night.
True that Odysseus for once
stopped thinking as the sight
and thunder of those moon-
pale horses
took his breath away, nearly.

Some left though for whistling
low to Diomedes, busy with tackle.
Made him look up.

SALLY CRAWFORD

Woman in a Public Garden

She seeks the breath of gardens, sees,
on the lower branches of that pine,
two seed cones
reach their ripening.

Collected there, in stillness,
she feels the tree's line lengthen,
winding her back
to the deep time of its origin

before the apple ever was
let alone the serpent.

JOHN F DEANE

Canvas

I had been reasoning with myself, had grown
angry, resolving nothing; thought of this charnel earth,
its sodden meadows, its daub, heard how it cries
come! put your hand here and feel my wounds!

Times like this, fretful, I long to glide
from the rim of the turning wheel, down the long spoke
to the centre of peace. I remember how father's
quick-lifted hand would cross a blessing on his life

before a journey and how, coming out of church,
his fingers sprinkled a tiny mist of thanks
from the stone stoup; that same big hand
would soothe me, mornings, into wakefulness;

and how I was hurt when he found that centre
where he is at rest. My own warm fingers
touched his frosted forehead and I wished him
every possible blessing on that journey. A small

message of rain has riddled across the rooftop
and evening sunlight touched the floor; I looked up
and saw how the legs of the swift tuck tightly in;
I watched through the skylight where clouds

puckered and shoved, assuming spaces, shapes;
sometimes a rook came black against the darkening sky
and once a heron passed, like one of those heaving crates
from an old war; above me then the world

was a Botticelli masterpiece, allowing
mystery its scope till I flung wide the skylight,
inhaling all God's bitterness and dalliance
and the curious slow turning of the stars.

SEAN ELLIOTT

Long Distance

I end my shift and catch the night bus, lapse
to blankness while the amber lights play on
the dug up streets; I watch the lorries turn
for new supplies and taste our near collapse.

No living contact and the silence saps
our resolution; now your parents phone
suggesting you'd go further on your own,
each gentle sentence starting with Perhaps...

They'll say that you were right to finish this,
congratulate you on the wisest choice
and they'll be wrong. Perhaps no one could miss

my lack of money or my lost career;
you'll find your plenty elsewhere. But my voice
will break your sleep, distant and always near.

Mother Kindness

Mother kindness, rough red hands,
a house as dizzy as a cold,
your mole dark rooms and snuffling humour,
your creaking swing where I lost my hold.

I stalked my cousin through the grass
and in our green and clumsy bed
travelled the brightness of her legs
while treetops hissed above my head.

Mother kindness, rough red hands,
you shouted down your cats and birds
and scrubbed my face with mother-spit,
I gagged and laughed and screamed for words.

From the Chapel

Almost eleven and the station fills
with couples staring down the lines of track,
a soldier strokes his girlfriend's back,
waiting in frost to hear the whining wheels,

a drunk is swearing with deliberate care
and from the chapel, bright, large-hatted, black,
three women dizzy on a gust of prayer
sing Jesus, Jesus on the brittle air.

A small man reads the news and mouths each word,
his lips consume a famine and a war
and still the women sing, each nodding head

dazed with a vision of that joy deferred
beyond the graves of their impoverished dead
while we, the other travellers, numbly stare.

JANE FRASER ESSON

Andre Parissy
(1908–1945)

In bronze, you shine against the stone
almost covered now with ivy;
I stand and gaze at your coronal
set up by local villagers.

In the sunshine, flowers bloom –
Normandy is sweet, this autumn;
you never saw the peace you fought for –
what can be said, that could atone?

SALLY FESTING

Leaf

As is the life of the leaves, so is that of men.
                                        Iliad

Rumpled jumpers peeled off, piled on a bed,
colours of reaped fields, bracken-gold,
a T-shirt next, then tight-drawn skin,
her back unspools
her dark head each time new.

Can't you see she is dancing with death,
said Bourdelle's wife of Isadora,
Don't be afraid
she is making way
for Spring.

Picture a leaf air-born,
vague as racketing memory,
soft as a moth in all its veils;
upside-down, on spirals,
helpless.

Paring is compulsive;
dragged between the nails,
crêpy tissue concertinas
until its quick release strips
space round the ribs,

light as leaf while I am burdened;
there is no protection –
art, travel, starving,
lay in childhood's forest
and made up rhymes.

It is near the end of September
and we know she is leaving soon;
she and life weaving together,
I will be earth,
she can slip back in.

JOHN E. FIELD

Two Letters

Abandoned

I search the wind and rain, but you are not there,
neither on the shore, nor amongst the
fishing boats, sprouting masts which beat time
to the tempest, like disorderly metronomes.
Perhaps you have faded into the tide
to be cast on remote beaches,
sea turned and diminished.
Skies harvest thunder and lightning,
squandering their burden fretfully
as the crippled harbour, feeding the marshlands,
persuades the billowing waves into ripples.
Their crests flash quiescence across the darkness,
then slither into sedge and saltwort at my feet.
Squalls support then spin me into shifting
sands, bordering marsh and sea.
Blackness and misadventure are my companions,
courting me along that invisible
no-man's land beside the tide's edge.
Scattered dwellings lean into the storm,
well versed in the night's catechism
as they peer blindly, sieving glimmerings of light,
to guide me back into their warmth.

A Death in Primrose Time

You are gone, yet you remain ever present.
I recall your essence in the smell of
spring flowers and cut hay
when you gave me life,
your healing mouth pressed to mine.
A sigh from the breeze that teased
your body drapes my shoulder in loneliness.
Distant voices, calling faintly across evening's
birdsong, chime our destiny.
Night brings her companions of solitude and
peace to share my memories.
But such conceits enshrine absences
or evoke images of distant happiness.
I need a livelier presence:
your voice and laughter, the burn of your touch,
your breath's intimacy.
May I breathe deeply tonight, and slumbering,
will my dream become reality?

GREY GOWRIE

Marches

Imagine a wood
in Wales, virtually in England
a mile away as the crows who nest in it
fly. The wood is small and scruffy.
Sheep can get in; a cow from time to time
disrupts the undergrowth, the private life.
The wind makes the noise winds always make in Wales
with one difference: it sounds like Ireland
when in from the west.
Laid up in London you weather yourself
against pain and pain's narrow horizon
by learning the wood by heart: from memory,
from articles on coppicing or fungi.
Imagine negotiating an overdraft
in a soft wind with rain, in late autumn,
to purchase a wwood you are unlikely to wander.
Naturally, the purchase is value-adding
as you live by the wood and mean to live by the wood
forever, gifted to an environment.
But in memory's eye and almost dead centre
of the wood lies a pool, mud with water on it,
which hides like a lost coin the mind's secret:
to live, live, walking against a wind
in Wales, in the mind, which lets you live in Ireland.

Birthday Song

Listen: she has leapt
from the impeccable water
into an air where words
make the right sound for her
without worrying: heartless: for her entirely.

Where is love? morality?
Two by two they are twining
a wavelike arabesque
white as the vacant, turning
scallop that brought her here. They fix the horizon.

The world has become an ocean:
shoreless, but held together
by a girl whom stars put
out of reach of worldly weather.
The moon is a cold shield; her wars are still far away.

Sea wind, curtain her day
old, completed body
by playing tricks with her hair.
We have too much to bear
as it is. We have seen her. She will not let go of her prey.

JOHN GREENING

Tribute

*Fotheringhay is the birthplace of Richard III
and where, on February 8th 1587,
Mary, Queen of Scots, was executed.*

At Fotheringhay, she's
thrown a swan's feather
into the Nene,
not to say 'coward',

not for those mute
numbers migrating
and breeding in Iraqi
airspace, but as her

tribute (like this
wreath here, freshly
laid, its ballpoint
message targeting

'murder') to the one
fragment that would not
be moved by a bullying
dynasty. It is still

February. The river,
however, is king
of spin and makes
my daughter's offering

an accusation, turning
a hunched back
away from us and
on to March

to advance in ruled
straight lines
towards the empire
of the Wash, her feather's

opinion, like her father's,
caught by the downing
thistlebeds and banks
of oil-stained bush.

February 21st, 2003

After the Mahler

After the *Symphony of a Thousand*
I am woken by the solitary
figure of my father walking

along a lonely road, just as
he was before he died.
I shout to stop the car,

leap out and embrace him
feeling the stubble and warmth
of his presence. Where we were

going, where the road
was winding to in my dream
I do not know. But years ago

we reeled out of a Prom,
where I had been standing
in the arena and he was sitting

somewhere up in the gods,
to meet at the bus-stop and rejoice
in what we had heard:

Veni Creator Spiritus . . .
Blicket Auf . . . as Faust
is raised to the empyrean.

Lines for Dennis O'Driscoll

I think of you as one of these cranes
rooted in the centre of Dublin –

yellow power grid of trinities,
meccano Book of Kells, lit at night

by a moonglow title on the sky
and a single bright red pulsing star.

You swing above the networking streets,
a grey set of tombstones on your back,

concrete counterbalance that gives you
the light touch, pirouetting to a

wittily apt angle, a deftly
bowed answering theme. Why do they wear

hard hats in your company? Because
you like to wind up big hollow pipes

and drop them back where they ought to be,
then raise with your few taut lines a skip

full of the dark, and carry it off.

October 2001, Dublin

HARRY GUEST

Light

for Lynn

Moonrise and the reddest flowers
turn silver.

       You pause before a mirror
where sunshine at two removes
provides a synopsis of your beauty.

        till daybreak . . .

(yes, there's always
the possibility of candleshine
or the flick for a sixty-
watt bulb to shed false radiance
but we'd surely plump for day
as the true referee of light)

         . . . till dawn, then,
limns you with appropriate gold
conceding your loveliness
to space, movement, colour
and my arms.

DAVID HARSENT

At the Roadside

If I pull over just here, I'm a hundred miles from you
and a hundred miles from the place I'm going to,
up on the hard shoulder with the artics slamming past
on one side, on the other a field of barley or some such,
the roadside row bearing a hard dark crust
of crud, bearing also the high bright stench
of diesel and oestrus: nose-to-tail trucks, creatures nose to tail
who might be the last of their species, hunting the nightspill for
food and each other, all their instinct and guile
come down, in these final days, to fuck and kill.

The wide black skidtrack snaking into the scrub,
the chunk of tyre with its inch-deep cleats,
a fan of feathers, a fist of claws, the blind O of a hub-
cap ... Hieroglyphs of terra incognita. Count the beats
of the slow-lane slipstream: you seem to get the bass
blur of the theme from that film where he's out of rehab
and driving home, when he catches the neon splash
of a sky-high logo featuring the ace
of spades, whereupon he pulls over at once and starts a tab he
knows full well he can never back with cash.

Folie circulaire, you said; *love or, leastways, love-and-hate* ...

Sun-and-cloud/side winds/rainfall; the trick is to sit tight
and the weather will come to you along that ten-county strip,
yourself a slim silhouette, the radio growing faint,
your breath misting the windscreen, and a hint
of something sour mixed in with your body heat
... or mine, as it happens ... while the last airwave lets slip
news of the planet rendering down to crap.

I could read the owner's manual. I could clock-watch. I could sleep.
Breaking all rules, I could walk at dusk through the hip-
high barley, or whatever it is, and come to the Travel Lodge
by way of a farther field, by way of a hawthorn hedge,
by way of the car park, by way of the wheelie bins and air-
conditioning units, and take a room and go down to the bar

my purpose, of course, to pick up the Playtex rep,
already half-cut, to catch her eye, to catch her on the hop,
to pin her down with a heartfelt pledge
that will turn on the verb 'to cherish', to watch her drop everything,
down to the fluffy red cache-sexe
she filched from stock . . . And at three a.m. to get up
and find my way back in the dark with only a slop
of lights for guidance, which could be the lights of wrecks
out there on the strip, or that self-same line of trucks,
shining blind as they barrel down the blacktop.

All Hallows

On that day we go to the graveyard with eggs and plaited bread,
with candy and candles, with bucket-brewed liquor,
and talk to each other, and talk to the long-time dead.
Which is how they found us, gathered there
in our suits and silks, the whole village, as if we'd been led
by a taste for death, by a whiff of death in the air.

They must have been glad of a square
meal, given the distance they'd covered, given the hard
road they'd travelled; they must have been glad
of something to cut the dust, of a chance to rest,
what with the promise of bad
weather backing from the west, with an all too rare
sight of ourselves caught between prattle and prayer;
and they must have been pressed for time, given their speed
with rope and wheel, as they showed us St Stephen, St Eulalia,
St Nicomedes, St Kilian, St Catherine, St Euphemia, St Jude.

What to say but that the women cut their hair
next day and threw the tresses in the yard, and fetched blood from
their cheeks; what to say but that we tore
all pictures from the walls; what to say but that we wore
ashes and clay, that some of the men went back with food,
as before, to recover the lost, to leave the raven's share.

from Legion

Piss-pail

We were dug in, just light of an apple orchard. You got
a faint scent from whin until the dew burned off, and bird-song out of the
branches, or else a bullet.
One went up for a look-see, then another, then a third
which was long enough for the trickster in the tree to draw a bead
and clip, as if he'd meant to, the piss-pail that stood
on the lip of the trench, which rose in the air and flipped like a lucky bet
once, then again, to come down flush over the third man's head
who buckled and blacked out, thinking he'd been hit.

We laid him under a flag. Kyrie eleison we sang,
Christi eleison, until the earthworks rang,
and he opened his eyes to a world of light
such as he'd never seen, the cryptic white-on-white
of clouds and sky, white of gunsmoke, white of the trench walls,
whites of our eyes as we knelt and called to bring him back,
of his wife's shift, her steady smile, the slack
of her breasts as she stopped and stooped to gather windfalls.

Daisychain

When we saw the smoke, we knew. The smoke was indelible
Some went to the lowland scrub, some to the sacred
sites. but some (some women, I mean) found another way, hard,
as if a word had been spoken, as if it might be infallible,
as if, last night, it had come to them in dreams,
the blade going from hand to hand, each making the second cut
on the one before in case she couldn't, in case it came to that.
Others were ashamed and did what they did in private
coming to light later, some in the orchards, some from house-beams.

Well, they must have gone round us. We sent men out
next day and the day after that, but the world was empty, it seems;
of that smoke, not a trace; of that word, not a syllable.

FRIEDA HUGHES

Fingers

His fingers' thought rose
From the hand that slept.
It met the woman's idea
Of her skin, as her eyes
Travelled the width of closed lids,
Seeing inwards.

The moment of contact
Felt by the nerve ending
In the landscape of her body,
At the point where hip met thigh,
Connected her to the thought
Of the man's fingers.

Attached to the thought
Came the sleeping hand,
Attached to the hand,
Now a palm's slow progress
Across the fields, was an arm.
Attached to the arm, curious
At the journey taken,
The body of a man,
Waking.

Court Green

The yellow of the daffodils did not
Surprise me in itself, the sheer
Vast number of the blooms
Was what made me gasp.
Their cool yellow pools spread out
Among the cherry trees. I waded
Knee deep in yellow,
Bunch-petals like butterflies
Struggling to escape their stems
And illuminate.

They will come again
My mother said,
When I saw them dead,
Encrusted at their stem-ends
Like desiccated dragonflies.
Then the lilacs bloomed,
White, purple, crimson red.

I would curl up among the daisies
And dandelions of the uncut lawn
And sleep, insects crawling over me,
The lilac scent as heavy as a blanket.

Until an earwig bedded
In the tunnel of my head,
And I was never so unconscious.

M.C. JONES

Phone Card

From farther sides of an estranging sea
Weekly we chat, briefly. Your voice with age
Has deepened, grown more gentle. Now, to me
Thirty years on, it's calmer – so much rage

Vanished. When we were rash and sharp and young
It was your voice that first evoked desire –
And where we shared, or suffered, pain or wrong,
(Or inflicted it), our voices stoked the fire.

Our private language, in a hostile world
A soundwall curtain, screening out the chill.
We find we utter shared ideas aloud,
In the selfsame words, like twins. Need I tell,

If death should cut the line, that, before I go
My voice will find you? You already know.

For a Departed Cyclist

As you go your way,
May no hurtling vehicle brush you,
No sudden door swing open,
No driver's curses follow.

May your wheels go spinning in a freewheel headlong
And the hills be kind.
Let the wind gather and speed you,
Like your father teaching you to ride when you were small.

May your brakes be sound and your saddle firm.
May no shards lie in wait for you –
All cycle lanes be taxi free.

Let boughs sway where you ride,
The sun be a mild bath, and the rain cool you.

May your paths lead where, in the glide of water
For ever
Giant beeches gaze.

Just After Midnight

For my mother EL, 23.10.02

Just after midnight long time gone
you set aside your slipper
onto the step of the house
and as you came into the
house, barefoot left it.

You would talk of your sleeping prince,
waking him with that kiss,
such whims in the garden maze,
a modern woman's pounce.
I walked in the sun of your walk.

Our tales hang by their cherry ribbons.
Silks and satins, cotton, rag.
How all the dazzlers danced
for you. How midnight
carried you off, brightest moon.

The Prince in His Sleep

For my father FL 3.08.01

I sat by you all day,
a most unfamiliar behaviour,
you deep asleep, the sleeping prince
returned to his beauty, my mother
would have said. Love in the mist,
poor thing, she could hardly see you.

Sometimes she stood and bent and kissed
your narrowing forehead and
called out loudly in her strong
deaf voice, 'My darling, I want to
keep you but I think God may want you.'
You narrowed and sank all day.

I saw your golden eyelids,
fragile, unwritten speech, smooth
as they hadn't been – Remembering
the months and years of a sad haste ...
Ten seconds to spare, you'd open
your blue eyes lazily and wide,

your blue eyes, good as a good child,
shy, sly at your chosen curious day,
your deeds; proud, modest. The space
of your life was wide. I rattled, fell
into your space regularly, but
we, or you, or I, smoothed out,

filled in, planted a sprig, a flag,
departed smiling. It never stopped,
your switchback and my small career
colliding and keeping up, laughing,
sometimes besides myself. Your eyelids,
closed, transparent, authoritative.

BRENDAN KENNELLY

Always

It will always go back
To a big man hunched in pain over a phone,
Smoking, waiting for news from Cork,
A brown envelope containing
Stamps of Sarawak,
Talk, on the landing near the room
Where I awoke, sweating,
Of freak weather hitting the South,
A forefinger touching a scar
Like a sign of friendship
Made after war,
The first taste of blood in the mouth.

It will always go forward
To a man standing over a grave
Acknowledging a woman,
A woman standing over a grave
Acknowledging a man,
Both rotten, having remembered
The privilege of being forgotten
By children, friends, the faithful stone,
The patient acre fertilising every sin,
The river joining the sea's voice
Like the pair of them standing at the door of the house,
'You're welcome, welcome! Come in! Come in!'

Calling Home

'Shakespeare's forehead is a map of the universe'
she said, rifling her pockets for coins
to pay for the phonecall home to her father
who was developing an interest in dreams.

'It's the one map I never tire of seeing'
she said. 'It helps me to travel all
the shadowy corners of my being.
And there's that laughing light out of it as well.'

She inserted the coins, talked, listened, talked, smiled
at her father, far away, into dreams, on his own now,
                old king, old fool.

Or was he? Was he not back at school
learning again to dreamthink, causing her to smile,
turning rusty decades into a limber style?

MIMI KHALVATI

Magpies

I have one tree in my garden
and two magpies in it;
two magpies in a yard
growing greener by the minute.

I have two kids by one father,
three husbands I regret;
the tree that was my grandmother
is dying in my head.

Everywhere is shrinkage but
you've heard that all before;
everywhere the censors cut
the truth about the war.

In black and white, the magpies come,
two cut-outs in a tree;
in coat-tails and as handsome
as black and white can be.

The first sign of spring is children
yelling in the street;
by *Eid* they will have killed them
before the killing heat.

What season shall we pray for now
when we know what March will bring?
In a mass of green on every bough,
the weapon that is spring.

I have one tree in my garden,
two magpies in it;
two magpies in a yard
growing greener by the minute.

The Servant

Ma'mad, hurry, water the rose.
Blessed is the English one that grows
               out in the rain.

Water is scarce, blood not so.
Blood is the open drain that flows
               out in the rain.

Bring in the lamp, the olive's flame.
Pity the crippled flame that blows
               out in the rain.

Where are the children? What is the time?
Time is the terror curfew throws
               out in the rain.

Hurry, Ma'mad, home to your child.
Wherever my namesake, Maryam, goes
               out in the rain.

JOHN KINSELLA

You'll Have to go to the Dead Place

You'll have to go to the dead place
intent on healing to find me there,
and as the salt – white irony – disappears,
all trace of me will evaporate

then condense on the leaves of trees
planted for recovery, or damp spots
on the sun's surface so minute
they will always evade detection:

black spots white as salt, destructive
as chlorine in the lungs, explosive as sodium
and water, air. Here growth is luxuriant –
red as blood gone into scarified soil,

run into layers of rock too far down
to be polluted. Contact me in those places,
because the air is solid, and I can't move there,
roots and branches tangled, leaves like eyelids

shut over wells burning for light,
for those black spots of sight
where reflections are absorbed like grace
and plough discs deflect contact in waves.

Exchange – Vit. D Hunger

Because I don't live through summers
every strand of sunlight is absorbed
    and collected; the intricate
    workings of bees, tactile
and tenacious movements of thornbills
registered, locked up outside electrodes

and x-rays, and garbled in nightmares
or under hypnosis; what's not taken, a chemical
    pattern that through heat and reaction
    will be changed, will make something
else out of the spectrum. If this is prayer,
then winter warmth and an air marred

only by floating tissue and the cold static
of unremembered strings and sequences
    drive it inside out, an exchange
    of colour, blood sprayed
into the spectrograph, that no pollution can entirely
obscure. The formula: the wing, the prayer.

MICHAEL KIRKHAM

Disquiet

You wake, wondering – it is still dark: you think
it's the basket chair easing itself with
discreet little cracks. But is it? You peer
into nothing, listening ... and you hear
pins of hail pricking the quiet, pecking
at the glass: all round, at every window
a space of sound extends, room after room,
floor below floor, in layered recession:
volume of black night opens to the ear.
Out there's soundless, but you imagine the
pock, pock of the tiny ice-pellets in
the snow-crust: a world becalmed in snow has
heaved and flaked – ice-fretted, wind-raked and -curled
into sculpted surf, a scarred and pitted
moonscape. A round, plump-packed, velvet silence –
domestic calm at the thimbled finger –
the house feels now like a pin-cushion, pin
after pin piercing the unpuckered skin
as if punctures cannot hurt. You lie tight,
fit your knees into the crook of her knees,
knowing you are safe, and wait out the night.

A Death and After
A Sequence

I Aubade

In the dead light
before dawn
bright notes
bubbling from
dark throats.

The first robin
twiddles his tune
again and again
making sweet
monotony.

This dawning the dying
woman listening
life
      is
again
      unending.

II Last Rites

Death lodged in the blocked bowel,
earth cannot feed you: liquid
life dribbled into the vein:
worn down to bone, past pain,
must bear the full stress of your
mortality: this cell fetches
no deliverance; here, love's
suffering buys no reprieve.

Mornings we tend the body. The nurse
will anoint and dress the bedsores
of exasperated flesh. I soap
the slack skin and with soft cloth
and circling hand stroke the remembered
slopes of neck and shoulder, back and thigh:
preparing each last day.

And now the last of last days
(there is nothing here for doctor or priest):
the last touch and taste of life's savour.
I touch your mouth with mine. You taste
(again, remembering) wine.

III The Gift of a Ring

We had talked. Afterwards I would wear your ring,
the broad band of worn silver we had preferred
to bright gold. It was old when bought, and now,
older by thirty years, its dull sheen mists
the tale of scratch-lines – an etched history,
with light and dark passages, sealed in time:
we wear, are worn by, a bond of love, of life.
Such things were said, or thought. There were fewer words
and longer silences of shared intent;
and at the last, almost the last breath,
snatched from its finger, your bequest of the ring.

As willed I wore it, and in due course our daughter,
to seal her marriage vows, tied her life
within its circle. And now I wear another.

This is the aftermath: time's returns.

IV Self-less

You come in the night, known unknown to me
(grief not for you, but the loss of you),
with a look of reproach for things done undone by me.
Grieve for the self closed and close to me.
'Selfless and gracious/In dying as in living' –
of whom are they true, words graved instead of you,
as true and as false as words are?

'Naught but bone, bone' and beautiful
you said: Don't make a poem of me.
You are self's sealed self:
I have made nothing of you.

JEHANE MARKHAM

Fear of Falling

The sea is washing its sheets.
Through closed eyes
I hear the slap and suck
of it beating the fabric of itself,
its elastic wetness
pulsing against the rocks.
Glass that melts
over and over the rocky ledge,
hissing out a lacey frill,
a liquid edge.
Nothing on the surface
but sunlight and the slant of depths.
A rocking horse ocean
rocking the deep.
A sofa without a seat,
if I'm not careful,
I'll fall right through,
knocked out by emerald knuckledusters,
the weight of water,
electric blue.

GLYN MAXWELL

The Generations

[for Les Murray]

It was hard to see how even the *crême* of the young
could prosper in the kingdom we had talked of,
had swallowing alluded to on the shoreline
as we watched them paddle, float out, stand, sail,
give five on little islands.

Candidly, it was hard to see what they had
that might be what was asked. It was hard also
to put ourselves through imagining that scene,
where they offer up with genuine doey smiles
such sorry minimums.

We didn't want to say so, and indeed
we didn't, except here, when they donned shorts
and splashed out to be giants, leaving us here,
giants instead. We didn't want to be using
our giant voice, though.

Nor did we hope that in joyous estivations
of bliss and bop they'd assay the impossible:
actually hearing. They all believed in a silence
we were in on. But we'd been telling them jokes
they die before they get.

Because, back here, there were many becoming lively,
wise and rested, sundried from being
out in the open, motionless, sure of their footing,
and those stood near to us, by the stiff trees
chained into sandplots.

Back here there were bulging hearts Scotch-taped with
    marriage,
livers plump with feeling, teeth arranged
for puzzling old beliefs, and there were eyes
like the coelecanth, extinct then not, like someone
got overruled somehow.

Back here there were broken ones with cutting edges,
or blown and sanded ones with nothing wasted,
them with arms grown thin by taking nothing,
fat ones lost to envy. And they were back here,
coughing up the damage.

All in all there was with these a certain
readiness to be done. And against these
the young began to seem somehow at a mercy
that wasn't what it used to be. We sighed
at the pity of those changes.

PATRICK McGUINNESS

'Death Whispers Softly'

Death whispers softly 'I am no-one,
I do not even know myself:
the dead do not know they are dead,
nor even that they are dying –
children at least, or heroes, the sudden deaths.

My beauty is made up
of last moments – lucidity, a face –
the beauty of what would be me
without me. For as soon as I am
(that one dies) I cease to be.

Thus I am made of forebodings,
intuitions, supreme shudders.
I am not except in idea.

As for the others, for the living,
their tears etc., that is just
my shadow clothing them in black'

(From Mallarmé's notes for *Anatole's Tomb*)

Sign

Speaking with their fingers, their words are shapes
that tumble from their open hands like dice.
Words pass like knots along the guyrope
of their muteness. They have made a silence

happen at the centre of our noise, language
made from what denies us ours:
silence open at both ends, language
starting out from what precedes and follows

language. The eye mishears, one gesture slurs
into the next; some words are so quiet they're
invisible, planed to a whisper; others
need a hand to ease them through the air,

words that move in space, that turn in it like worlds.

JAN MONTEFIORE

Mysteries

Darkness lies inside a hedge of thorns
lovingly etched, where you drew my birthday candle
spreading its glassy teardrop light
over your gift-wrapped continents.
There are many mysteries in the dark

This year no card of course
and your phone switched off till nightfall.

I watch my life pass away
Look how candle-smoke spreads
into blackening wings, how wax spills liquidly over
the dissolving contours.

Feathered the Bed of Nightmare

Feathered the down that fills the quilt
that covers the bed of nightmare.

Feathered the bird whose death is guilt
that shed the down that fills the quilt
that covers the bed of nightmare.

Feathered the sky with icy down
as light as mist and as cold as stone
that fills the air when the bird has gone
the fluttering bird whose death is guilt
plucked of its feathers to stuff the quilt
that covers the bed of nightmare.

Feathered the pane of icy glass
covered with fronds of branching frost
that blanches breath and brings down cloud
to flake and drift in a pale soft shroud
that climbs the wall to the window-sill
filling the room with deadly chill
where the sleeper shudders beneath the quilt
stuffed with the barbs of mortal guilt
that lies on the heart of nightmare.

Feathered the breast all white and warm
of the bird that flew in the howling storm
that darkened the sky that froze the cloud
that covered the world in the cold white shroud
of the innocent bird whose life was spilled;
feathered the arrow that maimed and killed
piercing the flesh as the marksman willed
and the wounded breastbone bled and thrilled
of the warm white bird whose death is guilt
that shed the down as soft as silk
that smothers the bed of nightmare.

Feathered and sharp the grey goose-quill
dripping its ink like a greedy bill
that drew the crossbow aimed with skill
and feathered the arrow that pierced and killed
the bird whose breast is bloody and chilled
and feathered the sky with drifting down
as white as mist and as cold as stone
and feathered the pane of icy glass
with abstract patterns of branching frost
that bleaches breath and thickens cloud
to crystallise in a colourless shroud
that lies on the heart all cold with guilt
that feathered the down that fills the quilt
that covers the bed of nightmare.

MICHAEL O'HIGGINS

Rooks in a Country Churchyard

The rape of air by cawing rooks
Breaks the calm of this quiet
Planted lovingly with the long dead.

Old headstones tilt precariously
Over the mounds.
The trees whisper sibilantly
In a stiff breeze, as though at prayer.

The place is like a garden overgrown.

Lichen stains the headstones
With small grey maps of time.

An open grave yawns invitingly:
Someone's final parking place.

Isolated and alone,the graveyard
Jealously guards its privacy,
Except for the raucous rooks.

Who, each Spring,
Religiously build their nests,
Prepare for new life
In happy ignorance
                    Of the sad function

Of their habitat.

WILLIAM OXLEY

Familiar Stranger

Where the evening spreads across the sea
and darkens waves' wild tracery;
where greyest streets are soon dismissed
and the awkward day dissolves in mist

you can sense a presence past decay.
For mind shakes out its atoms in this way
to become a room dusted of despair
leaving its own windowed image there:

a second-self of inward sight. Here
where moving sands and solid stones near,
there's something closer still – it can
only shine or speak through words of man.

So in loss that's evening you may find
not only fading sunsets but your mind –
that shadowy orchard where day by day
a familiar stranger comes to stay.

MARIO PETRUCCI

Black Box

I was raw data. His something-for-nothing box.
  Caught him watching me as I slept – a cold

forensic look. He favoured a bed with bones
  that clicked. Wanted to see if my face was

different from the rest in the act of love.
  He'd inquire over dinner – jaw set in intense

nonchalance he thought I couldn't decipher –
  So. *What colour did it burn? What colour*

precisely? I turned the tables. Kept a diary
  of the way his dessert spoon would hover mid-

slurp with each counterfeit story I slipped him –
  noted the lustre in those coins of eyes as he

made the base salute of a shirtsleeve dragged
  across lips, excused himself to the bathroom

to lick his stub of pencil, spend a breathless
  minute spawning apocrypha in that journal

jammed behind the cistern. God knows I tried–
  one dusk as the moon rose, thin as rice-paper

I ran true. Told him what I had seen there. Seen
  with my mind – that freedom is not an absence

of control. But he just leant closer as I blanched
  a perfectly good chicken in salt water then

threw out the scum three times. Those monitor
    eyes widened. *Salt gets it out,* I told them.

I ditched him. Couldn't see then that he was right.
    The Reactor. I had it in me after all – a searing

rod of black so stuck in my crop it made me
    fall for someone like him – grim receiver who'd

piece together my pain and publish the results.
    Perhaps I'd hoped he would draw it out – bloody

from between my ribs. I'd rather he had shoved it
home. Quelled this constant rising drone in my brain.

CAROLINE PRICE

Sheafhayne

As the shadows lengthen
I see you standing by the low stone wall
at the garden's edge, gazing across
the folded fields of cows and hedges and struck trees
as if it is all yours, all this –
your own shadow stretching out behind
until it laps at the walls of the house, one elbow dipping
as you shade your eyes
into the still, green surface of a pond
that is full of mysteries, your other hand
brushing the trodden ground beneath the flaring chestnut
to sweep it free, or gather another conker
into the pile already there. To your side
a pair of pillars, chiselled stone
standing on their own, no gate, no wall,
that you might have come through
or be about to disappear through again,
choosing your moment with care,
just as that pheasant winds itself up
like a clockwork from your own childhood
and launches itself through them precisely –
not the usual oriental brilliance
but pale, white gold,
a sighting rare and precious.

The Day My Father Died

And what I can't get out of my mind
is the greenfinch one moment
chipping at the peanut feeder
and then, in the blind spot of an eye,
tricked away, a thud on glass,
the delayed action
of a few feathers drifting down.

It's lying on its back on the patio,
legs drawn up, a flicker
in a visible eye.
It is a breezy mild March day.
A sudden gust
rocks its tiny weight, blows its wings
half open – and at this reminder of flight

its feathers twitch, it turns its head
from one side to the other,
slowly shifts itself
a quarter-circle in the dust.
And if this struggle
is great, the next is even greater,
its breathing growing faster

until its whole body shakes
like a feathered toy wound up
and not released – and it stretches out
its legs and opens both wings
wide, like fans, and arches its back
in a gargantuan effort
to meet or resist the end

which comes then, the shuddering
stopping abruptly, wings
folding, eyes slipping shut.
It lies warm in my hand, almost
weightless, head lolling back
in the crook of my fingers, claws
still extended, stiffening

on something just out of reach.
I stroke the misty greengrey
of its breast, wipe away specks of peanut
still clinging round its bill.
Which was all I could do.
It was a mild day in March.
It was the sixteenth of September.

PETER ROBINSON

Ghost Characters

for David Taylor

I

Then at the end of a long weekend
(a day of marriage celebrations,
container ships standing off between islands)
we went where lido restaurants'
wall-high windows opened
onto waves and a trampled beach.
Vistas of the freshening breeze
hurried breakers towards that shore
and, though you'd think we were well out of reach,
some pursued us even here.

II

Ghost characters had accosted us
in shadowy corners of late-night bars,
written out ghost characters
who can't remember what they've done,
never knew the harm they caused,
bringing back a time with them
when nettled, half-ashamed by words,
I left; but their compounded hurts
still stick to us like burrs.

III

Talk would exorcise them, clear the air,
taking with it such a one
as that drunk character driving home
who scared the living daylights from us
at earliest morning near the door
to another of life's safe houses.

IV

There, you stir in the midday haze
absorbed by an authentic wall,
a spare room possessed by nothing at all,
empty of ghosts like the bed's foot skeleton
waking a new woman up in her futon
from 'The Former Wife's Return'.

V

From folds in the bedclothes they rise
with daylight, stubborn memories
of a misplaced past.

It's like glimpsing from a tour bus
stuck in traffic on some by-pass
people you have lost.

What do they come back for?
To deepen the morning? Make sure
you're alive at least?

VI

Others badly done by, all the more
prone to spoiling acts
would knock the stuffing out of us.
Yet seeing as how, at last, pursuers
left for other haunts and these
misplaced persons were spirited away,
in a hotel lounge I breathe again.

The blocks of neon sprawling below
turn to scenes of habit, signs
of some relief.
          But if content appears
and you've only competitive ears
to be heard by, how let anyone know?

VII

Distanced, they come back again,
ventriloquized familiars
from circles of gossip or rumour,
as doing the different voices
you hint the one thing worse than being
talked about is being here.

Noh masks, devils' heads, bogeymen –
you're giving vent to all of these
and me, I'm mesmerized,
dazed, quite ready to believe
that talking makes it so.

VIII

This exercised them, filled the air
with spectres of those characters
appearing to go along with us
like running jokes or sores,
or like the coast road's ghost hotels'
ranked, reflective windows
overlooking an islanded horizon –
vast, abandoned structures
from which the trade had gone
away to Hawaii or to Guam.

IX

No threat, they're almost missed.
'The curse of a half-decent memory,'
you say, 'I'm repossessed by them.'
Yes, and so you promise
to drive me out that way some time,
revisit those vast, abandoned
structures from the past.

X

Walking out towards North Beach,
an angular coast of flat reclaimed land
in a Sunday blur brought back
the dome, hotels, apartments, far-fetched
landmarks, local habitats
overwhelmed with so much sky;
and I saw at last how grounds of habit
could alter the possible aired by
words – words letting us understand
they're not only what comes with the territory,
but what you do about it.

XI

Now in the small streets, smells of drains
assail like mildness as passersby
bring to mind nobody else.
The currents form an ebb and flow
of diary entries, vanity mirrors,
dental floss, their *vitaes* of achievement
fading away with the sounding heels
under that expansive sky.

XII

So, at the end of a long weekend,
we went where lido restaurants'
wall-high windows opened
onto freshening breeze and overcast skies
failing to cut the day down to size.

Gesticulating palm trees
made themselves felt like an offered hand
which stretched to include us in its grip,
each breath of the air kept up
by an ocean skyline's low release.

SUE ROE

Wraith

In her dressing room drawer
She stores the smallest clothes
But sometimes when the wind beats
Fast advancing footfalls
She crosses all her dreams to watch
A pantomime of sea swell

It is the piano music
Like the ruined rooms of houses
That enters at her shoulders
Clings around her ankles

She hums it, folds small garments
For the life still not invented
And the sea fingers the *Gymnopedies*
Through the gaps in the cavity walls

She hears a small voice singing through
The cracks in her dressing room floor

STEPHEN ROMER

Figment

I bow to Him, and bow to Him;
for bowing breaks the thought stream.

The wind in trees. That is a beginning
& an end. Refuge on refuge.

Stopped at source. Not desire
but the knowledge of desiring.

I send the Sutras to all & sundry & preach
what I cannot practise.

*   *   *

The temptation of symbolic orders
came to me again,

a peacock imago on Shelley's page
where I read with jaundiced eye

how he meets, in human guise,
the moonlike idol of his thought,

there was this multicoloured creature,
woken from the dark, and sunning

beneath the scholar's lamp, Epipsychidion,
his love, his wraith, his mind.

A Presto?

It seems we were both waylaid
in the Vasari Gallery en route
for the Pitti
by the little chapel of Santa Felicità
where Pontormo's
elongated stary-eyed angels
in their pastel bodystockings
of pink and green
most elaborately depose
the Crucified.

It seems we both sat down
in the Piazza Santo Spirito
and then walked on
in the warm evening
to where the Duomo
shepherds her houses
and Africans fold and unfold
their cloths of merchandise
in a game of cat-and-mouse
with the languid police.

It seems we both deplored
Botero's squat Roman
baring his buttocks
at Verocchio's angel
but smiled inwardly
at the affront.
It seems, on the face of it,
with all this in common,
we might even meet.
What say you, Benedetta?

TATIANA SHCHERBINA

Last year's flame sustains today's discourse.

The oldest bridge in Paris is called 'New Bridge'.

I have seen it decorated with flowers: some festival, bankrupt, filed a petition, and the bridge, completely naked, bare-backed, sends my thought in the diection of the best dressed stones.

The ducal palace in Dijon – fancy that – is the architectural sibling of Versailles. I visit the two and I die of desire. I die, I die, I die, and finally I survive. Desire is what dies.

In a pitiless battle between desire and the rest of the world, the rest of the world remains, and desire goes away.

The rest of the world still remains, and desire, that pitiful homeless person, claims to be a ruined king, laying claim to his royal ruins.

I cannot make sense of this madman's words; he ought to be restrained; I am from the other side of the bridge, where no restitution is envisaged.

There is nothing like paper, it is the softest thing in the world. Paper wipes away your tears and everything you entrust it with. It accepts you, welcomes you, takes you over entirely while giving you as much freedom as you can cope with. If you possess a magical instrument, it is your fountain pen. And if you know how to transform your blood into ink.

The only thing on earth that is solid and reliable: your fountain pen. Who comes and stops some swine from torturing you? The pen. Who rises like a stake at the edge of the abyss and says to you: stop, speak to me? It is the ear of ears: your pen.

It serves you too as the measure of distance: 16 cms. The distance that must be preserved between yourself and life. When life touches you, it weakens you. Penetration is the worst thing of all. The fountain pen never attempts to penetrate you. It permits itself one gesture: to shake your hand.

Life still has some good things to offer: staple guns to strengthen you: you go well together. A memorandum book enabling you to start life in the morning, to make you eat regularly, and offering you all the diversity in the world. Open it and you will see that life does not end today: next week is full up.

And postcards greeting you all the time: Happy Christmas, Happy Birthday, I am thinking about you, I love you.

Long live stationery!

(Translated by Anthony Rudolf from the original French of a poet who usually writes in her native Russian.)

ROBERT STEIN

Salthouse

Two have slipped through the sky
On a yellow February.

Nothing but the raddled sea;
The mouth drained, the heart empty.

No apparition, no gold, no strange bird.
No stone mysteriously turned.

Nothing but the psalmody of villages:
Newgate, Kelling, Bodham Street.

Two men washed as if for sacrifice,
Laid on an opened sheet.

They will go back as usual,
Watching carefully the last boat in.

One boat fewer in the morning.
Nothing that the eye takes in.

DAWN SULLIVAN

I Will Thrive . . . . . !

(For Josie Russell and other survivors)

I will thrive because I will drive
my spirit fillies of the wind
who offer only their manes for reins:
careering across chasms of fear, their voices hear
me – the hammered child of Paradise survived!
And pyramids of stars will candle me
up from the blind bed of the dumb sea
I will be every merry tree
I who fell to hell through roaring waters of air
I fling my heart into the flame of every flower
prancing; I am the miracle dancing from the rock
of your despair

DAVID SWANN

Wednesdays

Somebody's left a piano
in a puddle by the bus stop down the hill.

They've felt-tipped a few shivery words
of explanation on a yellow post-it:

'Bin Men – Please don't take this piano.
It will be removed tomorrow.'

Tomorrow –
still there, rained on. And the next . . .

. . . and the next, and blotches in its wood,
and a thin wet dog sniffing the pedals.

I peek under the lid,
opening its wound to test the keys.

They're hard as teeth, and silent,
and drinkers are looking from the pub

so I rush away, to a train,
to another town, to my job,

but two days later, the piano's still missing buses
and the rain can't stop

and someone's loosened a side panel
with their toe-end or a brick.

But it takes them a while longer to find its ribs,
to slither its innards to the kerb,

it takes a week. And then –
there's not much more than a frame.

The day before it goes for good,
someone cuts a single word in the wood: 'ODIN',

name of the sky warrior who made music,
who was Othin who was Wotan who was Woden

whose wild hunts shook the forests,
whose only trace is Wednesdays.

RICHARD TAYLOR

Flamenco Dancer Dancing

For Jenny

Strike up and strum,
beat the antique drum;
fuse cultures, crescent shedding
light on cross
dressing down
topsy-turvy rhythmic enhance
the festive colours of gyrating belly dance
in market place of music
trading partners enthus-
iastic orgiastic navel display –
Midsummer Night's Dream to crown the doting day,
Radio Tarifa blending wordless breaths
of Moor and Spaniard to the death
of all hostility, song, sex and trance
crusading for the cause of measureless dance.

MICHAEL VENDITOZZI

Asking for Rain

The Japanese Buddhist pilgrim Jojin, passing through the Chinese capital in 1073, became the first Master from Japan to be commanded by the Emperor to pray for rain . . .

I

I will begin under the crab-apple
in September – half-green, half-red
with the unripe and the ripening fruits
and the delicate twine of clematis;
the grass at its foot littered with the apple stunts,
rotting, and the wasps rising off them –
there is incense burning somewhere, there is mist
coming down from the hills to the Emperor's garden,
and I am afraid.

II

I will pray here for thirteen days,
all the birds pray with me:
their Spring menagerie vye-and-echo calling.
I will learn their faculty for talking
to the clouds, for telling what will happen
with the weather and the chances for rain.

Their swopping blossom-tales I envy,
their presences in trees – between seasons
of the living and the dead – are alive
to something, in some way I know nothing of.
No, not nothing: I have my glimmers,
glimpses of what they might mean
and when I see them, I will write them down.

III

This tent is full of mysteries.
I lie awake and listen to the wind
and wonder if the rain will come tonight,
and whether it will stay long enough
for the Emperor to be pleased with my efforts
which he cannot govern, but
which I cannot possess alone;
he knows this, and I choose to be here.

Our conversations are all silence,
a history of listening from respective places;
his palaces are full of voices.
But sometimes when the wind drops
we can discern each other,
attending and immeasurably divine,
each in his own, and I know
he will permit himself a smile
in my direction.

IV

In the whole of the wet world
there is nothing like this mist
that sways over everything
so everything is seen –
the trees, the hut, the gardener's plot –
as if new-formed by looking,
the eye itself having found
its true object, learned its nature
in the nature of other things.

The body of the world breathes
and is saturated, laden with an air
that can change the shape of birdsong
and the calls of early risers
that float and twist and vanish
over the valley; its scent,
inborn and rich and palpable,
condensing over warm cheeks,
reaching the heart everywhere.

In the palace the Empress awakes
and seeks her favourite slippers,
faded beyond their value in embroidery;
slips on her gown and out
onto the balcony to let the air
wash over her, lip to thigh,
longing – only later – for the sun;
but I should not dwell with her:
the Emperor stirs by his favourite wife,

My master now, dreaming always of the rain.

V

Mistress, I use the lotus flower
        to make the rain,
a billion petals descending
to scent the driest parts of your kingdom:

        Honeysuckle
        Lobelia
        Coltsfoot
        Ladysmock
        Ladyslipper

and the ivies growing over the palace walls at dusk.

The lupins hold my secret in their bells,
bees turn silver in the rain pools:
and if you would only drink the drops that run
down the stems – let your lips drown! –
you too would understand the bees' wings,
the bees' words blurring as they sip the dew;
and the blackbird in your throat would sing
with a voice like blackbird honey,
make morning flute-long melodious
when the distant swans and noises
of the marsh crake
break the world awake.

     Red Dragon Lady
     Green Dragon Lady

Rise up to the sky!
From the corner of my eye
I see you and smile:
Mistress, ours is the oldest master of all.

JOHN WELCH

Valley

I stir for you
And I have to trust the words
More than I trust myself

On an evening of rainwet fractured light.
Sun-drops peopling each bush
We'll drive further into the valley

Where the quality of the late
Light is like a released ache,
Skin-near and the

Rooks lift from treetops.
The wind takes their cries.
Each leaf is the sum of light

And I wonder what this to-be-
held might be like in our quiet house
Over against the fall of dark

Parented

I

Somewhere between boredom and longing
Was where I'd felt I almost always was.
There was something that felt banished,
And in the end had moved
To its place of watching and waiting.
She was still there
With that smile of an all-knowing mothering sadness
As if she were light
        Singing in its grave.

II

Spring twilight, passers-by
Mere ciphers in the streets.
What the light finds it
Hides,
    My father walking into me.
Resemblance merges, fades.
'He You and I' – as if
A text of self were being made.

III

'I want to come to you', I'd said
'From the most enormous distance,
To be a visitor here,
Travelling shaft of light
That pauses for just a moment,

Faint twitch of a curtain, and then that slow
Gathering of sound as the
Car parked outside pulls away.'
So who is it lives in there now
As if baffled by his own absences –
What is it lives
In the spaces between each mouthful?

Breathing it lifts
Another page
And I can see it now.
It is the writing-self,

Me-not-me, in that
Perfected circle's pool of light –
'Left long enough in here', I thought.
'The books will all read themselves'

And looking in there I saw him.
It was Tantalus feeding.

Collected

'The Collected' was in
His glass-fronted bookcase,
My clergyman father
Who'd once quoted Prufrock
Standing there in the Vicarage study –
The words came with such sudden feeling
Like a glimpse of something, and later
There were those spectral encounters;
Stetson, the Fisher King
Or, walking to early communion,
The compound ghost's baked features
And day-trips to the country,
A moment when something briefly flares
Like sun on frozen water –
Somewhere between
My father and me
It is still there, the poem. It shimmers
Over a burnt-out landscape
And today as I am passing
One of those huge London churches,
St Pancras, which was my grandfather's
Parish, and I was baptised there,
I dart abruptly in,
Smell that cinammon and chrysanthemum smell,
A sense of being there and not-there
Among the flower-dust
And patient embroidery.
I have the bookcase now
Whose fringed shelves exhale
A polished mustiness
And I remember that gesture –
Him taking it down and handing it to me,
Eliot's Collected. Sometimes I feel

It was almost the only
Connection there was between us.
Being sixty years old I cannot
Help but start to imagine
Somewhere I might return to.
Hearing his voice that speaks, out of
A sort of hesitant stillness
I hover here, make myself other
Where reflections, branches and leaflight,
Like broken water are caught
In the bookcase's glass and the sunlight
Pours uselessly onto the page where I write.
My waste lands waited then
For impossible fertilities
And it is as if I'm still saying
Give me this, give me this, the
Love that blinds, and satisfies.

SUSAN WICKS

Birds at Dawn

They are taking possession,
their whole transparent world
displacing ours: so many audible voices
to chirp and twitter, the sudden creak
of high wings. And a sharp note like barking –
as if *they* might wake
to hear us calling at the fringes,
similarly strange, through the same dawn,
our songs translating themselves
into mud, into tree-skeletons,
craters where the bodies of birds
lay bleeding. Under its feather shield
a mind drifts, not grasping
what makes the metal sing,
how a man can inhabit
such treeless spaces.

Through Glass

A country of dark islands
where trees reach in the wind
and ivy shimmers, marooned

behind flawed glass.
Look at it long enough
and faces grow in the bark,

a withered finger beckons
from the fork of a branch
the sky inhabited.

Across this frozen liquid
wings leave a spreading wake –
as if simply by looking

you could learn to see
a giant thumbprint,
a signature on the grey.

But there is one pane
your eyes are drawn to,
newer, clear as the air

where the trees stand
neither drowning in bright haze
nor abandoned.

ANNE WILLIAMS

Condolences

'I know that it is the last page, and yet I turn it over'
(Leonard Woolf – April 1941)

After the rush and noise of grief . . . Silence
Like a splash of water settles patiently
On her last words. They swim through
Once dark spaces, blurred memory channels
To reach him. Again, he searches the
Familiar print for meaning. The green ink
Smudged in places reminds him of weeds.
The river's edge; this morning like no other.
Closing his eyes brings her to him. He is her.
Wasted pages crumpled in his fist. Wet ink.
A draft as always, those long stained fingers.
He can see the pen, her wrist, bent at the strap,
Time itself ticking. Her arm resting on the table
He sits at now. Feeling the helplessness of love.

Anyone with even a passing interest in poetry knows that *Agenda* is one of the most reputable of literary magazines. Under William Cookson's editorship, it followed its own path without concession to fad or fame. It is that integrity of approach, that unwavering belief in his own taste that marked *Agenda* out as essential for both readers and poets. William, like Alan Ross at *London Magazine*, nurtured the publication throughout his life. It was a struggle financially but he kept going. Poetry is the better for him and the sadder without him.

Gary McKeone
Literature Director
Arts Council of England

Poets and reviews/essayists in the South/South East Region in this Issue

Peter Abbs
Lucy Calcott
Peter Carpenter
Matthew Chapman
Peter Dale
John E. Field
Judith Kazantzis
Glyn Maxwell

Jan Montefiorè
Caroline Price
Sue Roe
David Swann
Susan Wicks
Anne Williams
Patricia McCarthy
Sam Milne

Many of the Broadsheet 1 poets are from this region also.

Forthcoming Issues:

Double Irish Issue: Special focus on
John Montague
Vol 40 Nos 1–2   Winter 2003/4

Australian (Double) Issue, guest edited by
John Kinsella
Vol 40 Nos 3–4

General anthology issue, Special
focus on US poetry
Vol 41 Nos 1–2

Special Issue on Carol Ann Duffy,
reviews by women writers, general
anthology section for women poets
Vol 41 No 3

Submissions invited for the above, and for the Broadsheets.